WHAT HAPPENED IN HISTORY

Professor V. Gordon Childe, D.LITT., D.SC., F.S.A., F.B.A., was born in Sydney, Australia, in April 1892. He was a graduate of Sydney and Oxford Universities, and from 1919 to 1920 he held the post of Private Secretary to the Premier of New South Wales.

In 1927 he was appointed the first Abercromby Professor of Prehistoric Archaeology in the University of Edinburgh, and directed numerous excavations in Scotland and Northern Ireland, but notably at the wonderfully preserved Stone Age village at Skara Brae in Orkney. From 1946 to 1956 he was Professor of Prehistoric Archaeology and Director of the Institute of Archaeology in the University of London.

Among the sixty-odd distinguished scientists and men of letters invited from all over the world to address the Conference of Arts and Sciences organized by Harvard University to celebrate its Tercentenary in 1936, Childe was selected to represent prehistoric archaeology and was awarded the honorary degree of Doctor of Letters, while the University of Pennsylvania conferred upon him an honorary Doctorate of Science in 1937. He was Visiting Professor at the University of California during the summer session of 1939, and in 1940 was elected a Fellow of the British Academy. His own University of Sydney awarded him an honorary LITT.D. in 1957. He died that year.

Professor Childe was the author of several well-known books which include *The Dawn of European Civilization, The Most Ancient East, The Prehistory of Scotland, Man Makes Himself, Prehistoric Communities in the British Isles,* and *Social Evolution.*

GORDON CHILDE

WHAT HAPPENED IN HISTORY

WITH A NEW FOREWORD
BY PROFESSOR GRAHAME CLARK

PENGUIN BOOKS

Penguin Books Ltd, Harmondsworth, Middlesex, England
Penguin Books Inc., 7110 Ambassador Road, Baltimore, Maryland 21207, U.S.A.
Penguin Books Australia Ltd, Ringwood, Victoria, Australia

—

First.published 1942
Reprinted 1946, 1948, 1950, 1952
Revised edition 1954
Reprinted 1957, 1960, 1961
Reprinted with foreword and footnotes 1964
Reprinted 1965, 1967, 1969, 1971

—

Copyright © Estate of V. Gordon Childe, 1942
Foreword and footnotes copyright © Grahame Clark, 1964

—

Made and printed in Great Britain
by C. Nicholls & Company Ltd
Set in Monotype Baskerville

CONTENTS

FOREWORD by Professor Grahame Clark   7

AUTHOR'S PREFACE   11

1. ARCHAEOLOGY AND HISTORY   13

2. PALAEOLITHIC SAVAGERY   33

3. NEOLITHIC BARBARISM   55

4. THE HIGHER BARBARISM OF THE COPPER AGE   77

5. THE URBAN REVOLUTION IN MESOPOTAMIA   97

6. EARLY BRONZE AGE CIVILIZATION IN EGYPT AND INDIA   121

7. THE EXPANSION OF CIVILIZATION   138

8. THE CULMINATION OF BRONZE AGE CIVILIZATION   159

9. THE EARLY IRON AGE   193

10. GOVERNMENT, RELIGION, AND SCIENCE IN THE IRON AGE   213

11. THE CLIMAX OF ANCIENT CIVILIZATION   240

12. THE DECLINE AND FALL OF THE ANCIENT WORLD   270

MAPS   293

INDEX   297

FOREWORD

by Professor Grahame Clark

PROFESSOR V. GORDON CHILDE, who died in the Blue Mountains of his native Australia in 1957 soon after retiring from the Directorship of the London University Institute of Archaeology, was one of the great prehistorians of the world. More perhaps than any other man he showed how by using the data won by archaeologists and natural scientists it was possible to gain a new view of what constituted human history. Inevitably some of the books in which he summarized, with brilliant mastery of detail, the current situation in different fields of prehistoric archaeology have begun to lose something of their value for modern students. The general works in which he opened up new and often vast perspectives on the other hand are in many cases classics that repay constant re-reading and are likely to retain their value for a long time to come. Of these one of the most important is the present volume, originally published in 1941 and last revised in 1954.

In approaching this book it is important to remember two important facts about the author. Ever since he went up to Oxford he was fascinated, as perhaps only one could be who came from a different continent, by the unique quality of European civilization: to understand his approach to prehistory we must accept his word, printed after his death, that he took up the subject precisely to find an answer to this question. The scope even of a work as comprehensive as *What Happened in History* is bound up with and limited by this concern: the New World, like Australasia, is omitted and only glancing references are made to the great focus of civilization in the Far East. Childe's concern was confessedly with what, from a European point of view, is the 'main tradition', from its sources in Egypt and Mesopotamia to the confluence of these in the Hellenistic

Mediterranean. His book begins with the Old Stone Age and ends to all intents and purposes with the collapse of the Roman Empire.

A second point to remember is that he made no secret of his interest in Marxism. He found it useful to suppose that societies at each phase of social evolution rested on definite productive forces which shaped their lives, but which harboured contradictions that in due course compelled the emergence of new productive forces and a new cycle of social evolution. He thus found a model which not merely accounted for the way in which societies functioned at any particular time, but, what was even more important in some respects, provided some explanation for the dynamism of the historical process. Childe had a great contempt for what he called 'postage-stamp archaeology' and a corresponding predilection for a model that enabled him to handle in a meaningful manner the myriad facts gathered by archaeologists and historians. He was profoundly impressed by the limitations imposed on societies at the level of savagery by the low density of population and uncertainty of food-supply normally associated with reliance on hunting and gathering. Conversely he tended to lay special stress on the liberating effect of the domestication of animals and plants, the basic achievement which underlay his Neolithic Revolution. Neolithic barbarism in turn he saw to have been handicapped by a surplus too small to withstand natural disaster and by a self-sufficiency which meant that expansion could only be achieved by enlarging the area of settlement, a solution inherently wasteful since it could only be achieved in the end through conflict. This is why he stressed the importance of achieving a surplus which was reliable and large enough to support urban life and the employment of specialists like metal-workers, priests, and rulers, an achievement which for him constituted a veritable Urban Revolution. But the urban civilizations of Egypt, Sumer, and the Indus Valley were no more immune from the effects of inborn contradictions than the Neolithic peasantries had been: to mention only two, the concentration of purchasing power in comparatively few hands prevented an adequate expansion of the market, and the divorce between craftsmen and literate members of society constituted an effective drag on technical advance. The fundamental importance of the adoption of iron for tools and weapons, in place of the relatively much more expensive copper and bronze, lay in the fact that it so to say democratized basic activities like agriculture, industry, and warfare: if, to begin with, cheap iron weapons allowed relatively barbarous societies to topple over ancient civilizations, iron tools ultimately made possible the emergence of Classical civilization and so in due course of our own.

Such a bare outline gives no adequate idea of the range of material presented, and no intelligent reader can read this exciting book without being led to question the model which the author is at no pains to conceal. Certain factual revisions are needed especially for the earlier prehistoric period in which research has recently been so rapid. Certain of these are listed as footnotes in the text, in the knowledge that the author himself went to the greatest pains to keep his works up-to-date.

AUTHOR'S PREFACE

How has Man progressed during the several hundred thousand years of his existence on the Earth? That is the question to which this book offers an answer which does not pretend to be exhaustive. It is thus an extension of the account of Man's progress in the long ages before the dawn of written history advanced five years ago in *Man Makes Himself* (Watts & Co.); indeed in Chapters 2–5 I have had to recapitulate in a compressed form many events and conclusions set forth more fully there. But in other respects I have had to amplify what I then wrote to adjust it to the wider perspective. For in the subsequent chapters I trespass upon the domains of literary history in which written records disclose aspects of human endeavour that can only be inferred speculatively by prehistoric archaeology. Yet here, too, I have tried to keep in the foreground the concrete archaeological facts of the same kind as those available in prehistoric times. Finally, if only for considerations of space, I have focused attention on what seems from the standpoint of Europe and America in 1941 to be the main stream of human progress and even so have had to close my account some fifteen hundred years ago.

V. Gordon Childe

Edinburgh, October 1941

In the twelve years that have elapsed since the first publication of this work a remarkable number of new archaeological discoveries have enriched the picture of man's cultural development, particularly in its earlier stages, without, however, modifying the general outlines of the scene. The most relevant and exciting of these new results have been included in the present edition, but no substantial rewriting has been needed nor attempted.

March 1954

I

ARCHAEOLOGY AND HISTORY

WRITTEN history contains a very patchy and incomplete record of what mankind has accomplished in parts of the world during the last five thousand years. The period surveyed is at best about one hundredth part of the time during which men have been active on our planet. The picture presented is frankly chaotic; it is hard to recognize in it any unifying pattern, any directional trends. Archaeology surveys a period a hundred times as long. In this enlarged field of study it does disclose general trends, cumulative changes proceeding in one main direction and towards recognizable results.

Aided by archaeology, history with its prelude prehistory becomes a continuation of natural history. The latter studies in the geological record the 'evolution' of various species of living creatures as the result of 'natural selection' – the survival and multiplication of those bodily adapted to their environments. Man is the last great species to emerge; in the geological record his fossil remains would occur in the topmost layers, so that in this literal sense man is the highest product of the process. Prehistory can watch the survival and multiplication of this species through improvements in artificial and detachable equipment that secure the adaptation of human societies to their environments – and of their environments to them. And archaeology can trace the same process in historical times, with the additional aid of written records, as well as in regions where the dawn of written history has been retarded. Without any change of method it can follow down to the present day the working out of trends discerned already in prehistory.

Our species, man in the widest sense, has succeeded in surviving and multiplying chiefly by improving his equipment for living, as I have explained at length in *Man Makes*

Himself. As with other animals, it is chiefly through his equipment that man acts on and reacts to the external world, draws sustenance therefrom and escapes its perils – in technical language adapts himself to his environment or even adjusts his environment to his needs. Man's equipment, however, differs significantly from that of other animals. These carry their whole equipment about with them as parts of their bodies; the rabbit carries paws to dig with, the lion claws and teeth for tearing his prey, the beaver carpenter's tusks, most beasts hairy or furry coats to keep in warmth – the tortoise even carries his house on his back. Man has very little equipment of this sort and has discarded some that he started with during prehistoric times. It is replaced by tools, extracorporeal organs that he makes, uses, and discards at will; he makes picks and shovels for digging, weapons for killing game and enemies, adzes and axes for cutting wood, clothing to keep him warm in cold weather, houses of wood, brick, or stone to provide shelter. Some very early 'men' indeed had projecting canine teeth set in very massive jaws that would be quite dangerous weapons, but these have disappeared in modern man, whose dentures will not inflict mortal wounds.

As with other animals, there is of course a bodily physiological basis to man's equipment. It may be summed up in two words, hands and brains. Relieved of the burden of carrying our bodies, our forefeet have developed into delicate instruments capable of an amazing variety of subtle and accurate movements. To control the latter and to link them up with impressions from outside received by the eye and other sense organs we have become possessed of a peculiarly complicated nervous system and an exceptionally big and complicated brain.

The detachable and extracorporeal character of the rest of human equipment has obvious advantages. It is more convenient and more adaptable than other animals' equipment. The latter fits its possessor for living in a particular environment under special conditions. The mountain hare passes the winter comfortably and safely on the snow-clad

hills, thanks to his changeable coat; he would be danger-
ously conspicuous in the warmer valleys. Men can discard
their warm clothing if they move to a hotter climate and can
adjust their costume to the landscape. A rabbit's paws are
good digging tools, but cannot compete with a cat's as
weapons, while feline paws are poor spades. Men can make
both tools and weapons. In brief, an animal's hereditary
equipment is adapted to performing a limited number of
operations in a particular environment. Man's extracorporeal equipment can be adjusted to an almost infinite
number of operations in almost any environment – 'can be',
note, not 'is'.

As against these advantages man has to learn not only to
use but also to make his equipment. A chick soon finds
itself equipped with feathers, wings, beak, and claws. It
certainly has to learn their use – how to keep its feathers
clean, for instance. But this is very simple and will not take
long. A human infant arrives with no such outfit and it will
not grow spontaneously. The round pebbles on the ground
do not in themselves suggest knives. Many processes and
stages must intervene before the wallaby's skin can be
transferred to the child's back as a coat.

Even the simplest tool made out of a broken bough or a
chipped stone is the fruit of long experience – of trials and
errors, impressions noticed, remembered, and compared. The
skill to make it has been acquired by observation, by recol-
lection, and by experiment. It may seem an exaggeration,
but it is yet true to say that any tool is an embodiment of
science. For it is a practical application of remembered, compared, and collected experiences of the same kind as are
systematized and summarized in scientific formulas, descriptions, and prescriptions.

Happily the individual infant is not left to accumulate in
its own person the requisite experience or itself to make all
the trials and mistakes. A baby does not indeed inherit at
birth a physical mechanism of nerve-paths stamped in the
germ-plasm of the race and predisposing it to make automatically and *instinctively* the appropriate bodily movements.

But it is born heir to a *social tradition*. Its parents and elders will teach it how to make and use equipment in accordance with the experience gathered by ancestral generations. And the equipment it uses is itself just a concrete expression of this social tradition. A tool is a social product and man is a social animal.

Because it has so much to learn, a human infant is peculiarly delicate and helpless, and its helplessness lasts longer than with the young of other animals. The physical counterpart of learning is the storing of impressions and the building up of connexions between the various nerve-centres in the brain. Meanwhile the brain must keep on growing. To allow of such growth the skull-bones protecting the infant's brain remain very loosely joined together; only slowly do the junctions (or sutures) knit up. While the brain is thus unprotected it is very vulnerable; an infant can be killed terribly easily.

Helpless infancy being prolonged by these interrelated causes, if the species is to survive, at least one social group must keep together for several years until the infants are reared. In our species the natural family of parents and children is a more stable and durable association than among species whose young mature faster. In practice, however, human families seem generally to live together in larger societies comparable to the herds and packs of gregarious animals. Indeed, man is to some extent a gregarious animal.

Now in human, as in animal, societies the elder generations transmit by example to the younger the collective experience accumulated by the group – what they in turn have learned in like fashion from their elders and parents. Animal education can all be done by example; a chick learns how to peck and what to peck at by copying the hen. For human infants who have so much to learn the imitative method would be fatally slow. In human societies instruction is by precept as well as by example. Human societies have gradually devised tools for communication between their members. In so doing they have brought forth a new sort of equipment which can conveniently be labelled *spiritual*.

Owing to the structure of the larynx, tongue muscles, and other organs human beings, in common with some other creatures, are capable of emitting a very large range of noises that are technically called *articulate sounds*. Living in societies and possessing expansive brains, men have been able to invest these sounds with *conventional meanings*. By agreement sounds become *words*, signals for action and symbols for objects and events familiar to other members of the group. (Note, incidentally, that gestures too can be given meanings in the same way, though less conveniently.) The cries of birds and the bleats of sheep have meanings in this sense; on hearing the signal all members of the flock act in the appropriate way. It means to them at least action and provokes an appropriate response in the creatures' behaviour. Among men spoken words (and of course also gestures) fulfil the same function, but on a tremendously richer scale.

Men's first words may perhaps have carried their meanings on the face of them. Our word 'peewit' simulates the cry of the bird thus named. Paget suggests that the shape assumed by the lips in pronouncing a word may pictorially mimic the thing indicated. In any case such self-explanatory noises would not carry us very far. Most words used even by the lowest savages bear no recognizable similarity to what they denote. They are purely *conventional*; that is, meanings have to be attached to them artificially by some sort of tacit agreement between members of the society using them. The process becomes explicit when a conference of chemists agrees on the name for a new element. It is usually far more subtle.

It is just because the meanings of words are thus conventional that children have to be taught to talk. Learning to talk means essentially learning what meanings the society to which the child belongs attaches to noises that it can make. Incidentally this is a substantial addition to the formidable list of things a poor human infant has to learn. It certainly has a physical counterpart localized in well-defined tracts of the brain. (When these are injured the victim cannot understand what is said to him, i.e., cannot remember the meanings attached to the noises he hears.) Even the earliest 'human' skulls bear marks of a swelling of the brain in the speech regions, so that language seems as old and universal a human trait as tool-making.

Language transforms the process of social tradition; precept accelerates education. By example a mother can show her offspring what to do when a savage beast appears. But many young things find such concrete lessons fatal! By precept, she can explain in advance what to do if the savage beast does appear – a method of instruction much more economical of life! In general by imitating your fellows you learn how to act in a concrete case actually present. With the aid of language you can be taught how to meet an emergency before it arrives. Language is the vehicle for the transmission of the social heritage of experience; by its means experience – the results of trials and errors, what may happen and what to do – is collected and transmitted. Through social inheritance the young partake not only of the experience gained by their physiological ancestors – which might conceivably be transmitted 'in the blood' by biological inheritance – but also that of all their group. Not only can parents describe to their descendants the crises of their lives and how they countered them; all the members of a society using the same conventions in language can tell their fellows what they have seen, heard, suffered, and done. Human experience can be *pooled*. In learning to make and use your equipment you are being initiated into this pooled experience.

Language is more than a mere vehicle of tradition. It affects what is transmitted. The socially accepted meaning of a word (or other symbol) is almost necessarily somewhat *abstract*. The word 'banana' stands for a *class* of objects having in common certain visible, tangible, odorous, and above all edible qualities. In using it we make abstraction of, that is, we ignore as irrelevant, details – the number of spots on its skin, its position on a tree or in a trap and so on – that are qualities of any real individual banana. Every word, however gross and material its meaning, possesses something of this abstract character. By its very nature language involves classification. On the practical side, by example you learn to imitate accurately and in detail a particular set of manipulative movements. By precept you can be taught the sort of movements to perform, but you are still left a little room for variation. In engineering the contrast between apprenticeship and a university education really goes back to this. Language makes tradition rational.

Reasoning has been defined as 'the ability to solve problems without going through a physical process of trial and error'. Instead of trying to do a thing with your hands and perhaps burning your fingers, you do it in your head using *ideas* – images or symbols of the actions which would be involved. Other animals than men certainly behave as if they reasoned in this sense. Faced with a banana midway up a tube, open at both ends but too long to reach up, a chimpanzee discovered how to push the banana with a stick from one end and then grab it from the other, without going through a number of futile movements, by sitting and 'reasoning'. The ape must have imagined the banana in various non-existent positions before it hit upon the trick. But it did not have to go very far from the concrete situation with which it was actually confronted. What is distinctive of human reasoning is that it can go immensely farther from the actual present situation than any other animal's reasoning ever seems to get it. In this distinctive advance language has surely been a very great help.

Reasoning and all that we call thinking, including the chimpanzee's, must involve mental operations with what psychologists call *images*. A visual image, a mental picture of, say, a banana, is always liable to be a picture of a particular banana in a particular setting. A word on the contrary is, as explained, more general and abstract, having eliminated just those accidental features that give individuality to any real banana. Mental images of words (pictures of the sound or of the muscular movements entailed in uttering it) form very convenient counters for thinking with. Thinking with their aid necessarily possesses just that quality of abstractness and generality that animal thinking seems to lack. Men can think, as well as talk, about the class of objects called 'bananas'; the chimpanzee never gets further than 'that banana in that tube'. In this way the social instrument termed language has contributed to what is grandiloquently described as 'man's emancipation from bondage to the concrete'.

To reason is to operate with symbols 'in the head' and not with things or actions in the external world. Conventional words are symbols, though by no means the only kind. You can put such symbols together and combine them in all sorts of ways in your head without moving a muscle. The term 'idea' is generally used for what words and other symbols denote, mean, or refer to. In a sense 'banana' does not refer to anything you can see, touch, smell, or even eat, but only to an idea – the 'ideal banana'. Still this idea is happily represented by plenty of substantial edible bananas, even if none of them quite comes up to the standard of the ideal banana. But in society men make names for and talk about ideas which cannot in fact be seen, smelt, handled or tasted like bananas – ideas such as two-headed eagle, *mana*, electricity, cause. All these are social products, like the words that express them. Societies behave as if they stood for real things. In fact men seem to be impelled to far more strenuous and sustained action by the idea of two-headed eagle, immortality, or freedom than by the most succulent bananas!

Without going in for any metaphysical subtleties, socially approved and sustained ideas that inspire such action must be treated by history as just as real as those which stand for the more substantial objects of archaeological study. In practice ideas form as effective an element in the environment of any human society as do mountains, trees, animals, the weather and the rest of external nature. Societies, that is, behave as if they were reacting to a spiritual environment as well as to a material environment. To deal with this spiritual environment they behave as if they needed a spiritual equipment just as much as they need a material equipment of tools.

This spiritual equipment is not confined to ideas which can be – and are – translated into tools and weapons that work successfully in controlling and transforming external nature, nor yet to the language which is the vehicle for ideas. It includes also what is often termed society's ideology – its superstitions, religious beliefs, loyalties, and artistic ideals. Apparently in pursuit of ideologies and inspired by ideas, men perform actions of a kind never observed among other animals. At least 100,000* years ago those strange-looking creatures termed Neanderthal men ceremonially buried their dead children and relatives, and provided them with food and tools. Every known human society today, however savage, performs rites – often quite painful – and abstains from pleasures that are available to them. The motives for – and stimuli to – these actions and abstentions today, and presumably in the past too, are socially sanctioned ideas of the sort denoted by our words 'immortality', 'magic', 'god'. Such actions are strange to the rest of the animal kingdom, presumably because brutes do not use a language symbolism and hence cannot form such abstract ideas.

Flints over a hundred thousand years old seem to have been fashioned with more care and delicacy than was requisite for mere utilitarian efficiency. It looks as if their author had wanted to make an implement that was not only serviceable but also beautiful. More than 25,000* years ago people began painting their bodies and hanging round their necks shells and beads made with considerable labour. Today all over the world we find people knocking out their teeth, binding their feet, deforming their bodies with corsets, or submitting to some other mutilation in obedience to the dictates of fashion. Such behaviour again seems peculiar to

*Radio-carbon analysis suggests a revision of certain dates, viz. 50,000 for 100,000 and 30,000 for 25,000. – J.G.D.C.

the human species. It results from and gives expression to an ideology.

So with the aid of abstract ideas men have evolved and come to need new stimuli to action beyond the universal urges of hunger, sex, anger, and fear. And these new ideal motives come to be necessary for life itself. An ideology, however remote from obvious biological needs, is found in practice to be biologically useful – that is, favourable to the species' survival. Without such spiritual equipment not only do societies tend to disintegrate, but the individuals composing them may just stop bothering to keep alive. The 'destruction of religion' among primitive peoples is always cited by experts as a major cause in their extinction in contact with white civilization. Of the Eddystone Islanders Rivers wrote: 'By stopping the practice of head-hunting the new [i.e. British] rulers were abolishing an institution which had its roots in the religious life of the people. The natives have responded to that by becoming apathetic. They have ceased to increase sufficiently to prevent the diminution of the island's population.'

Evidently societies of men 'cannot live by bread alone'. But if 'every word that proceedeth out of the mouth of God' does not directly or indirectly promote the growth and the biological and economic prosperity of the society that sanctifies them, that society and its god with it will vanish ultimately. It is this natural selection that guarantees that *in the long run* the ideals of a society are 'just translations and inversions in men's minds of the material'. The religion of the Eddystone Islanders provided a motive for living and kept an economic system functioning. But in practice head-hunting kept down the numbers of the islanders. So it made improvement in material equipment superfluous, and eventually left the islanders a prey to British conquerors. It is from the standpoint of the social group that an ideology is judged by historical selection. But the verdict may be long delayed.

An ideology is evidently a social product. Not only are the words which support its ideas produced by life in society and unthinkable apart therefrom; the ideas, too, owe their reality, their power to influence action, to their acceptance by society. Seemingly absurd beliefs can win and maintain credence provided every member of the group accepts them and has been taught to believe in them from childhood. It will never occur to anyone to question a belief universally held. Few of us have any better grounds for believing in germs than for believing in witches. Our society inculcates the former belief and ridicules the latter, but other societies reverse the judgements. Of course a number of acknowledged experts have seen germs under the microscope. But still more experts in medieval Europe and in Negro Africa have seen witches functioning. The superiority of our belief is in the long run established if antiseptics and vaccines succeed better in preventing deaths, and so permitting social growth, than do incantations and witch-burnings.

Not the least important function of an ideology is to hold society together and lubricate its workings. And in this guise at least ideology reacts on technology and material equipment. For, like spiritual equipment, material equipment is a social product not only in the sense that it springs from social tradition. In practice the production and use of tools also requires cooperation between members of a society. Today it is self-evident that modern Europeans and Americans get food, housing, clothing, and satisfaction for other needs only as a result of the cooperation of a vast and highly complicated productive organization or *economy*. Cut off from this we should be very uncomfortable and should probably starve. Theoretically 'primitive man', with simpler wants and more rudimentary equipment, could shift for himself alone. In practice even the rudest savages live in groups organized to cooperate in getting food and preparing equipment as well as in performing ceremonies. Among the Australian aborigines, for instance, we find a division of labour between the sexes in hunting and gathering as well as in making implements and vessels. There is also a division of the product of this cooperative activity.

Even the student of material culture has to study a

society as a cooperative organization for producing means
to satisfy its needs, for reproducing itself – and for producing
new needs. He wants to see its economy working. But its
economy affects, and is affected by, its ideology. The
'materialist concept of history' asserts that the economy
determines the ideology. It is safer and more accurate to
repeat in other words what has been stated already: in the
long run an ideology can survive only if it facilitates the
smooth and efficient functioning of the economy. If it
hamper that, the society – and with it the ideology – must
perish in the end. But the reckoning may be long postponed.
An obsolete ideology can hamper an economy and impede
its change for longer than Marxists admit.

Ideally social tradition is one: the man of today is
theoretically heir to all the ages, and inherits the accumulated experience of all his forerunners. This ideal is, however, far from realization. Mankind does not form one
society today, but is divided into many distinct societies;
all the available evidence suggests that this division was not
less but even greater in the past as far as archaeology can
penetrate. Each society may have not only different language conventions, but also equally different conventions
about spiritual and even material equipment; for each has
preserved, transmitted, and built up its own peculiar tradition.

The babel of tongues is painfully obvious today; it will
suffice here to recall that each language is the product of a
social tradition, and itself reacts upon other traditional
modes of behaving and of thinking. Less familiar is the way
in which divergences of tradition affect even material culture. Americans use knives and forks differently from
Englishmen, and the difference in usage finds concrete
expression in subtle differences in the shapes of the knives
and forks themselves. In Ireland and Wales rural workers
use long-handled shovels; in England and Scotland the
handles are much shorter. The work accomplished is in each
case the same, though the handling of the tool is, of course,
different. The differences are purely conventional. They

reflect divergences in the social tradition. As such divergences are concretely expressed in the forms of the tool employed, they fall within the purview of archaeology, and can be followed into a remote past when no written records permit the recognition of linguistic differences.

Man-like creatures appear some four to five hundred thousand years ago dispersed from England to China, and from Germany to the Transvaal. We can only assume that they lived in social groups and that these were small, sparsely scattered, and mutually isolated. Under such conditions we should expect that each would develop rather different traditions in accordance with the varying climatic and other environmental conditions with which it had to contend. And, in fact, among the earliest undoubted products of human handiwork in the oldest certain tools, regional differences in the methods of shaping stones and in the forms given to the resultant implements can be detected. They are seemingly arbitrary, not conditioned either by the nature of the material or by the use to which the product must be put. Like knives and forks in England and America, and shovels in England and Wales, these differences in technique and form must correspond to divergent traditions developed and practised by distinct societies – bands, hordes, troops, clans, tribes, or what you will. As time goes on and the archaeological record becomes fuller, more and more differences can be detected and affect an ever widening range of concrete products. One of the principal aims of prehistoric archaeology has been to define the several social traditions expressed in the differences among their relics.

Archaeologists classify the objects of their study not only by function into knives, axes, huts, tombs, and so on, but also into different 'types' of knives, axes, dwellings, and graves. The several types of knife or tomb each fulfil roughly the same function; the differences between them repose upon divergences in the social tradition prescribing the methods of their preparation and use. In each functional class archaeologists can distinguish a variety of types current over a restricted area at a given period in archaeological

time. The totality of recognized types current simultaneously in a given area is termed a 'culture'. Archaeology is
liable to become a study of cultures rather than of culture!

The variety of types is testimony to the multiplicity of
social traditions governing their manufacture and employment. The remarkable uniformity of types in a given local
and chronological group or 'culture' just discloses the
uniformity and rigidity of the traditions actuating their
makers. As the peculiarities of the component types are
determined by convention rather than by function, the
culture must correspond to a social group which sanctifies
the distinctive conventions and carries the social tradition.
It would be rash to try to define precisely what sort of social
group corresponds to the archaeologist's 'culture'. Since
language is such an important vehicle in the formation and
transmission of social tradition, the group distinguished by
possession of a distinct 'culture' might be expected also to
speak a distinct language.

Now it is *a priori* likely that divergences in linguistic
conventions are at least as old as divergences in material
equipment or burial rites. The extraordinary multiplicity of
distinct languages or mutually incomprehensible dialects
among savages who have remained near the economic level
of pleistocene men gives some positive justification for this
assumption. The aboriginal Australians, estimated as some
200,000 in all, spoke no less than five hundred languages.
In the 150,000 square miles of California Kroeber dis-
tinguishes thirty-one families of languages and at least 135
dialects. Again, when the first written documents begin to
reveal men's speech, we find several widely divergent
linguistic traditions established in the tiny areas we can at
first survey – Egyptians, Sumerian, Semitic (Akkadian),
and Elamite, with hints of others in personal and geographical names. As writing spreads, ever new tongues are
revealed – Nasili, Luvian, Hurrian, Proto-Hattic, Pheoni-
cian, Chinese, Greek, Persian, Urartian, Etruscan, Latin,
Celtic ... to name only the most notable. The tendency
for the traditional conventions of language to diverge is still

observable even where the English language is standardized by a widely-circulated printed literature. 'Next Friday'
in England becomes 'Friday first' in Scotland; when you
cross the Atlantic 'lorry' must be translated 'truck'. The
tendency which can resist the standardizing effect of writing
and the unprecedented facilities for travel, must have
worked more rapidly and more effectively before writing
and regular means of communication were available.
Linguistic divergences must be just as old as the cultural
divergences traceable directly in the archaeological record.

Nevertheless culture and language need not coincide. The
differences in equipment between Denmark, England,
France, and Germany are insignificant in comparison with
the differences between Danish, English, French, and German. Material equipment is more permanent than spoken
words; its preparation and use can be learned by example
as well as by precept. Useful devices can – and do – keep
linguistic frontiers. But if the culture does not necessarily
represent a linguistic group, it is generally a local group
occupying a continuous geographical area.

Regarding cultures as geographical units, the differences
between them appear less arbitrary and more significant.
They can be partially explained as adjustments to different
environments. The various species of lower animals are
generally adapted to life under particular conditions of
climate, soil, and plant-life; many of their differentiae, the
features that distinguish one species from another, have
been established by natural selection precisely because they
proved favourable to survival under such a specific set of
geographical conditions: that, for instance, is obviously
true of the mountain hare with his variable coat, and the
lowland hares that do not turn white in winter. The human
species is not physiologically adapted to any particular
environment. Its adaptation is secured by its extracorporeal equipment of tools, clothes, houses, and the rest. By
devising suitable equipment a human society can fit itself
to live under almost all conditions. Fire, clothing, houses,

and an appropriate diet enable men to endure arctic cold and tropic heat equally well.

Material culture is thus largely a response to an environment: it consists of the devices evolved to meet needs evoked by particular climatic conditions, to take advantage of local sources of food and to secure protection against wild beasts, floods, or other nuisances infesting a given region. Different societies have been prompted to invent different devices and to discover how to use different natural substances for food, fuel, shelter, and tools. Forest dwellers can develop wood-working, carpenters' tools, log-cabins, and carved orna-ments; steppe folk must make larger use of bone, basketry, and leather, can do without axes and dwell perforce in skin tents or in subterranean shelters.

In response to the promptings of its own peculiar environment, each society may be expected to evolve distinctive processes and devices. But luckily the appropriate inventions and discoveries are not confined to the regions where they were evolved. Societies may migrate to regions which have evoked other responses in other societies. The migrant society does not throw away its traditional equipment to adopt that appropriate to its new home; more usually the immigrant and the native traditions blend. Again inventions and discoveries do transgress the boundaries of locality and linguistic convention; they can be – and are – *diffused* from one society to another, despite all obstacles of space and language. The richness of our own cultural tradi-tion is due very largely to diffusion, to the adoption by our progressive societies of ideas created by many distinct groups in response to the diverse conditions and oppor-tunities of many regions. For instance, as staple vegetable foods we have added to the wheat, barley, and fruits of Hither Asia, rice from East Asia, maize, potatoes, marrows, and other plants from North America, bananas from tropi-cal Africa, and so on; our alimentary tradition has been enriched from every quarter of the globe.

Prehistory and history do indeed show how culture grows more and more diversified through the differentiation of societies in response to special stimuli – geographical, technical, or ideological. What is, however, even more striking is the growth of intercourse and interchange between societies. If the streams of cultural tradition go on multiplying they none the less tend to converge more and more, and to flow into a single river. A main stream with ever-growing emphasis dominates the whole drainage system to canalize the waters of fresh springs. Cultures are tending to merge into culture.

If our own culture can claim to be in the main stream, it is only because our cultural tradition has captured and made tributary a larger volume of once parallel traditions. While in historical times the main stream flows from Mesopotamia and Egypt through Greece and Rome, Byzantium and Islam, to Atlantic Europe and America, it has been repeatedly swollen by the diversion into it of currents from Indian, Chinese, Mexican, and Peruvian civilizations, and from countless barbarisms and savageries. Chinese and Indian civilizations have indeed not failed to absorb currents from one another and from farther west. But, on the whole, they have hitherto discharged these into placid unchanging backwaters. The civilizations of the Mayas and the Incas, on the other hand, have ceased to run altogether, save in so far as their waters are carried on in the main stream of modern Atlantic civilization. In the sequel we shall be frankly concerned primarily with the course of the main stream, even though we have to diverge from time to time to trace its enrichment from lateral tributaries.

If the whole long process disclosed in the archaeological and literary records be surveyed, a single directional trend is most obvious in the economic sphere in the methods whereby the most progressive societies secure a livelihood. In this domain it will be possible to recognize radical and indeed revolutionary innovations, each followed by such increases in population that, were reliable statistics available, each would be reflected by a conspicuous kink in the population graph. These revolutions can accordingly be used to mark off phases or stages in the historical process which may be summarized in advance as follows.

(1) The story begins perhaps 500,000, perhaps 250,000 years ago, with man emerging as a rare animal and a *food-gatherer*, which lived like any other beast of prey, a parasite on other creatures by catching and collecting what food nature happened to provide. This *gathering* economy, corresponding to what Morgan terms *savagery*, provided the sole source of livelihood open to any human society during nearly 98 per cent of humanity's sojourn on this planet throughout the whole of what archaeologists call the *Palaeolithic* or *Old Stone Age*, and geologists name the *pleistocene*. It is still practised by a few backward and isolated societies in the jungles of Malaya or Central Africa, in the deserts of north-western Australia and South Africa, and in the Arctic regions.

(2) Perhaps not more than 8,000* years ago, some societies, first apparently in the Near East, by actively co-operating with nature began to increase the supplies of food available by cultivating plants and often also by breeding domestic animals. The new *food-producing* economy is distinctive of what Morgan calls *barbarism*, and is represented in its simplest form in what archaeologists term the *Neolithic* or *New Stone Age*. But in the economic sense, at least, neolithic does not correspond to a period of time, since the Maoris of New Zealand were still neolithic in equipment and economy in A.D. 1800. Moreover, many societies that economically are still barbarian have learned to use iron or bronze tools and weapons, although the full industrial use, at least, of bronze was possible only after the next economic revolution.

(3) This was initiated in the alluvial valleys of the Nile, the Tigris–Euphrates, and the Indus about five thousand years ago, with the transformation of some riverside villages into cities. Society persuaded or compelled the farmers to produce a surplus of foodstuffs over and above their domestic requirements, and by concentrating this surplus used it to

*For 8,000 years, read between 10,000 and 12,000 years. – J.G.D.C.

support a new *urban* population of specialized craftsmen, merchants, priests, officials, and clerks. Writing was, as will be shown, a necessary by-product of this urban revolution which ushers in *civilization* and initiates the historical record.

(*a*) The first two thousand years of civilization coincide with what archaeologists describe as the *Bronze Age*, because copper and bronze were the only metals used for tools and weapons. Both are so expensive as normally to be available only to gods, kings, chiefs, and the employees of temples and States. The social surplus, derived primarily from subsistence agriculture by irrigation, was concentrated in the hands of a relatively narrow circle of priests and officials, whose limited expenditure limited also the growth of the urban industrial and commercial population.

(*b*) The *Early Iron Age*; initiated by the divulgation of an economical method of producing wrought iron about 1200 B.C., meant the popularization of metal equipment. At the same time in the Near East the invention of an alphabetical script popularized writing, which had hitherto been a mystery confined to a small class of learned clerks, while after 700 B.C. small change in coined money facilitated retail transactions. In the *Classical* or *Greco-Roman* economy, using these popular innovations combined with the facilities for cheap transport offered by the Mediterranean, the surplus, now partly derived from specialized farming, was more widely distributed among an upper middle class of merchants, financiers, and capitalist farmers. This permitted a notable growth of population, at least in the Mediterranean basin, which was, however, ultimately checked by the relative impoverishment or actual enslavement of the primary producers and artisans.

(*c*) Feudalism in Europe tied to the soil the hitherto semi-nomadic barbarian cultivator, ultimately increasing the productivity of the temperate forest zone. But it emancipated him from chattel slavery of the Roman pattern, while the *guild system* secured to the artisan as well as to the merchant not only freedom but an unprecedented economic status. So eventually trade and industry, superimposed upon a more intensive and settled agriculture and now using water power, promoted an unparalleled growth in the European population.

(d) Finally the discovery of the New World and of seaways to India and the Far East opened to Atlantic Europe a world market. In exchange for mass-produced popular goods, societies on the Atlantic seaboard were enabled to draw upon the food stock of the whole world, itself augmented by an increasingly scientific rural economy. The sharp upward bend of the population graph in England between 1750 and 1800 not only testifies to the biological success of the new *bourgeois capitalist* economy, but also justifies applying the term industrial revolution to its first phases.

2

PALAEOLITHIC SAVAGERY

THE first chapter of human history is still interwoven with natural history. Prehistoric anthropology studies what is to be known of man's physical evolution, the bodily changes in the human animal. Prehistoric archaeology shows how man became human by labour and studies the improvement of his extracorporeal equipment. Both the anthropological and the archaeological records cover a span of time roughly a hundred times as long as that covered by the oldest written record. The emergence of man and the manufacture of the first tools may be put somewhere about five hundred thousand years ago. That is the age assigned on one view to the beginning of the pleistocene epoch, the last volume in the geological record before the holocene or recent, which may begin ten thousand years ago and is far from ended.

Such figures are only approximate and are in any case so large that they mean relatively little to most people. What is more certain, and perhaps more helpful, is that man witnessed very substantial changes in the landscape and the configuration of his planet's surface. For instance, during part of the pleistocene Britain was joined to the continent of Europe. Much of what is now the North Sea must have been dry land, and men could have followed the equivalent of the Thames till it joined an early Rhine. Though the chief mountain ranges had already been uplifted before the first 'men' began to make tools, men lived to see quite important hills thrown up by the folding of the earth's crust. One school, indeed, holds that such gigantic cracks as the Rift Valley in Africa opened up when men were already inhabiting that continent.

Catastrophic changes in climate undoubtedly affected the whole earth; three or four Ice Ages followed one another in high latitudes, and were accompanied by periods of torrential rain in now arid sub-tropical zones. The snow caps and glaciers that today cover the high Norwegian mountains grew slowly bigger, crept down the valleys, and eventually spread out in a huge ice sheet over the plain of northern Europe. Ice caps developed on the Scottish Highlands, too, and thence ice sheets spread out over Ireland and over England to join the Scandinavian ice sheet to the east. The Alpine glaciers likewise crept downstream. The Rhône glacier that now terminates high above the Lake of Geneva flowed down till it reached almost to Lyon in France. Now glaciers are not rivers that have frozen, but rivers of ice that flow at not more than ten or twenty feet a year. In Greenland and Antarctica we can still see ice sheets like those that covered England and northern Europe in the pleistocene; they 'flow' at the rate of about a quarter of a mile per annum. So one can guess how long it took for the Scottish ice to reach Cambridge or the Scandinavian ice to cover Berlin. And the process of retreat, the melting of the huge ice masses, was almost as slow.

But melt they did. The climate grew warm enough for hippopotami and tigers to live in Norfolk, and for rhododendrons, now at home in Portugal, to grow in the Tyrol. And then the ice spread once more, only to contract again. Indeed, most geologists admit four major Ice Ages or glacial periods separated by three inter-glacial warm intervals. Some authorities would, in fact, admit a still larger number of glacials and inter-glacials.

Meanwhile man witnessed new species of animals emerge and become established by natural selection, sometimes only to die out. In the first inter-glacial some very curious creatures – the sabre-toothed tiger, the little three-toed horse, and the southern elephant – survivors from the pliocene, were still competing with newer varieties that eventually replaced them. To withstand the cold of the ice ages species of elephant and rhinoceros – the mammoth and the woolly rhinoceros – acquired hairy coats. Such variations were presumably established by a process of natural selection extending over many generations – and elephants are notoriously slow breeders.

The most curious of all the species emerging was, however, Man himself. The first 'men' differ so radically in their bony structure from any race living today that zoologists classify them in distinct species or genera and refuse to them the scientific name for modern man, *Homo sapiens*. Such can be called *hominids*,* 'man-like creatures', or just 'men' in inverted commas. The oldest fossil hominids exhibit many 'simian traits', features proper to apes that modern men can do without for reasons hinted at on p. 20 and more fully explained in *Man Makes Himself*.

> *Pithecanthropus*, the ape-man of Java, had a very thick but very small skull with a cranial capacity varying from 1,100 to 750 cubic centimetres – on an average about midway between that of chimpanzees and modern man. His forehead sloped back behind a bony visor or torus that protected the eyes and supported the massive architecture of skull and jaw. But a rudimentary swelling over the area devoted to speech in

*The picture of hominid evolution has undergone major changes in recent years. So far from there being intermediate links between apes and men, it begins to look as though we must go far back in geological time to find their common prototype.

Much more clearly defined notions exist about the hominid forms present in the Villafranchian or early pleistocene and in the middle pleistocene periods. Great attention has been paid to the Australopithecines, which combine small brains with an upright posture, since their forelimbs would have been free to manipulate tools. On the other hand the discovery in bed I at Olduvai in east central Africa of part of the skull of a large-brained hominid casts doubt on the idea that *Australopithecus* stood directly in the line of human descent and made the tools with which its remains have occasionally been associated.

Middle pleistocene deposits have yielded a much more convincing body of hominid fossils in the *Pithecanthropus* group having brains of between 1100 and 750 cubic centimetres capacity. The association of Pithecanthropine remains with artifacts has not yet been established in Java where the group was first found, but discoveries in north Africa and at Chou-kou-tien in north China leave no doubt about the essentially human character of *Pithecanthropus*. – J.G.D.C.

our brains shows that Java man was already talking and investing sounds with socially approved meanings. But his jowl was disproportionately large and his jaw chinless. *Sinanthropus*, the generic name for the hominids found in the cave of Chou-kou-tien, near Peking, exhibits the same sort of peculiarities.

Thus in lower pleistocene times the anthropological record disclosed, as might be anticipated, the emergence of species and genera intermediate in some ways between apes and men in the full sense of that term. The extreme rarity of documents illustrating this phase of evolution is significant. In digging drains or railway cuttings or other excavations through the gravels of ancient rivers or the debris of pleistocene ice-sheets, or where erosion has laid bare old seashores and river banks, the fossilized bones of sabre-toothed tigers, rhinoceros, and mammoth may often be picked up. But down to the approach of the last ice age only four incomplete fragments of fossil hominids are known in the whole of Europe, although scientists and amateurs are everywhere on the look-out for 'missing links'. Four fossils to represent the hominid population of our Continent during say 200,000 years! Asia has proved more productive. Java men and China men combined now take us into the twenties. Still the rarity of human fossils does justify the conclusion that during the first millennium or so of their existence 'men' were rare animals. The minute groups of hominids cannot have seemed dangerous competitors to the contemporary mammoths, cave-bears, tigers, and hippopotami.

This conclusion is not really falsified by the evidence of archaeology. It is true that cartloads of tools, made by early hominids, can be picked up on the high veldt where once the Vaal and Zambesi flowed. Admittedly museums' cellars in France and England are crammed with implements dug up in equally ancient gravels. But a single hominid might in a day make, use, and discard three or four such tools. The many tons of them spread over a couple of hundred thousand years of 365 days do not attest a vast multitude of tool makers.

They do tell all that is to be learned directly of the development of that extracorporeal equipment that was to make its users masters of all the brutes. Admittedly the first beginnings of that development elude the grasp of archaeology. A critical moment was when men learned to control and later to initiate the chemical process of combustion – to use the terrible red flower from which other jungle dwellers flee in terror. But evidence for the use of fire is unobtainable in the conditions under which the oldest archaeological remains are normally unearthed. Still in the earliest known 'home', the cave of Chou-kou-tien, near ꞈking, charred bones indicate that even that odd hominid *Sinanthropus* was controlling and using fire. Similarly the first tools must have been natural objects only slightly modified to serve human needs. In so far as they were of wood, these have perished irretrievably. Those made of durable stone are so like natural chips as to be scarcely recognizable. The archaeological controversy about what are termed 'eoliths' centres around just such doubtful products.

When in lower,* or on a modern view only in early middle, pleistocene times unmistakable tools, stones patently shaped in an intelligent and purposeful way, do appear, their use is still uncertain. Probably each had many uses; tools were not yet specialized as with us to specific ends, but the same roughly-chipped flint served all purposes from dispatching a tiger to scraping the hairs off his hide or digging up roots. Gradual improvements can be detected as traditional skill was slowly accumulated; instead of just knocking off coarse chips by banging one stone against another, some men found out how to detach neater flakes by

*The earliest well-defined stone industries yet recognized, those from Villafranchian deposits in northern and east-central Africa, comprise chopper-like tools made by detaching a few flakes from one or two directions to form an irregular working edge. – J.G.D.C.

blows with a billet of wood. And we can observe methods of flint working diverging in different areas as divergent traditions grow up among distinct social groups.

Throughout Africa, in western Europe, and in southern India the favourite and most carefully shaped tools were made by knocking bits off a large lump or *core* till this was reduced to one of four or five standard forms. The products can all be classified as *core tools* and are currently designated hand-axes. In Europe during the ice age and in northern Eurasia we meet on the other hand almost exclusively what are termed *flake-tools*. Their makers do not seem to have cared much what shape was ultimately assumed by the parent lump or core; they were primarily interested in the flakes detached and trimmed these up to form implements, less rigorously standardized than hand-axes. Finally the tools made by China man and the earliest implements (termed Soan) from northern India and the Malay Peninsula cannot be classed as either core or flake tools, but are regarded as representative of a distinct 'chopper' or 'pebble' cycle.

The divergent traditions thus revealed no doubt reflect different responses to differing environments. But they are essentially conventional and conditioned by distinct social traditions. No factor of climate or habitat obviously obliges a tool maker to choose the core rather than the flakes detached from it. And no less striking than the divergences between the main cycles are the uniformity and continuity within each. Notably in the core-tool province the same peculiar forms were given to hand-axes from the Cape of Good Hope to the Mediterranean and from the Atlantic coasts to central India. For a couple of glacial cycles we can detect only minor variations and improvements on a small assortment of traditional forms. And in each part of the province these variations succeed one another in the same order. It looks as if some sort of intercourse were being maintained among the widely-scattered groups so that ideas were interchanged and technical experience was pooled.

Finally, many of the later tools, particularly of the hand-axe class, display extraordinary care and delicacy of workmanship. One feels that more trouble has been expended on their production than was needed just to make them work. Their authors were trying to make something not only useful, but also beautiful. If so, the tools in question are really works of art, expressions of aesthetic feeling.* But this expression was conditioned by the traditions of the group that used hand-axes. Some not quite unambiguous indications (an imperfect jaw of doubtful geological age from Kanam in Kenya and the occipital bone of a skull found in a gravel pit at Swanscombe, Kent) suggest that the hand-axe makers may have been more like ourselves than *Pithecanthropus* or *Sinanthropus*; they may have been our evolutionary ancestors, a status some would deny to the fossil men of Asia and even to *Homo heidelbergensis*, the proud but unhappily unknown possessor of a massive fossil jaw found in a deep sandpit at Mauer in Württemberg.

It may be assumed that all early hominids were just gatherers. Hand-axes would serve as well for digging up edible roots as for hunters' weapons. *Sinanthropus* was almost certainly carnivorous; the animal bones from his cave seem to have been split deliberately by the hominid. Among the bones thus treated are those of hominids too. So *Sinanthropus* may have been a cannibal. Probably all hominids were in fact omnivorous; they ate whatever they could get. Not the least important lesson they had to learn by experience and transmit by social tradition was what was safely edible and what was poisonous. Their mistakes are not recorded in the archaeological record, but the

*The new skull from bed II at Olduvai, which yielded hand-axes, had pronounced brow-ridges and stood in an evolutionary sense somewhere between *Pithecanthropus* and *Homo sapiens*. The skull from Steinheim, Germany, had pronounced brow-ridges and that from Swanscombe, England, which closely resembled it, was deficient in the frontal region. The brain size of the Steinheim and Swanscombe skulls fell within the range of modern men. It looks as though the hand-axe people, though retaining some Pithecanthropine traits, showed a marked development in brain size. – J.G.D.C.

simplest surviving savages have learned the necessary
lessons and embodied them in their traditions. The determination of edible plants and animals, the discovery of
ways of collecting or catching them, the recognition of the
appropriate times and seasons were steps towards science.
In jungle lore lie the roots of botany and zoology, of
astronomy and climatology, while the control of fire and
the manufacture of tools initiate the traditions that emerge
as physics and chemistry.

Only towards the close of middle pleistocene times, on
one chronology about 140,000 years ago, does the archaeologist's picture of hominid life become clear enough to
allow an economy to be tentatively sketched. As the last
great ice age was approaching, men were sufficiently well
equipped to evict other denizens and themselves to find
shelter in caves. There we find true homes.

The best-known groups thus inhabiting Europe all belong
to a curious race termed Neanderthal and perhaps specifi-
cally distinct from *Homo sapiens*. Though their brain-cases
are as capacious as those of many Europeans today, there
is a huge bony vizor or torus above the eyes instead of two
eyebrow-ridges; the forehead is retreating, the jowl enormous, a chin lacking. The head was so balanced on the
spine that it hung forward; the structure of legs and feet
permitted only a shuffling gait.*

Many authorities believe that Neanderthal man represents a distinct species of humanity specialized and adapted
for living under Arctic conditions and that the species
became extinct when those conditions passed away.
Whether any 'Neanderthal blood runs in the veins' of
Europeans or other modern races is doubted. Hominids
exhibiting many Neanderthal features, such as the supra-
orbital torus, retreating forehead and excessively heavy jowl,
have been found in recent years in Palestine, South Africa,

* It is important to note that re-examination of the skeleton of
La Chappelle-aux-Saints suggests that the individual in question was
distorted by arthritis. It is now maintained that healthy Neanderthal
men stood upright. – J.G.D.C.

and Java. While some anthropologists incline to regard
these as representing in a general way a stage in the
evolution of *Homo sapiens*, others regard most of them as
aberrant branches from the main human stem that had
gone up an evolutionary blind alley and then died out.
But some of the Palestinian fossils admittedly exhibit traits
such as a rudimentary chin that suggest at least hybridiza-
tion with *Homo sapiens*, and men of the latter type did exist,
making flake tools, during the last interglacial.

Whatever their biological status, Neanderthalers and
their other middle palaeolithic contemporaries must be
credited with positive contributions to human culture. All
possessed a more varied and differentiated equipment than
their predecessors. It includes specialized weapons (represented by spear-heads), as well as distinct tools for scraping
and chopping. Most of these are made from flakes. Rarely
in Europe, regularly in Hither Asia and Africa these are
made by an ingenious process, known as the Levallois
technique, requiring much foresight and scientific planning
ahead; for the desired shape was blocked out on the core
before the flake was detached.

In the case of the European Neanderthalers we know a
good deal of their economy and culture as well as of their
skeletons and implements. They lived by hunting, principally the mammoths, woolly rhinoceros, and other thick-
skinned beasts that browsed on the tundras along the
margins of the European ice-sheet and in Siberia. Evidently
such big game could not be pursued profitably by isolated
families. The Neanderthalers must have hunted together as
organized packs, and, however small these may have been,
their economy required some social organization.

For all their primitive bodies they needed a spiritual
culture too. For their dead relatives they devised and
socially sanctified burial rites which they perhaps fondly
hoped would somehow reverse or cancel death. They buried
the bodies in specially excavated graves, sometimes placing
stones to protect them from the pressure of the earth. The
graves were normally dug in the caves that the living used

for homes. Sometimes they are situated near to hearths as
if in the hope that the fire's heat would restore to the cold
corpse the warmth of life. The bodies are placed in deliberately chosen attitudes, generally doubled up. In one
grave the skull had been separated from the trunk. Joints
of meat and implements were regularly buried with the
corpse. Neanderthalers must have imagined that life somehow continued so that the dead experienced the same needs
as the living. From middle palaeolithic times ceremonial
burial can be traced continuously, till today the wreaths,
the nodding plumes, and the wake embody a complex of
ideas which, however much altered in the transmission, are
at least a hundred thousand years old.

This was not all. In some Alpine caves heaps of bones
and skulls, particularly of cave bears, have been found
deliberately, one might say ceremonially, arranged. The
arrangement suggests the rituals still performed by hunting
tribes in Siberia to avert the wrath of the bear spirit and
ensure the multiplication of bears to hunt. Perhaps then
we have here proof of hunting magic, if not worship, before
the last ice age. In any case even the rude Neanderthaler
had an ideology.

Despite the seemingly unfavourable conditions prevailing
we get the impression that humanity had multiplied. In
any case we have from Europe at least five times as many
middle palaeolithic as lower palaeolithic skeletons, though
the phase lasted perhaps only a fifth as long. But the
Neanderthal stock and its industrial traditions too seem to
vanish abruptly from Europe at the close of the first phase
of the last ice age. In the more genial interval which ensued
modern men appear already fully formed and with skeletons
at least that would be hard to distinguish from recent
specimens in an anatomical museum.

Men of modern type, fully fledged 'wise men', appear
in the anthropological record much about the same time
not only in Europe but also in North and East Africa,
in Palestine, and even in China (in an upper cave at
Chou-kou-tien). They emerge already differentiated into

several distinct varieties or races. Even in Europe anatomists distinguish the faintly negroid *Grimaldi* race, the tall *Crô-Magnon* stock, a shorter *Combe Capelle* variety sometimes round-headed, perhaps a Brûnn type exhibiting possibly Neanderthaloid traits, while a later skull from Chancelade is said to resemble that of modern Eskimos. Such variety among the earliest modern men enhances the plausibility of the theory that direct ancestors of *Homo sapiens* had been evolving earlier in the pleistocene, even though most earlier fossil documents so far authenticated are more like Neanderthalers.

In the archaeological record modern men appear in the upper palaeolithic enormously better equipped than any group so far distinguished in lower or middle palaeolithic times. The new equipment is found from the first differentiated by divergent social traditions, doubtless in response to varying environments, so that archaeologists can henceforth distinguish several cultures corresponding to several social groups. The best-defined of these* are (1) the Châtelperronian of France; (2) the Aurignacian found in Hither Asia, the Crimea, the Balkans, central Europe and, after the Châtelperronian, in France; (3) the Gravettian of the north Pontic zone, which succeeds the Aurignacian in central Europe and France and spreads to England and Spain (all the foregoing used to be treated as mere phases of a single culture termed Aurignacian); (4) the Aterian of Africa; and (5) possibly later the Capsian in North Africa. Subsequently other local cultures crystallize out, notably the Solutrean and the Magdalenian in western Europe (these are strictly local cultures, though their names, like Aurignacian, are used in the older text-books to designate periods within the upper palaeolithic). None of these social groups defined by archaeology demonstrably coincides with any of the races distinguished by anatomists; for instance,

---

*More precise information is available about the upper palaeolithic cultures. The Gravettian for example is strongly represented in Italy. The Capsian has been shown by radio-carbon analysis to be of mesolithic age. – J.G.D.C.

Grimaldians and Crô-Magnons alike used a Gravettian equipment in the famous Grottes de Grimaldi near Mentone.

Common to all these upper palaeolithic societies are the use of bone and ivory for tools and distinctive traditions in flint-work. All had learned how to prepare a lump of flint or obsidian so that a whole series of long narrow flakes, termed blades, could be struck off a single core once the long preliminaries had been executed. The method was more economical in material and, in the long run, in labour too than even the Levallois technique, which, however, was still employed extensively by the Aterians and other societies in Africa, Siberia, and China. Moreover, common to all upper palaeolithic groups in the Old World is an ingenious instrument termed a *burin* or graver – a blade pointed by removing a facet along one edge in such a way that it can be repeatedly repointed by simply removing another facet.

Economically upper palaeolithic societies must still be designated savage inasmuch as they relied for a livelihood on hunting, fishing, and collecting. But their methods and equipment have undergone an almost revolutionary improvement. From the collective experience of ancestral generations they have learned how to take full advantage of natural conditions and how to manufacture ingenious new engines.

The several hunting communities who occupied Europe had still to brave the severities of a subarctic climate; for the great ice sheet still covered the northern plains, though the mountain glaciers had retreated, albeit only temporarily. But, equipped to support these disabilities, they entered a land of steppes and tundras where vast herds of mammoths, reindeer, bison, wild cattle, and horses offered an easy prey to organized hunts. On the plains of south Russia and central Europe the Gravettians pitched their camps along the routes the herds of big game must follow on seasonal migrations from winter to summer pastures. Along the Don the sites were cleverly chosen in river valleys which provided shelter against blizzards but adjacent to the mouths of lateral gullies which could be used as natural corrals to trap the herds. Immense piles of bones testify to the success rewarding the choice of such locations.

Artificial protection against the cold was provided by tents, presumably of skins, or even by substantial 'houses', dug in the soft loess soil and roofed by skins and turfs similar to those inhabited by arctic hunters today. As wood was scarce the hunters burned bones to keep them warm – the bone heaps may take the place of wood-piles – and could construct fireplaces provided with sunken flues to supply a draught to this fuel. They made clothes of skins, since the scrapers for preparing these and needles for sewing them together are found. A statuette from Mal'ta in Sibera seems to be clad in a trousered suit of furs such as Eskimos wear.

In the Dordogne and on the slopes of the Pyrenees and Cantabrian mountains ample caves offered shelter to Aurignacians and Gravettians who hunted on the adjacent plateaux and plains. Yearly the salmon ran up the rivers to breed, and the Magdalenians at least had learned to catch the fish with hook and line or spear them with 'harpoons' of reindeer antler.

Upper palaeolithic hunting tackle had been enriched by many fresh inventions. The Aterians and Capsians in Africa certainly, their European and Asiatic contemporaries probably, employed the bow,* the first composite mechanism devised by man; the total energy gradually expended by the archer's muscles is stored up in the bent wood or horn so that the whole can be concentrated at one point and released simultaneously. The Magdalenians and probably also other upper palaeolithic societies used the spear-

*The first certain evidence for the use of the bow consists of wooden examples from the mesolithic of northern Europe, but notched wooden shafts from a reindeer-hunters' site in Schleswig-Holstein suggest that the device had probably come into use before the end of the Ice Age. The Aterians of North Africa made barbed and tanged points that resemble arrow-heads, but there is no direct evidence of how they were propelled. – J.G.D.C.

thrower, another mechanical device for increasing the range of a missile and the accuracy of its aim.

Specialized tools were needed and used for manufacturing this tackle and for satisfying the new needs for housing, clothing, and adornment. Men were no longer content to extemporize tools to meet immediate needs, but had the foresight to make tools for making tools – secondary and tertiary tools, in fact. In addition to wood and stone, men had now secured mastery over other materials, notably bone, antler, and ivory. For sharpening these a new process was employed – polishing, which applied to stone used to serve old-fashioned archaeologists as a criterion of the new stone age. Moreover antlers, bones, and even flat stones were sometimes perforated with circular holes. If not requiring the use of a drill, perforation seems to imply some application of rotary motion, so preparing the way for such critical inventions as the wheel.

The pursuit of large gregarious animals by Aurignacians, Gravettians, and the rest required the cooperation of a group larger than the natural family, even more certainly than among Neanderthalers. But speculations as to how such groups were organized are hardly profitable. Some division of labour between the sexes may be deduced from modern analogies, but each 'family' or 'household' could probably manufacture its own equipment. And each group could be self-contained and self-sufficing.

Yet there are indications of interchange of products – in fact of a sort of 'trade' between distinct communities, though the articles traded were normally luxuries not indispensable. Mediterranean shells have been found in the caves of the Dordogne (west-central France). Some of the flint found at Gagarino on the Don seems to have been brought from exposures more than seventy miles down stream, perhaps at Kostienki, where there was another large camp. Finally, the bones of sea-fish are so common in Magdalenian refuse heaps in the Dordogne that it looks as if there may have been a regular interchange of commodities between coastal and inland communities living in France contemporary with mammoths and reindeer. Such intercommunal specialization can be illustrated among recent savages on the same economic plane as the Magdalenians. Evidently upper palaeolithic groups were not entirely isolated from one another. The interchange of material objects attested by archaeology gave opportunity also for the pooling of ideas.

Upper palaeolithic societies had further elaborated that spiritual equipment already vaguely attested among Neanderthalers and earlier. Dead Grimaldians and Crô-Magnons were interred with even greater ceremony than Neanderthalers. Their graves were furnished with food, implements, and ornaments. Often the bones are found reddened with ochre. The mourning relatives had sprinkled the corpse with the red powder, surely in the pathetic hope that by restoring to the pallid skin the colour that symbolized life they would also restore the missing life itself. Such a confusion of the symbol with the thing symbolized lies at the root of 'sympathetic magic'. It is symptomatic of the tenacity of tradition that the practice of sprinkling the dead with ochre persisted for 20,000 years, long after experience should have convinced everyone of its futility.

Magic rites to ensure the food-supply, to promote the multiplication of the hunted game, and secure success in the chase, were also devised. The Gravettians used to carve little figures of women out of stone or mammoth ivory, or model them in clay and ash. Archaeologists term these Venus figures (Venuses). But they are generally hideous; most have no faces, but the sexual characters are always emphasized. They were surely used in some sort of fertility ritual to ensure the multiplication of game; Zamiatnin suggests puppet plays imitating and so magically causing the generative process. In any case they must mean that the Gravettians grasped the generative function of women, and sought magically to extend it to the animals and plants that nourished them.

In France Gravettians and their Magdalenian descendants elaborated other rites. In the deep recesses of limestone caverns, perhaps two miles beneath the earth, the impenetrable gloom lit only by the feeble flame of fat burning in a stone lamp with moss wick, and often on rock surfaces accessible only by standing on a helper's shoulders, artist–magicians painted or engraved the rhinoceros, mammoth, bison, reindeer, that they must eat. As surely as a pictured bison was conjured up on the cave wall by the master's skilful strokes, so surely would a real bison emerge for his associates to kill and eat. The beasts are always highly individualized, actual portraits not abstract shorthand symbols (p.26). They reflect minute and deliberate observation of real models. But the models so carefully studied and so accurately reproduced were very likely dead beasts.

In fact, so important was this magic art in the estimation of upper palaeolithic society that the artist–magicians may have been liberated from the exacting tasks of the chase to concentrate on the reputedly more productive ritual; they would be assigned a share in the proceeds of the hunt in return for a purely spiritual participation in its trials and dangers. At least, the pictures are so masterly that they seem to be the work of trained and specialized craftsmen. In fact, from the Magdalenian site of Limeuil (Dordogne) we possess a collection of stone slivers and pebbles on which are scratched what look like small-scale trial pieces for the cave pictures; some show correction as if by a master's hand. The collection may be scraps from the copy-books of a school of artists. Thus we dimly discern the emergence of the first specialists – the first men to be supported out of a social surplus of foodstuffs to collecting which they had made no direct contribution. But of course the Magdalenians regarded their magical contributions as just as important as the acumen of the tracker, the precision of the archer, and the valour of the huntsman.

The economic prerogatives of the specialized magician are based upon socially sanctioned superstition. But the surplus that the magician thus appropriated was available only because just at this time the hunting grounds and rivers of France were exceptionally well stocked with game and fish. When forest invaded the steppe at the end of the ice age, magic was of no avail; bison, reindeer, and mammoth vanished, and with them the Magdalenians and their art.

At the close of the last ice age, when the tundra zone was shifting north, the reindeer migrated, too, and men followed them. Every summer a band of hunters from farther south used to repair to Holstein and encamp beside a little mere at Meiendorf, not far from Hamburg. They succeeded in slaughtering hundreds of reindeer. But the first kill of each season was not eaten. Its body, weighted with a stone, was cast into the mere, presumably as an offering to the spirit of the herd or the genius of the land. If this interpretation be correct, the idea of sacrifice and some correlative conception of spirits to be placated and conciliated had been reached by these rude savages at least 10,000 years ago. So even in the savagery of the Old Stone Age we can discern the germs of religion, the propitiation by a collective social sacrifice of spirits, conceived as having human emotions and desires, in contrast to the vaguer and impersonal forces that magic is supposed to 'control', often for individual rather than social ends.

Art, too, enriched the spiritual culture of upper palaeolithic societies. The engravings and paintings in the French caves are admired as beautiful by artists today. If they were executed for prosaically utilitarian magical purposes, that did not debar the artist from an aesthetic satisfaction in making his drawing beautiful, even though he could see it no more than Beethoven could hear the Ninth Symphony. Music, as well as graphic art, may have played a part in Magdalenian magic, since bone pipes and whistles have been found in the caves.

With the same duality of motive, hunting tackle was embellished with life-like carvings and engravings of animals by the Gravettians and Magdalenians of France and Spain. All upper palaeolithic peoples tried to increase their beauty and enhance their personalities by mutilating their bodies or decking them with ornaments. In Africa a tooth was knocked out – at the behest of fashion, no doubt, but also as a ritual act. Everywhere shells or animals' teeth were collected, pierced, and strung together to serve as necklaces. But they were not only personal ornaments but also charms. Cowrie shells were so highly valued as to be brought from the Mediterranean to the Dordogne; they were valued because they resemble the vulva and therefore confer fertility. Bracelets might be made from mammoth's tusks. One from Mezin in the Ukraine is carved very beautifully with a purely 'ornamental' geometric pattern – the meander. But to Australian black-fellows patterns equally devoid of representational content have a meaning, tell a story, and work magic. Art and fashion are as definitely rooted in the Old Stone Age as magic and superstition. They were as necessary socially then as now. It is permissible to doubt whether the 'Highland Cattle' on the sitting-room wall or the diamond necklace on the dowager's throat be an advance on the bison in the limestone cave or the shell necklace of the Crô-Magnon savage.

In Ice Age Europe savagery produced a dazzling culture and, judging by the relatively numerous skeletons that survive, supported a substantially increased population. But this cultural efflorescence, this expansion of population were made possible by the food supply bounteously provided by glacial conditions and an economy narrowly specialized to exploit these. With the end of the ice age these conditions passed away. As the glaciers melted, forest invaded tundras and steppes, and the herds of mammoth, reindeer, bison, and horse migrated or died out. With their disappearance the culture of societies which preyed upon them also withered away. In early holocene times, during what archaeologists term the *mesolithic* phase, we find instead of the Gravettian and Magdalenian cave-men small groups scattered about in the vast forest in open glades, on the shore of sea or meres, and along river banks, hunting and snaring forest game, wild fowl, and fish.

By contrast to what had passed away, the mesolithic

societies leave an impression of extreme poverty. Nevertheless, all seem to have enjoyed one advantage: in mesolithic sites in Portugal, France, the Baltic region, and the Crimea, bones of dogs are first found. Now it is precisely in hunting red deer, wild boar, hares, and similar game that dogs could help men. The wolfish or jackal ancestor of the domestic dog may have begun hanging round camp fires, a tolerated scavenger, much earlier. In mesolithic Europe he is first disclosed as a partner in man's food quest, exploiting man's superior cunning, but helping in the hunt and rewarded with offal from the catch.

Again the mesolithic societies inhabiting the wooded plain extending from the central English Pennine chain to the Urals seem the first in Europe to have devised any equipment for dealing with timber – and the forest was the outstanding factor differentiating the holocene from the late pleistocene environment. Beginning with splitting tools – handle wedges – of antler, such as had been employed already in late pleistocene times in south-eastern Europe (Rumania and Hungary), the mesolithic forest-folk armed their wedges with blades of flint or of stone, sharpened like the antler tools by grinding. Eventually they thus created a regular kit of carpenter's tools of axes, adzes, and gouges with which, among other achievements, they could solve the problem of transport over snow and ice by making sledges. (Runners of sledges found embedded in mesolithic peat in Finnish bogs are, perhaps, the oldest surviving vehicles.)

Savages, in fact, could – and did – advance after the end of the Old Stone Age, though remaining savages. But within the limits of savagery the scope for progress was very small, and its pace as slow as in the pleistocene period. Some societies, by an economic revolution, emerged from savagery and progressed much faster. So it would be tedious, were it possible, to enumerate the timid steps forward made by savage societies from the end of the Ice Age till the present day.

The fate of the most brilliant savagery of the past – the Magdalenian cultures of France – will have sufficiently disclosed the biological limitations of that economy. A happy conjunction of circumstances, quite outside their own control, provided the Magdalenians with sufficient food to support a growing population, obtainable with so little effort that they had leisure to embellish life with a brilliant spiritual culture. But the magic superstructure did nothing to increase the supplies of food which, after all, were not inexhaustible. So population was limited and eventually waned with the specially favourable conditions.

The same conclusions could be drawn from an ethnographic study of modern savages. Red Indian tribes on the north-west coast of America, by exploiting salmon runs and similar resources as the Magdalenians had done, attained an even richer culture and were relatively very numerous. Kroeber estimates that the population density in the more favoured regions was as high as 1.7 to a square mile. But that is quite exceptional for savagery. Even on the Pacific coast the same author puts the density in other regions as low as 0.26 per square mile, while on the prairies the hunting population would not have exceeded 0.11 per square mile. In the whole continent of Australia the aboriginal population is believed never to have exceeded 200,000 – a density of only 0.03 per square mile.

However approximate such estimates may be, they give a fair idea of the inherent defects of savagery as an economy. It led to an impasse – a contradiction – and, had that contradiction never been surmounted, *Homo sapiens* would have remained a rare animal – as the savage in fact is.

Still, on the margins of tropical jungles, deserts, and ice-fields, isolated tribes have continued to eke out an existence with a palaeolithic economy long enough for recent anthropologists to be able to study their spiritual culture. From the reports of these observers it is possible to deduce what sort of ideology effectively lubricates the operations of a food-gathering economy. Such deductions cannot disclose with scientific precision what savages in the Old Stone Age actually believed, or how Moustierian or Gravettian societies were organized – that is unknowable – but are relevant inasmuch as 'survivals' from inferentially savage ideologies seem to clog the workings of barbarian and civilized economies.

Contemporary savage tribes are generally groups of *clans* which, being more stable, overshadow or even replace the family *as an institution*. All clansmen are regarded as related in virtue of mystical descent from a *totem* 'ancestor'. The totem is generally an edible animal, insect, or plant, important in the tribal economy, more rarely a natural phenomenon, a feature of the landscape, or a man-made implement. 'Descent' is reckoned sometimes in the male, sometimes in the female, line. The system of kinship which determines the mutual rights and duties of clan-members and, in particular, who may marry whom, is frequently 'classificatory'. Not only the natural father, but also all paternal (or maternal) uncles, etc., are classed as 'fathers', first and second paternal (or under a matrilinear system, maternal) cousins are classed as brothers, and so on. Membership of the clan is theoretically based on 'blood', practically on ceremonial initiation at puberty. While 'kinship' guarantees the 'right' to initiation, the same rites may secure adoption into the clan. Hence the relationship of clansmen may be more or less fictitious.

Hunting and fishing grounds, and the food obtained therefrom, are generally owned and enjoyed in common. But something like personal property in weapons, vessels, and finery and even in spells or dances may be recognized.

Old men generally enjoy authority and prestige that entitles them to a major share in women or any other sort of 'wealth'. But, particularly in America, these privileges have often been monopolized by hereditary 'chiefs' who can sometimes accumulate considerable wealth. Occasional or endemic warfare between tribes or even between clans is reported even in Australia, and more often in America, where it serves to enhance the prestige of chiefs.

The ideology of savages seems to be expressed in words (spells) and imitative actions, *rites*, that symbolize changes in the real world that society wishes to bring about. Each totemic clan performs periodically dramatic ceremonies supposed to ensure the multiplication of the ancestral animals or plants. It looks as if the symbol were confused with the result. The savage behaves as if he thought that with spells and rites he can control natural phenomena that we now hold cannot be controlled by these means, if at all. All such operations are here termed *magical*. But it must not be assumed that they are, in fact, performed for any such clearly formulated reasons. That would be no more legitimate than if a Negro in A.D. 2050 inferred that Europeans of 1950 wore white collars to avoid sore throats. Nor can it be assumed that, besides magically 'controlling' nature, savages do not ever also invoke the interposition of supernatural beings that might be termed 'personal' and divine. On the contrary, Australian aborigines and others tell stories or *myths* about such beings. The impersonation of the totem by clansmen might lead to the personification of the ancestor. The word-book to a dramatic ceremony may become a myth.

Finally magic, though it cannot produce the results its practitioners are supposed to desire, can be biologically useful. Totemic ceremonies and abstinences, for instance, promote not only social solidarity but also the efficiency of the hunter both by giving him confidence, and by familiarizing him with the habits of the totem. Moreover, the clansmen's abstinence from the totem as food does, at least, retard the destruction of this source of livelihood for the rest of the tribe.

The foregoing remarks are not intended to define the religion or the social organization of all savages. There is, in fact, as much variety of spiritual and of material culture among modern savages as there was at least of material culture among the men of the Old Stone Age described more fully in this chapter.

3

NEOLITHIC BARBARISM

THE escape from the impasse of savagery was an economic and scientific revolution that made the participants active partners with nature instead of parasites on nature. The occasion for the revolution was the climatic crisis that ended the pleistocene epoch; the melting of the northern ice sheets not only converted the steppes and tundras of Europe into temperate forests, but also initiated the transformation of the prairies south of the Mediterranean and in Hither Asia into deserts interrupted by oases. The revolutionaries were not the most advanced savages of the Old Stone Age – the Magdalenians were all too successfully specialized for exploiting the pleistocene environment – but humbler groups who had created less specialized and less brilliant cultures farther south. Among them while men hunted, women – we must suppose – had collected among other edibles the seeds of wild grasses, ancestral to our wheat and barley. The decisive step was deliberately to sow such seeds on suitable soil and cultivate the sown land by weeding and other measures. A society that acted thus was henceforth actively producing food, augmenting its own food supply. Potentially it could increase the supply to support a growing population.

This was the first step in the neolithic revolution, and suffices to distinguish barbarism from savagery. In the archaeological record it is, perhaps, illustrated in certain caves in Mount Carmel and elsewhere in Palestine. The Natufians, as the caves' inhabitants have been named, hunted with an equipment of flints very similar to those current among mesolithic peoples in Europe. But they used some flints, mounted in rib-bones, as *sickles* for cutting grass stems or straw; a peculiar lustre on the flints proves this, but unfortunately does not disclose what sort of grass was cut, still less whether it were cultivated or wild.

Many barbarian societies known to ethnographers today have gone no further than the cultivation of some cereal or other plant. But the neolithic societies of Hither Asia, the Mediterranean region, and cis-Alpine Europe, whose culture we inherit, also domesticated certain food animals. It happens that just in those regions of Hither Asia where ancestors of wheat and barley grew spontaneously, there lived also wild sheep, goats, cattle, and pigs. Now the hunters whose wives were cultivators had something to offer some of the beasts they had hunted – the stubble on grain plots and the husks of the grain. As suitable animals became increasingly hemmed in to the oases by the desert, men might study their habits and, instead of killing them off-hand, might tame them and make them dependent. One school of ethnographers holds that stockbreeding arises directly from hunting without the intervention of cultivation. Mixed farming would be due to the conquest of cultivators by pastoralists, producing mixed or stratified societies. But the oldest neolithic societies known to the archaeological record consist of mixed farmers who have already domesticated some or all of the beasts named above. Their abstinence and their foresight in finding water and pastures and warding off beasts of prey allow the flock and herds to multiply. Their accumulated observations on their charges have perhaps already disclosed that the latter can not only be tame game, reserves of food and skins, but also living larders and walking wardrobes. Cows, goats, and ewes can be induced to provide food in the form of milk without being killed; selected varieties of sheep grow yearly a woolly fleece (wool sheep seem to be the result of selective breeding; in most wild sheep the coat is hairy and only a thin down represents what becomes wool).

The new aggressive attitude to the environment did not stop short at producing new food supplies. Most known neolithic societies and most neolithic barbarians of recent times also created new substances which do not occur ready-made in nature. By heating friable and plastic clay, the farmer's wife can induce a *chemical* change (driving out the 'water of constitution' from the hydrated aluminium silicate that is the principal component of clay) and produce *pottery*, a substance with quite different sensible qualities – no longer plastic and no longer disintegrated by water. By the rotary motion of spinning she can convert certain natural fibres – wool and flax, later also cotton and silk – into threads by a still mysterious rearrangement of the molecules.

From their plastic clay the potters built up with skilful hands new shapes, suggested, indeed, by older vessels cut out of wood or soft stone or gourds, but still free constructions that allow some play for the constructive fancy. From their threads the womenfolk wove fabrics, using an elaborate mechanism – the loom. The new ideas of construction were applied to habitations, too; neolithic households normally live in built huts of mud, reeds, logs, stone, or withies plastered with clay. To assist them in these activities neolithic societies manufactured a greatly enlarged assortment of specialized tools. Among these an axe-head, made from fine-grained rock sharpened by grinding, is generally, but not universally, conspicuous. Archaeologists take the polished stone axe as the hall-mark of a neolithic equipment. But it is not quite unknown to savages and not invariably employed by barbarians whose economy is or was neolithic.

The foregoing incomplete inventory (which may be supplemented by reference to *Man Makes Himself*) will show how enormously neolithic equipment was richer than that of any palaeolithic or mesolithic savagery. Barbarism results from applying a regular complex of scientific discoveries and inventions. In the archaeological record, as in ethnography, most of the traits just enumerated are found already fully developed and applied. But they are applied in different ways and to the production of distinct forms in each province and by each society that can be distinguished. Archaeology reveals no single neolithic culture, but a number of distinct cultures. These may have been differentiated by divergent applications of common basic traditions, adjusted perhaps to varying local opportunities and needs. Such is the contention of the diffusionists. If it be accepted, it follows that the 'neolithic revolution' began a very long time ago.

On the other hand, no trace of the revolution's effects has yet been detected in any geological deposit assignable to the pleistocene. Within the succeeding holocene, the geological present, its antiquity can best be inferred in the east Mediterranean area. There the early invention of writing provides a horizon, datable by historical records, about 3000 B.C. There, too, communities were forced to live on the same site for many successive generations. The clustered huts of reeds or mud would decay with the passage of time, but new structures would be built upon the ruins. Eventually the accumulated debris forms a regular hill or *tell*. The valleys and coastal plains of Greece, the plateaux of Asia Minor (Turkey) and Iran, the steppes of Syria and Turkestan are studded with thousands of such tells. In Hither Asia and Iran a 'historical horizon' – street levels and house floors on which have been dropped objects fashionable about 3000 B.C. – can often be recognized high up in the mounds. Working back from this level by dead reckoning, the depth of the underlying deposits gives a rough indication of the age of the oldest village on the site.

More accurate indications have been given since 1950 by 'radio-carbon dates' based on the amount of the radio-active isotope, C^{14}, still left in organic substances that have ceased to absorb fresh supplies from the atmosphere. An unexpected antiquity, about 7000 B.C.,* has been thus attributed to the earliest farming settlement thus dated – the oasis village of Jericho in the Jordan valley. The village was surprisingly large – perhaps 8 acres in area – and, still more surprisingly, was defended by a rock-cut ditch, 27 ft wide

---

*Recent work in Kurdistan, notably at Shanidar, has thrown clearer light on the beginning of incipient domestication. Radio-carbon analysis suggests that this had occurred by the ninth millennium B.C. – J.G.D.C.

and 5 ft deep, and a stone-built rampart. Its earliest inhabitants supported themselves by hunting and collecting, but also by growing crops, watered by a perennial spring, and grazing sheep and goats, but probably not kine, on irrigated meadow land. But in contrast to later, more familiar villagers, they used no ground stone axes and did not convert clay into pottery by firing. So Jericho I is said to illustrate a *pre-pottery neolithic* stage. The same stage is represented in a second village, Jericho II, built on the site a thousand years later by a fresh people, and still later, about 4750 B.C., at Jarmo in Kurdistan. The farmers of Jarmo were cultivating cereals that still show clear traces of their origin in the wild grasses of the region, but bred cows as well as sheep and goats. They did use axes, or rather adzes, of ground stone and made unbaked clay figurines of women. But they made no pottery, and used instead, as even the Jerichoans had done, vessels of stone and doubtless also of wood.

The next stage can be illustrated by the village at the base of a tell at Sialk on the western edge of the Persian desert near Kashan. Here, as at Jericho a perennial spring would not only attract game and wild fowl, but provide water for the irrigation of small plots. The builders of the first village at the base of the tell hunted with slings and clubs the game that congregated round the waters. But they bred cattle, sheep, and goats. They grew cereals by irrigation and reaped them with sickles of bone armed with flint teeth like the Natufians'. They spun and wove some undetermined fibres and made vases out of stone and pottery. They even knew how to decorate their pots with patterns painted in dark colour on a background that after firing was pale pink and thus enhanced the likeness of the vases to the plaited-grass baskets which had suggested many of the shapes.

West of the Nile small communities settled about 4300 B.C. on the shore of a lake that then filled the Fayum depression to a height of 180 feet above the level of the present lake. All that remains of the settlements are middens – the heaps of food-refuse left by the settlers. The debris from their repasts, as well as immense numbers of flint arrow-heads, bone harpoons, and bone dart-heads prove that the Fayumis hunted the game that watered at the lake and the wild fowl that nested on its reedy banks, and speared the fish swarming in its waters. But bones of cattle, sheep or goats, and pigs, presumably domestic, occur with remains of game in the middens. Near-by straw-lined pits were found filled with grains of emmer wheat and barley. From the volume of the grain that could be stored in the silos it has been deduced that the cereals alone could not have supported the community; they must have provided, rather, a reserve supply of food and supplemented a diet consisting mainly of game. On the other hand, the grains are already definitely cultivated forms, many stages removed from wild grass seeds; the barley from the Fayum is, indeed, almost identical with that now cultivated by the barbarous societies of North Africa.

Moreover, granaries were dug and lined with straw to preserve the crop. Special tools – sickles consisting of flint teeth mounted in a straight wooden handle – were made to reap the crop and stone querns to convert it into flour. Society's equipment has been enriched with new artificial materials – pottery for vessels and linen for clothing – and new implements, axe-heads sharpened by grinding and polishing, spindles, looms.

On the western edge of the delta a few miles north of Cairo, Austrian excavators at Merimde explored a village of flimsy huts sprawling over some six acres. Again, the food refuse and relics of equipment for hunting and fishing demonstrate the predominant importance of hunting, fowling, fishing, and gathering. But bones show, too, that pigs, cattle, sheep, and goats were bred. Beside each hut site were granaries containing barley and emmer, and remains of threshing floors where the grains were separated from the chaff. All the new equipment found at the Fayum sites recurs at Merimde, too. Moreover, here the arrangement of the huts in regular rows, along streets in fact, reflects a recognized social order and organization of the communal life.

In Europe the neolithic economy could be illustrated more fully from a great variety of well-excavated sites. While these disclose a bewildering variety of distinct cultures, often more primitive – that is to say, poorer – in equipment than those of the Near East, the oldest all show a significant divergence from the economy just described. In the oldest neolithic settlements so far known north of the Alps the productive activities of grain-growing and stock-breeding are so far dominant that hunting has been relegated to a secondary role. They no longer represent a 'mixed economy', properly so called.

For instance, all over central Europe from the Drave to the Baltic and from the Vistula to the Meuse, where patches of loess offer easily cultivated soils neither swampy nor densely forested, we find what are termed Danubian villages and cemeteries, In all, remains of wheats and barley, stone hoeblades, sickles and querns, as well as their locations, emphasize the importance of cereal cultivation. Bones of cattle, pigs, and sheep occur, too, but in relatively small numbers. Bones of game, on the contrary, are practically non-existent and hunting tools extremely rare. Over this vast territory the Danubians' equipment is astonishingly uniform: pots, axes, ornaments everywhere preserve the same traditional shape. They must be the products of a single people who had spread. As their pots seem to imitate vessels made from gourds, it is inferred that the Danubians themselves came from a warm southerly region where gourds will harden, as they will not north of the Hungarian plain. They seem, moreover, to have brought with them from the south a superstitious attachment to the shells of a Mediterranean mussel, *Spondylus gaederepi*, which they imported even into central Germany and the Rhineland for ornaments and amulets.

The process of Danubian expansion has been illustrated by the excavation of a complete village at Köln-Lindenthal, near Cologne. The settlement at one time consisted of 21 gabled long houses, neatly grouped parallel to one another in a fenced area of 6½ acres within which were enclosed various irregular hollows, dug originally to provide clay for house walls and pots but later converted into rubbish-pits, pig-sties or working places. Some houses measured as much as 100 feet in length with a width of 20 feet, enough to accommodate a clan rather than a single natural family. But after perhaps ten years these were deserted; the villagers left the site, only to return again after an indeterminate interval. Presumably they had found they could no longer secure decent crops from the exhausted plots round the village and had shifted bag and baggage to fertile virgin soil.

The Danubians were adopting what seems the simplest device for escaping the effects of soil exhaustion through repeated cropping. It is a solution adopted still by barbarian cultivators in Africa, Assam, and elsewhere. But the Danubians had found out that if they let the brushwood grow over their deserted plots and then burned down the scrub, they could then reap good crops once more; the ashes from the fresh clearance would in fact return to the soil much of its lost virtue. So the village was rebuilt on the old site, with a slightly different alignment of its houses, and then again deserted for a while.

After several repetitions of this cycle the Danubians, whose fashions in pottery decoration had meanwhile changed somewhat, were obliged to surround the latest village with a defensive ditch and rampart to exclude human foes – apparently a new people, the so-called Westerners, whose earlier settlements are known in Switzerland, France, Belgium, and Britain.

These settlements emphasize another aspect of neolithic economy. The Westerners, too, cultivated cereals and also flax, and, perhaps, apples. But cattle formed the staple source of food; in their kitchen refuse the bones of cattle far outnumbered those of any other animal. The bones of game are relatively scarce – in Switzerland only 30 per cent, in Normandy as little as 2.5 per cent, of the total food animals. So in western Europe, too, the productive activity of the herdsman had ousted the gathering of the huntsman from its primacy in the social economy of the earliest neolithic communities.

But while pastoralists, these Westerners were no more nomadic than the Danubians. On the shores of the Swiss lakes they laboriously built wooden houses raised on piles. On the south English downs and on hills overlooking the Rhine they encircled encampments with multiple ditches quarried in the solid chalk and supplemented by stockades. Their equipment was of the same kind as the Danubians', but the forms of the individual tools are quite different. They preferred axes for carpentry while the Danubians relied exclusively on adzes. Their pots seem to imitate leather vessels. These and other articles in Western equipment are so strongly reminiscent of those used at Merimde and in the Fayum that the Westerners' traditions seem to derive from North Africa. They may have been gradually spread by a quest for fresh pastures comparable to the Danubians' search for virgin soil. But in each case the gathering economy that must still have been dominant in the first phases of the revolution had been largely discarded to make way for a purer neolithic food production.

These five concrete examples must suffice to suggest the complexity of the neolithic revolution, the expansion of its results, and the divergent applications to which it could give rise. These points could be amplified by further reference to the archaeological record or by ethnographical citations. Four thousand years ago archaeology discloses societies practising a neolithic economy dispersed over Eurasia from Ireland to China. Barbarian communities on a comparable level live, or lived quite recently, in parts of Africa, round the Pacific, and in the Americas. All shared such basic arts as the cultivation of plants, manufacture of pottery, construction of houses, and sharpening of axe-heads by grinding; only the Amerinds lack a true loom, but stock-breeding had a more restricted vogue outside Eurasia and was practically strange to America. However, the concrete application of the principles diverges enormously.

Our debt to preliterate barbarians is heavy. Every single cultivated food plant of any importance has been discovered by some nameless barbarian society. So we find neolithic peoples relying not only on wheats and barleys, but on rice, millet, and maize, or even on yams, manioc, squashes, or other plants that are not cereals at all. The methods of cultivation found appropriate for each species are naturally different. Even for cultivation of the same species – wheat and barley, for example – different geological and climatic conditions impose corresponding differences in method. Particularly in arid regions like Iran natural or artificial irrigation is the normal procedure. In a well-watered temperate zone like Europe rain will supply the necessary moisture, but a plot will not yield a decent crop for more than two or three successive years. The simplest escape from this dilemma is to clear a new plot every year and, when all the land round the village has been used up, to shift bag and baggage and start again on virgin soil. This was the solution adopted by the Danubians in prehistoric Europe and still applied by some African tribes, such as the Lango, by the hill tribes of Assam and other peoples. Its former prevalence helps to explain the worldwide expansion of neolithic cultures.

Such agricultural nomadism is a bar to any luxury in domestic architecture and household furniture, but these inconveniences might be overlooked as long as land seemed unlimited. But even in prehistoric times some societies were finding out ways of restoring fertility to exhausted plots or preventing exhaustion. If a plot be allowed to go back to bush and then cleared again by burning, the ashes will have restored to the soil much of its lost virtue. Mixed farmers can graze stock on plots they have cleared for crops, and then the droppings of the flocks and herds will serve as fertilizers and permit of a new crop being grown in time. Or human excreta or animal manure can be deliberately collected and applied to exhausted fields, effecting a more rapid regeneration. One or other of these devices must have been employed in Greece and the Balkans in late neolithic times, for there we find successive settlements built upon the same site just as much as among the irrigation cultivators of Hither Asia.

To accomplish the neolithic revolution mankind, or rather womankind, had not only to discover suitable plants and appropriate methods for their cultivation, but must also devise special implements for tilling the soil, reaping and storing the crop, and converting it into foods. For breaking up the ground the commonest implement used by modern barbarians is just a pointed stick that may be weighted with a perforated stone near the point. But most African tribes prepare the ground with a hoe, and hoes were demonstrably used by the prehistoric Danubians, and probably by other European and Asiatic peoples. Cereals were first reaped with sickles composed of flint teeth set in a straight wood or bone handle, as among the Natufians and Fayumis, or in an animal's jaw-bone or a wooden imitation thereof.

It is an essential element in the neolithic economy that sufficient food shall be gathered at each harvest and stored to last till the next crop is ripe, normally in a year's time. Granaries or storehouses were accordingly a prominent feature in any barbarian village, and have been identified in such early prehistoric settlements as Merimde, the Fayum, and Köln-Lindenthal. Wheat and barley need to be separated from the husk by threshing and winnowing, and then ground into flour. The grinding could be done by pounding in a mortar, but the standard procedure was to rub the grains on a saucer-shaped or saddle-shaped stone with a bun-shaped or sausage-shaped rubbing-stone. Such *querns* must, however, be made of tough stone, or the meal will contain as much grit as flour.

The flour can be easily converted into porridge or into flat cakes, but to make it into bread requires a knowledge of some biochemistry – the use of the micro-organism, yeast – and also a specially constructed oven. Moreover, the same biochemical process as was used to make bread rise opened to mankind a new world of enchantment.

All modern barbarians prepare some sort of fermented liquor. By the dawn of history beer was being brewed in Egypt and Mesopotamia and it was already established as the appropriate drink to stimulate the oldest Sumerian gods to potent beneficence. By 3000 B.C., indeed, intoxicants had become necessities to most societies in Europe and Hither Asia, and a whole service of jars, jugs, beakers, strainers, and drinking-tubes had come into fashion for their ceremonial consumption.

All the foregoing inventions and discoveries were, judged by ethnographic evidence, the work of the women. To that sex, too, may by the same token be credited the chemistry of pot-making, the physics of spinning, the mechanics of the loom, and the botany of flax and cotton. On the other hand, in the prehistoric societies we have cited and in others like them in Europe and right across Asia to China, the feminine achievements have been welded into a single economy with others attributable to men. For among modern barbarians the care of flocks and herds and the processes and equipment pertaining thereto fall to the men. In the archaeological record the neolithic economy is an economy of mixed farming, and we must now see how such an economy works.

The neolithic populations of Europe and Hither Asia are normally found living in small communities – villages or hamlets. When fully explored these have been found to cover areas from $1\frac{1}{2}$ to $6\frac{1}{2}$ acres. The community that lived at Skara Brae in Orkney comprised not more than eight households; in central Europe and southern Russia twenty-five to thirty-five households seems to have been a not uncommon number.

Such spatial aggregates formed social organisms whose members all cooperated for collective tasks. In the western villages on Alpine moors the several houses are connected up by corduroy streets, at Skara Brae in Orkney by covered alleys. Such public ways must be communal not individual works. Many neolithic villages in western Europe and in the Balkans are surrounded by ditches, fences, or stockades, as a protection against wild beasts or human foes, and these, too, must have been erected by collective effort. It has been calculated that to dig the defensive ditch round the latest village at Köln-Lindenthal must have taken nearly three thousand man-days of labour. The arrangement of the dwellings along definite streets noticed already at Merimde in Egypt again gives expression to some form of social organization, and a similar orderliness has been reported in some Western villages from south-western Germany and again in south Russian settlements.

But there is no need to assume any industrial specialization within the village apart from a division of labour between the sexes. On the analogy of modern barbarians each neolithic household would grow and prepare its own food, make its own pots, clothes, tools, and other requisites. The women would till the plots, grind and cook the grain, spin, weave, and manufacture clothes, build and bake the pots, and prepare some ornaments and magic articles. Men on the other hand may have cleared the plots, built the huts, tended the live-stock, hunted, and manufactured the needful tools and weapons.

Moreover each village could be self-sufficing. It grew its own food and could make all essential equipment from materials locally available – stone, bone, wood, clay, and so on. This potential self-sufficiency of the territorial community and the absence of specialization within it may be taken as the differentiae of neolithic barbarism to distinguish it from civilization and the higher barbarisms of the Metal Ages. A corollary therefrom is that a neolithic economy offers no material inducement to the peasant to produce more than he needs to support himself and his family and provide for the next harvest. If each household does that, the community can survive without a surplus.

Probably no known neolithic community conformed strictly to these standards. Even in the earliest neolithic villages and graves archaeologists have found materials brought from long distances. Shells from the Mediterranean and from the Red Sea were strung on necklaces by the

Fayumis. At Sialk and at Anau (in the Merv oasis) small ornaments were made from native copper and semi-precious stones that had been transported a hundred miles or so. The Danubian peasants in Hungary, Bohemia, central Germany, and the Rhineland wore bracelets and beads made from shells of *Spondylus gaederopi* imported from the Mediterranean.

Imports were not entirely restricted to such luxury articles. Neidermendig lava from near Mayen on the Moselle, a good tough stone, was used for querns by the Danubians even in the Meuse valley in Belgium and perhaps even by the Westerners of southern England. Good cutting stones – obsidian in Hither Asia and central Europe, high-grade flints and attractive greenstones for axe-heads – were transported quite long distances. Even pots, presumably containing something, were brought from the Main valley to Köln-Lindenthal, fifty miles down the Rhine, and were often interchanged between neolithic villages in Thessaly. Ethnographers have described quite intensive trade over long distances between barbarians whose equipment is still formally neolithic.

Moreover, the neolithic economy seems to have found room for some rudiments of intercommunal specialization, even in early prehistoric times. In Egypt, Sicily, Portugal, France, England, Belgium, Sweden, and Poland neolithic groups were mining flints. The miners had evolved a quite elaborate technique for sinking shafts through the solid chalk and cutting subterranean galleries to exploit seams of good nodules. From their winnings they manufactured axes, which are found distributed over wide areas. The miners were in fact highly skilled specialists. They almost certainly lived by bartering their products for the surplus corn and meat produced by farmers. In Melanesia and New Guinea today a very few villages specialize in making pottery and supply other communities over a wide area even across the sea.

Societies of savages continued and continue to exist side by side with food-producers. The latter now barter farm produce with hunters and gatherers in exchange for game and jungle products. The same complementary relationship may have existed in the past. The neolithic herdsmen and miners of the English South Downs used vast quantities of stags' antlers as picks, though bones of deer are not conspicuous among the refuse from their repasts. The antlers may have been supplied by descendants of mesolithic huntsmen who continued to live on the greens and country north of the Downs.

Now in pursuit of game hunters are wont to wander farther and more frequently than even the most primitive cultivators and herdsmen. They might profitably combine hunting trips with the transportation of those exotic substances that neolithic villages certainly did somehow obtain. In Britain the distribution to Wiltshire and Anglesey of axes made from Graig Llwydd rock at Penmaenmawr in North Wales appears to be associated with a type of pottery favoured by descendants of the native mesolithic stock as contrasted with the immigrant Western food-producers. In brief professional merchants may have been recruited in part from residual food-gatherers.

So the self-sufficiency of the neolithic community was potential rather than actual, just as such a community was seldom strictly sedentary. Intercourse with other groups was probably more frequent and more extensive than among palaeolithic food gatherers. The pooling of human experience had to that extent been accelerated by the neolithic revolution.

Nevertheless, fixed in an oasis in the desert, huddled in a valley bottom between rugged mountains, or hemmed in by trackless forests to a glade, neolithic villagers enjoyed only occasional contact with the outside world. For the greater part of the time they were engaged in adapting their economy and their equipment to a strictly specialized and localized environment. The latter would offer each society its own distinct opportunities for discoveries and inventions. So each group would develop peculiar traditions appropriate to its own circumstances. This is just what archaeology and ethnography reveal.

There is no 'neolithic culture', but a limitless multitude of neolithic cultures. Each is distinguished by the varieties of plants cultivated or of animals bred, by a different balance between cultivation and stock-breeding, by divergences in the location of settlements, in the plan and construction of houses, the shape and material of axes and other tools, the form and decoration of the pots, and by still greater disparities in burial rites, fashions in amulets, and styles of art. Each culture represents an approximate adaptation to a specific environment with an ideology more or less adequate thereto. The diversity results from a multiplicity of minor discoveries or inventions, at first purely local and conditioned by geological or climatic or botanical peculiarities, or from arbitrary, i.e. unexplained, idiosyncrasies.

Hence we cannot speak of 'neolithic science', but only of 'neolithic sciences'. Barbarian societies had at their disposal and successfully applied a richer stock of scientific traditions, based often on more active experimentation, than ancestral savages. They included indeed new sciences such as the chemistry of potting, the biochemistry of baking and brewing, agricultural botany, and the like, quite unknown in the Old Stone Age. But these traditions were handed on and enriched by each society in its own way. There was, for example, no universal potters' lore, but as many traditional recipes as there were societies. Even though such traditions seem to us only variations on a single theme, the women who transmitted them can hardly have discriminated between the essential theme and its accidental embellishments. The practical technical prescriptions of barbarian science were, for sure, inextricably entangled with a mass of futile spells and rituals. Even the intelligent and highly civilized Greeks still feared a demon who used to crack the pots while they were being fired, so they affixed a hideous Gorgon mask to the kiln to scare him away.

Nevertheless the intercourse that demonstrably took place between neolithic societies did involve some interchange of technical ideas. In this process comparison would help to sift out non-essentials. The subsequent history of science is largely taken up with the diffusion of useful ideas beyond the environment that originally inspired them and with the selection of the effective processes from among the traditional rituals in which they were once embedded.

Still less would it be legitimate to speak of 'neolithic religion', though barbarian societies behaved and behave as if they needed ideological support no less than savages. Most neolithic societies buried the dead (either in regular cemeteries or under and beside their houses) with still more pomp than had palaeolithic hunters. In the Mediterranean world, indeed, mortuary traditions inspired the excavation with terrific labour of subterranean replicas of the deceased's house; in western and northern Europe these were reproduced in gigantic stones and artificially put under ground by burial under enormous cairns at the cost of still greater social effort. That the dead so reverently committed to the earth were supposed somehow to affect the crops that sprang from the earth is for some societies a plausible inference that cannot, however, be generalized. Ritual burial is not practised by quite all barbarians and has not yet been demonstrated archaeologically for all neolithic societies in Europe.

Female figurines were moulded in clay or carved in stone or bone by neolithic societies in Egypt, Syria, Iran, all round the Mediterranean and in south-eastern Europe, and occasionally even in England. Such figurines are generally interpreted as images of the 'Mother Goddess'; it is inferred that the earth from whose bosom the grain sprouts has been imagined as a woman who may be influenced like a woman by entreaties (prayers) and bribes (sacrifices), as well as 'controlled' by imitative rites and incantations. These figurines in fact seem in some cases to be the direct ancestresses of images of admitted goddesses made by historical societies in Mesopotamia, Syria, and Greece. The male partner in fertilization is, however, represented only by phalli of clay or stone that were carved in Anatolia, the Balkans, and England.

Now magic must have still been practised in neolithic

times despite the enlarged real control over nature possessed by barbarian societies. We have direct proof of this in the *amulets* made by neolithic peoples all round the Mediterranean and already at Merimde (p. 65); there, for instance, miniature stone axes were perforated for hanging on a necklace, presumably in the belief that such a model would confer upon its wearer something of the queer power or *mana* inherent in the new tool. Indeed Thurnwald asserts that 'it is above all in societies where skill in craftsmanship is highly developed that importance is attached to magical precautions and ceremonies'. Naturally the magic of barbarians as of savages would find expression. In particular a ceremonial union of the sexes would symbolize and so 'cause' the fertilization of nature. But among grain-growers at least the fertility drama has to assume a more individualized form than in savage rituals. From a cycle of myths and cult practices widespread among the ancient peoples of Hither Asia and the Mediterranean basin, it has been inferred that the ceremonial marriage became restricted to a selected pair. For the male actor impersonates the grain (or vegetation in general) and assumes for a time a leader's role: he becomes a 'corn king'. But like the grain he must be buried and rise again. In mortal society that means he must be slain and replaced by a young and vigorous successor. In such actors the productive forces of nature assume personal forms and become 'goddesses' and 'gods'.

But if society be persuaded that the corn king's death can be replaced by the slaughter of a captive or made purely symbolical by magic rites, the 'corn king' would be on the way to becoming a temporal king too – a transition which would be facilitated had he also functioned as a war chief. This is one way in which 'divine kings' such as we meet at the dawn of history *may* have arisen. Whether such kingship or chieftainship actually had arisen in neolithic times in Hither Asia or Europe cannot be directly established. In Egypt and Mesopotamia and Greece historical kings did perform many of the functions in fertility rituals attributed to the hypothetical corn king. Many modern barbarians acknowledge hereditary chiefs whose authority is as much magical as military. In neolithic Europe a single house marked out by its greater size and central position in some Western villages has been explained as the residence of a chief. The great stone tombs of the Atlantic coasts and the vast long barrows of Britain have been interpreted as chieftains' sepulchres. But not even German believers in the 'leadership principle' have been able to detect any indications of chieftainship in a Danubian village like Köln-Lindenthal.

In any case it may be assumed that the clan structure and community based on 'kinship' survived the neolithic revolution unscathed. Among barbarians today land is normally held by the clan in common. If not tilled collectively, plots are allotted to individual 'families' for use only and are generally redistributed annually. Pastures are of course commons. Among pure cultivators, owing to the role of the women's contributions to the collective economy, kinship is naturally reckoned in the female line, and the system of 'mother right' prevails. With stock-breeding, on the contrary, economic and social influence passes to the males and kinship is patrilinear.

The neolithic revolution was vindicated biologically by the numerical increase in the species, *Homo sapiens,* that followed it. Small though they were, neolithic communities were substantially larger and far more numerous than palaeolithic or mesolithic groups. From Hither Asia, Egypt, and Europe literally thousands of skeletons have survived from the period between the neolithic revolution and the urban revolution or the transition to a Bronze Age economy, as against the few hundred human fossils from the whole of the Old Stone Age. Yet the Old Stone Age must have lasted ten to fifty times as long as the New!

The growth of neolithic population was eventually limited by contradictions in the new economy. The expansion in numbers involved expansion in space. Additional families could be supported only by cultivating fresh plots and finding fresh pastures for growing flocks and herds. Food-producers within the limits of barbarism just had to spread. Each self-sufficing village must keep budding off daughter villages. The worldwide expansion of the neolithic economy bears witness to this process. In practice of course the food-producers often expanded at the expense of food-gatherers. And the latter did not always submit passively to expulsion or extinction; sometimes savages adopted and adapted the economy of encroaching barbarians. The neolithic cultures of northern Europe seem to be due mainly to mesolithic forest-folk who had secured stock and grains from advancing Danubians and other farmers and had learned from them how to make pots, spin, and weave. Such disciples swelled the flood of expanding peasantry and accelerated its advance. In the long run various streams met. Proximity gave opportunity for exchanging experience and pooling knowledge.

But contact is not likely to be always amicable. For each and all are competing for the same sort of land, and the supply is not unlimited. Such competition might of itself lead to war. The earliest Danubians seem to have been peaceful folk; weapons of war as against hunters' tools are absent from their graves. Their villages lacked military defences. It is no accident that the latest village of Köln-Lindenthal was defended by elaborate fortifications and that weapons were buried in contemporary graves. In the later phases of the neolithic period in Europe, armaments in the form of stone battle-axes and flint daggers became the most conspicuous items of funerary furniture.

In central and northern Europe we almost see the state of war of all against all arising as unoccupied but easily cultivable land became scarce. Elsewhere the same process is traceable, if less explicitly. In the successive layers of the settlement tells in the Balkans, Greece, Anatolia, Syria, and Iran we see radical changes in culture. Such abrupt changes are taken to symbolize the replacement of one society by another with different social traditions – in other words, the conquest, expulsion, or enslavement of one people by another. Such changes of population effected by war are a recurrent feature of barbarian life as described by ethnographers in North America, Africa, and the Pacific.

Naturally to seize the grain-plots and pastures that others have been cultivating and grazing allows no addition to the total population those lands supported; it is no solution to the contradiction. War and slaughter diminish rather than increase the human species.

Nevertheless change of culture in the archaeological record need not always mean the extinction of the older society; the result may be a 'mixed culture' in which items of the older equipment persist, implying the survival of some members of the society formerly established on the site. In central Europe late neolithic cultures exhibit some traits derived from the native Danubian traditions combined with others that had been developed on the wooded plains of the north. Some of the older Danubian stock must have been left alive even though they may have been enslaved by the Northerners. Mixed cultures may denote stratified societies divided into rulers and ruled. In any case they are richer than either of the component cultures in that they result from the blending of two social traditions evoked by distinct environments. They illustrate one of the most important processes in the pooling of human experience. Moreover, they probably symbolize the incipient break-up of the clan and 'kinship' organization of society.

A second defect in the neolithic economy was the very self-sufficiency the barbarian village prized so highly. Such a community had indeed far greater control over its food-supply and environment than any group of savages, and could reasonably plan ahead to meet future eventualities. But all its labours and plans might be frustrated by events still beyond its control: droughts or floods, tempests or frosts, blights, or hail-storms might annihilate crops and herds. And even a local failure might spell famine and annihilation for the self-contained and isolated community. Its reserves were too small to tide it over any prolonged succession of disasters or to let it take preventive measures on an effective scale.

The urban revolution eventually offered an escape from both contradictions.

4

THE HIGHER BARBARISM
OF THE COPPER AGE

THE worst contradictions in the neolithic economy were transcended when farmers were persuaded or compelled to wring from the soil a surplus above their own domestic requirements, and when this surplus was made available to support new economic classes not directly engaged in producing their own food. The possibility of producing the requisite surplus was inherent in the very nature of the neolithic economy. Its realization, however, required additions to the stock of applied science at the disposal of all barbarians, as well as a modification in social and economic relations. The thousand years or so immediately preceding 3000 B.C. were perhaps more fertile in fruitful inventions and discoveries than any period in human history prior to the sixteenth century A.D. Its achievements made possible that economic reorganization of society that I term the urban revolution.

The neolithic revolution took place in the grey night of remote prehistory. From a few peaks faintly lit by the reflected light of an archaeological sun and by inferences from the landscape subsequently revealed we have reconstructed very tentatively the course of this first revolution. The second takes place almost before our eyes in the full twilight of prehistory and reaches its climax only with the dawn of history. It must therefore be described.

Its theatre can be provisionally delimited; it is bounded on the west by the Sahara and the Mediterranean, on the east by the Thar desert and the Himalayas, on the north by the Eurasiatic mountain spine – Balkans, Caucasus, Elburz, Hindu-Kush – and on the south, as it happens, by the Tropic of Cancer. The geological, physiographical, and climatic conditions of this zone proved propitious to the revolutionary development. It provided the raw materials for the decisive discoveries. It offered inducements to intensive social organization and rich rewards for large-scale cooperation. It gave facilities for communications by which new knowledge might be pooled and essential materials collected and concentrated. Finally its cloudless skies presented nightly the impressive spectacle of the uniform motion of the heavenly bodies that in other latitudes is too often veiled.

The whole belt is relatively arid, though it was better watered in prehistoric times than today. Permanent settlement is possible only beside a river or a perennial spring. Agriculture is largely dependent on irrigation; though you may 'catch a crop' watered by showers in Palestine and Syria or from the flooding of a torrent even in Arabia, irrigation alone guarantees success. At the same time several varieties of fruit tree and the vine grew wild in the region; the prospect of a regular crop of dates, olives, figs or grapes every year is a powerful inducement to remain fixed where the plants grow. The orchardist must abandon the nomadism that may still appeal to the grain-grower.

The digging and maintenance of irrigation channels are social tasks even more than the construction of defensive ramparts or the laying out of streets (p. 66). The community as a whole must apportion to individual users the water thus canalized by collective effort. Now control of water puts in society's hands a potent force to supplement supernatural sanctions. Society can exclude from access to the channels recalcitrants who will not conform to rules of conduct generally approved. Banishment in an arid zone is a more drastic penalty than in a temperate or tropical clime where land and water are still relatively abundant.

The zone is interrupted by mountains and desert unfit for habitation. But around and between these are more hospitable steppes over which villages can be dotted not too sparsely and herdsmen may wander with their flocks, so that intercourse is on the whole easier than in forests and jungles. The western part of the crucial belt has been termed by Breasted the *Fertile Crescent*.

The Crescent's western horn is Egypt. There the narrow valley of the Nile forms a thread of greenery through the forbidding desert of the plateau. The annual flood irrigates a strip of either bank and the broad Delta to the north. At the same time the river affords a moving road on which even bulky goods can be transported between the First Cataract and the Mediterranean. The valleys and plains of Palestine and the narrow strip of coast land in Syria form a continuation of the Crescent where the rainfall is sufficient to allow even of dry cultivation. Thence east of Lebanon and Anti-Lebanon a broad belt of steppe extends to the Iranian mountains beyond the Tigris. Throughout this 'saddle' – the ancient Syria and Assyria (the Mosul vilayet) – the winter rains suffice to provide pasture for sheep and even to water precarious crops of corn. But permanent settlement is in effect restricted to oases and the banks of many streams issuing from the Armenian mountains – the Euphrates, Balikh, Khabur, Tigris, Zab. Finally the eastern horn is formed by the lower Tigris–Euphrates valley, in which the two rivers fulfil the function of the Nile in irrigation and transport.

Beyond its border chains the Iranian plateau is desert at the centre. But on the mountain slopes all round rise springs and streams sufficient to water fields and gardens. Finally beyond the mountains of Baluchistan lie Sind and the Punjab. Here Mesopotamian conditions recur on an immensely larger scale, with the Indus and six tributaries to irrigate and carry freight.

The archaeological record begins in small oases on steppes and plateaux. Despite the threat of drought the difficulties of taming the soil were less formidable there than on the flood plains of the major rivers. By small beginnings societies had the chance of learning the techniques of irrigation and drainage.

Such a society has been encountered already at Sialk in western Iran (p. 58). The earliest culture found there can be matched at other sites upon the plateau and northward up to Anau in the Merv oasis in Russian Turkistan

(Turkmenian S.S.R.). At Sialk a second phase can be seen in the villages built on the ruins of those described. The houses are no longer built just of packed clay (*pisé*), but of moulded bricks, dried in the sun. Gathering is less prominent in the communal economy; horses have been added to the domestic stock. Shells are brought across the mountains from the Persian Gulf. Copper is commoner, but it is still treated as a superior sort of stone worked by cold hammering. Equipment is made from local bone, stone, and chert supplemented by a little imported obsidian. But special kilns are built for firing pots.

Then with Sialk III the village was removed to a new site, close by the old and watered by the same spring. Equipment is still mainly home-made from local materials. But copper is worked intelligently by *casting* to make axes and other implements that must still be luxuries. Gold and silver are imported and lapis lazuli from northern Afghanistan. Potters appear who make vessels quickly on a fast spinning *wheel* instead of building them up by hand. And men use *seals* to mark their property. Finally Sialk IV is a colony of literate Elamites who have achieved civilization in the alluvial valley of the Kerkha and impose it upon the barbarian mountaineers about 3000 B.C.

The same sort of stages can be recognized in Syria and Assyria, though it cannot be proved that these are parallel in time with those disclosed at Sialk in Iran. From Ras Shamra on the coast of Syria (near Alexandretta) to Nineveh and Tepe Gawra, east of the Tigris, the village ruins at the bottom of the tells disclose a 'neolithic' culture, not identical with those of Iran and Egypt, but probably parallel thereto though still very imperfectly known. The next set of settlements, representing phase II, were built by people with different traditions from the first but surprisingly homogeneous throughout the whole belt. Archaeologists call them Halafians, after Tell Halaf on the Khabur, where their distinctive products were first identified. They too lived as mixed farmers and relied for their equipment mainly on local stones and bones. But even on the Upper

Khabur they received shells brought from the Persian Gulf while obsidian imported from the volcanic mountains of Armenia was extensively employed; indeed a Halafian village near Lake Van seems to have been inhabited by an industrial community engaged in quarrying the volcanic glass for export, like the neolithic flint-miners in England. Moreover the Halafians were almost certainly acquainted with metal, if not with intelligent metallurgy. Vases were superbly decorated with polychrome designs and fired in specially constructed kilns as if their makers were becoming professionals. Amulets were not only carved into the likeness of 'potent' objects, but were also engraved with equally magical patterns. So they could be, and were, used as seals: stamped on a blob of clay affixed to a jar-stopper or bundle the pattern and so its magic was transferred to the clay, put a 'taboo' on the object and marked it as someone's property. Finally the villagers cooperated in erecting shrines to local deities. And so did their contemporaries, the first colonists of lower Mesopotamia. For the first shrine of Ea at Eridu must have been founded in this phase.

In phase III the Halafian culture disappears to make room for another, presumably borne by new settlers and called, not very euphoniously, the al 'Ubaid culture, after a site in Lower Mesopotamia near Ur. The break in tradition is not indeed complete. The old shrines were reconstructed on a larger scale on their hallowed sites; so the old local gods survived and therefore some of the community of worshippers that had imagined them. The largest of three shrines grouped round a court at Tepe Gawra now measured over all 40 ft by 28 ft and was built of sun-dried bricks, painted on the outside. But in general domestic architecture declined. On the other hand metal was now worked intelligently by casting, though in Syria and northern Iraq the al 'Ubaid people seem to have been normally content to go on using local stone instead of organizing their economy to secure regular supplies of metal, while potters still made vases by hand. Nevertheless the amulets had been developed into specialized square or button seals with a loop on the back, and engraved on the face with animal figures instead of purely geometric patterns.

In Syria some sites were temporarily deserted after phase III, but some villages in Assyria, notably what was to become Nineveh and Tepe Gawra only 15 miles away, grew into regular little townships. At Tepe Gawra the shrines, whose repeated reconstruction on the same spot proves the continuity of tradition through all the drastic changes in material culture, have now grown into little temples built of kiln-burnt bricks and divided into several rooms. They still form a group of three round a court, but one now covers an over-all area of 57 ft by 43 ft. Clay models of carts and even covered wagons leave no doubt that wheeled vehicles were familiar. And pots are made on the wheel too. Objects of copper or even poor bronze are not very rare. But axes, sickle-teeth, and the rest of the industrial equipment and even weapons were still normally made of stone and other local materials. Lapis lazuli from Afghanistan, small manufactured articles from Sumer, and other luxuries are indeed imported. But fundamentally the self-sufficiency of neolithic economy has been preserved. Yet the imports from the south show that these Assyrian villages were contemporary with genuine cities in Lower Mesopotamia.

On the relatively well-watered steppes of northern Iraq arable lands and pastures were still so abundant that no overpowering need compelled villagers to transform their economy. It was simpler to use the plentiful local materials for equipment than to organize the importation of regular supplies of metal to replace them. First in the next phase, V, were elements of a new economy imposed in Assyria as at Sialk in Iran. But this imposition is almost historical. It can be better explained when the urban revolution has been examined in southern Iraq.

Communities like Sialk III and the comparable al'Ubaid villages in Syria, as well as others similarly equipped on the plateau of Asia Minor, in Cyprus, and in peninsular Greece, disposed of all the technical knowledge and apparatus of civilization. The economic organization and social framework were alone deficient. During the thousand odd years of the Chalcolithic Age the peoples of the Near East had made discoveries pregnant with revolutionary consequences – the metallurgy of copper and bronze, the harnessing of animal motive power, wheeled vehicles, the potters' wheel, bricks, the seal. Even before 3,000 B.C. these achievements were being diffused at least to the Aegean and to Turkistan and India. In a thousand years or so they will reach China and Britain. But, save for two localized centres of bronze working in Mexico and Peru, none reached the New World, Oceania, or Africa south of the Sahara till late historical times. The significance and nature of the advances noted above in the archaeological record must now be underlined.

The implications and revolutionary consequences of metallurgy have been explained in detail in *Man Makes Himself*, as well as in more technical books on archaeology. In practice it meant the combination of four major discoveries: (1) the *malleability* of copper; (2) its *fusibility*; (3) the *reduction of* copper from ores; and (4) *alloys*. Copper, native or produced by reduction, may have seemed a superior sort of stone that can not only be sharpened to cut like flint, but can also be bent, shaped by hammering, and even beaten out into sheets which can be cut up. This property seems to have been known and utilized in Sialk I, by the Badarians and Amratians of Egypt mentioned in the next chapter, and was familiar to the pre-Columbian Indians of North America. By itself it did not take man very far.

Secondly, when heated, copper becomes as plastic as potter's clay; nay, it will become liquid and will assume the shape of any container or *mould* into which it is poured. Yet on cooling it not only retains this shape, but becomes as hard as stone and can be given as good a cutting edge as flint. For tools copper possesses all the virtues of the older materials – stone, bone, wood – with others super-added. In fashioning a tool out of the old materials the only thing to do was to detach bits from a larger lump or matrix. An implement of copper, like a pot of clay, can be made by joining pieces together indissolubly; in practice, it is generally the mould, often made of clay, that is built up, liquid metal being then run in till the cavity is full. The sole limit to the size of the mould and therefore of the casting, the metal implement, is the operator's technical skill. And of course the shapes that can be given to the casting are equally unlimited. Moreover, the form of the casting can be further modified by hammering, as copper is malleable. Finally, a metal tool is more durable than one of stone or bone. A copper axe or knife neither cuts better nor keeps its edge longer than a stone axe or a flint blade. But, apart from a very limited amount of resharpening, once a flint or stone tool is broken not all the king's horses nor all the king's men can put it together again. A copper tool can not only be resharpened by whetting or hammer-ing; if broken, it can be recast with trifling loss and a new tool turned out as good as the old.

The utilization of these advantages required in practice a complex of ingenious inventions – a furnace with a draught to produce the relatively high temperature requisite for fusion (in the event bellows were invented, but their use is not directly demonstrated before 1500 B.C. in Egypt and 1000 in Europe), crucibles to contain the molten metal, tongs to lift them with, and above all moulds to confer upon the casting the desired shape.

Thirdly, this superior stone, that occurs very rarely in the metallic state in the Old World, can be produced artificially by heating with charcoal several much com-moner sorts of stone or earth, the ores we call oxides, carbonates, silicates, and sulphides of copper. None of these looks in the least like metallic copper nor possesses its desi-rable qualities, but they are fortunately brightly coloured and so the sort of stones early man looked for as pigments or charms. The discovery of the magical transubstantiation of these crystalline minerals into metallic copper unlocked adequate supplies of the metal. It had been made by the time of Sialk III and the al 'Ubaid phase in Syria. It was followed in the Near East by the reduction of other metals – silver, lead, and tin – and so led on to the fourth discovery that was certainly the latest in time.

Casting is easier, and the product is more reliable, if to the copper there can be deliberately added antimony, arsenic, lead, or, best of all, tin. By 3000 B.C. the advantages of an alloy of copper and tin had been realized in India, Mesopotamia, Asia Minor, and Greece; *bronze* had been discovered. (In the sequel bronze means this alloy of copper and tin unless otherwise stated.)

The sciences applied in metallurgy are more abstruse than those employed in agriculture or even pot-making. The chemical change effected by smelting is much more unexpected than that which transforms clay into pottery. The conversion of crystalline or powdery green or blue ores into tough red copper is a veritable transubstantiation. The change from the solid to the liquid state and back again, controlled in casting, is hardly less startling. The actual manipulations themselves are more intricate and exacting even than those involved in pot-making, spinning, or boat-building.

Hence it is not surprising that in the earliest historical societies, as among contemporary barbarians, metallurgists are always *specialists*. Probably from the first metallurgy was a *craft* as well as a technique. Smiths and miners not only possess peculiar skills, they have also been initiated into 'mysteries'. Presumably their craft lore was transmitted by the same concrete methods of precept and example as hunting lore or textile skill. But it was not divulged to all members of the community as these would be; not every clansman was trained as a smith. The operations of mining and smelting and casting are too elaborate and demand too continuous attention to be normally conducted in the intervals of tilling fields or minding cattle. Metallurgy is a full-time job.

These occupations are the first industries not normally conducted within the household to provide for domestic needs, but to meet the demands of others. The operators must therefore rely for their sustenance mainly on surplus foodstuffs produced by their customers. After the magicians, they may be the first class to be withdrawn from direct food-production. They are therefore not immediately dependent on the land for food; their livelihood depends upon the possession of portable skills, and generally also of portable goods, which they exchange for food.

Such craftsmen are therefore less amenable to social discipline than fishermen or farmers, less dependent on territorial society than even the magician; for his authority is rooted in the 'subjective' beliefs and superstitions of his fellow clansmen. But the craftsman might find a market for his objective skill and substantial wares even among strangers. The rare metal objects that we have encountered in the Copper Age villages were very likely made by itinerant smiths travelling about the country with ingots of metal and producing implements on the spot 'to order'. This was demonstrably the case in the European Bronze Age. It is the rule for iron workers in Negro Africa today. The tinker in rural Europe is a survival of the same system.

Now, as the craftsmen were the practical bearers of the scientific traditions of barbarism, their ability to migrate contributed materially to the diffusion of discoveries and the pooling of experience. The comparative uniformity of the very earliest metal products, anterior to the urban revolution, may be explained as the result of such diffusion. Metallurgical lore is the first approximation to international science. But it remains craft lore. All the practical science of the ancient smiths and miners was certainly embedded in an unpractical matrix of magic ritual. Assyrian texts, even in the first millennium B.C., contain hints of what such rituals may have involved – foetuses and virgins' blood. So do the remains of a bronze-workers' encampment in Heathery Burn Cave (Co. Durham) in England. Today barbarian smiths' operations are surrounded with a complex of magical precautions.

In the second place, the transmission of such lore by apprenticeship is largely imitative and therefore conservative. The processes need not be described in abstract terms. All the apprentice need do is to imitate as closely as possible every operation of the master. In so doing he has no opportunity of introducing a variation which might be beneficial.

Finally, craft lore is liable to be secret. It is passed on from father to son or from master to apprentice. Craftsmen thus tend to form *guilds* or clans which will guard jealously the mysteries of the craft. Among barbarians we find hereditary craft-clans organized on the same 'kinship' basis as savage clans.

The adoption of metal tools will thus make room for a new class that had no place in a pure neolithic economy. But it will at the same time destroy the self-sufficiency distinctive of that economy. The individual householder sacrifices his independence in so far as he regards as necessities metal tools that he cannot make himself but must acquire by barter from the smith. He must henceforth produce a surplus beyond his domestic needs to support specialists who produce not food but indigestible ores, ingots, and axes.

The neolithic village, too, will have to sacrifice its highly-prized self-sufficiency. Copper ore is by no means common: the lodes are generally located among infertile mountains; very few villages can have had a copper mine in the immediate vicinity. Nearly always the raw material at least will have to be imported; its regular use involves the organization of a regular supply – trade, in fact, and that no longer a luxury trade. As soon as metal is regarded as a necessity and no longer a luxury, the local unit becomes by that very fact dependent on imported materials. Society must intensify its production of foodstuffs to support the specialists engaged in mining, extracting, and working the newly necessary material.

Now, owing to the relative rarity of copper and the absolute rarity of tin (as soon as the alloy becomes the standard metal), and owing further to the difficulties of transporting heavy materials, the surplus required to support the essential specialists is large. Bronze equipment involves a great deal of social labour; it is inevitably expensive. The advantages enumerated on page 83 do not appear in themselves to have been sufficient to induce peasants to produce the requisite surplus, to stimulate an 'effective demand', as modern economists would say. Two factors seem to have contributed to that end, to convert metal into a necessity.

On the one hand, under the peculiar conditions of alluvial valleys like the Tigris–Euphrates delta, where even stone is scarce, the greater durability of copper or bronze tools may have made them actually more economical than stone or obsidian. On the other hand, in war, especially for in-fighting, a copper knife or dagger is much more reliable than a flint one; the latter may break just at the awkward moment when you must stab your enemy or perish. The first metal objects, apart from small trinkets, to be commonly or regularly deposited in graves are, in fact, weapons, not tools. In practice we shall find that such depositions are common only after the urban revolution in the alluvial valleys had produced a new economic order which made the demand effective. But in the meantime another series of independent discoveries and inventions had simplified the satisfaction of the demand by reducing transport costs.

Having tamed cattle to provide meat and then milk, some societies hit upon the idea of shifting to the shoulders of oxen part of the heavy burden of toil. The first step, perhaps, was to make a pair of oxen drag over a field a variant on the hoe that women had hitherto wielded – a plough. Besides the plough itself, a yoke and harness had to be invented, by means of which the beast's tractive power could be imparted to it. Fortunately the broad shoulders of the ox give purchase for the yoke without impeding the animal's movement or respiration. Ploughs being at first made entirely of wood, no direct evidence as to the invention's antiquity is available. Written or inscribed documents attest the use of ploughs in Mesopotamia and Egypt by 3000 B.C., and in India not much later. Soon after 1400 B.C. ploughing is similarly attested in China, and not very much later pictures of ploughs were carved on the rocks of distant Sweden. So by 1000 B.C. the plough, like bronze, had attained the limits of its ancient diffusion (p. 169).

The plough changed farming from plot cultivation to agriculture (the tillage of fields), and welded indissolubly cultivation and stock-breeding. It relieved women of the most exacting drudgery, but deprived them of their monopoly over the cereal crops and the social status that conferred. Among barbarians, whereas women normally hoe plots, it is men who plough fields. And in even the oldest Sumerian and Egyptian documents the ploughmen really are males. To support the heavy work plough-oxen need better fodder than can be got by grazing on the steppe; they are generally kept in stalls and fed on specially-grown hay, or even barley. So stall dung became available to fertilize the fields. But the most decisive innovation was that by harnessing the ox man began to control and use a motive power other than that furnished by his own muscular energy. The ox was the first step to the steam engine and petrol motor.

The new motive power could be applied in other ways. On the dusty plains of Hither Asia as on the snows of northern Europe heavy loads can most conveniently be transported on sledges. As a sledge was known in northern Europe in mesolithic times (p. 51), it was almost certainly known in Hither Asia before 4000 B.C. Of course, a yoke of oxen can pull a sledge as easily as a plough. The same harness will serve in both cases. There is no more evidence for prehistoric sledges than for ploughs, but sledges were still being used – at least for funerals – in Mesopotamia as late as 2600 B.C.

Long before that transport had been revolutionized by the application of rotary motion, by the invention of the wheel. There are ambiguous indications of its use in North Syria as early as the Tell-Halaf phase. In any case, the models from Gawra (p. 82) show two-wheeled and four-wheeled carts already in general use about 3000 B.C. From Sumerian sculptures and actual specimens from tombs of the third millennium the details of their construction can be deduced. The wheels consisted of three pieces of solid wood mortised together and bound with leather tyres attached with copper nails. The wheels turned in one piece with the axles, which could be secured to the body of the sledge-wagon merely with leather thongs.

Carts like these can still be seen in use in Sardinia, Turkey, and Sind. Though heavy and clumsy, they are durable, and denote an immense advance on porterage or sledge transport. They are, indeed, the lineal ancestors of the automobile. By about 2000 B.C. wheeled vehicles were in use from the Indus valley to the Syrian coasts. In Egypt, however, no wheeled vehicles were in use before 1600 B.C. But the invention had reached Crete by 2000 B.C., and before the end of the second millennium was known from China to Sweden. But in the interval, by crossing with other inventions, vehicular transport had been materially accelerated.

Man's (or generally woman's) shoulders were the oldest means of transport. But when animal motive power came into use, it was natural to transfer the pack to the shoulders of some dumb beast. For this purpose the ox is not well adapted. The oldest pack animal would seem to have been the ass, a native of East Africa. Before 3000 B.C. the tame ass was known in Egypt, and presumably used for transport. Asses were certainly so used in Syria and Mesopotamia early in the third millennium. But there was a wild ass, the onager, in Hither Asia which was domesticated, too, so that it is not clear how far the pack asses of the Orient were of African origin.

In the fourth millennium horses' bones have been found

at Sialk in Iran, and at Anau in Turkistan. A native habitat for horses lay probably in that direction, and the Merb oasis would be a quite likely centre for their domestication. But, of course, horses can be kept to provide meat and milk, as they were by the Mongols and the Scythians. Yet they can be used for riding, driving, and as pack animals. Riding as a means of accelerating travel and facilitating intercourse is a factor to be reckoned with, but the extent of equitation and of the use of horses in general before 2000 B.C. is still problematical.

That is all that can be said at the moment of the use of camels, too. Since 1000 B.C. transport and communication across the deserts of Hither Asia have depended on the 'ship of the desert'. But long before that, camel bones turned up in a layer at Anau, equated with Sialk I or II, while there is an isolated model of a camel from an Egyptian grave said to be a little older than 3000 B.C. So some societies may have disposed of this means of cross-country transport even in the fourth millennium.

In any case, travel by land had been accelerated by 3000 B.C. by harnessing Asiatic asses or horses, or both (for safety let us say 'equids', which embraces both species) to light two-wheeled cars or chariots. The harness (familiar from Sumerian pictures in the third millennium) employed was that already devised to control the ox. But as these unfortunate equids do not possess broad shoulders like the ox, tractive power was transmitted to the yoke by a breastband across the animal's throat against which it had to pull. In so doing the wretched beast was half-choking himself. Despite the loss of power thus caused, the Oriental harness was copied wherever the horse-chariot was adopted, and was not finally reformed till the horse-collar was invented in Dark-Age Europe somewhere about the ninth century A.D.

So before the end of the fourth millennium B.C. the strength of oxen, horses, and asses, and the wheel had provided Oriental societies with the motive power and equipment for land transport which were not superseded till the nineteenth century. And by 3000 B.C. wind was providing motive power for water transport, too. Even palaeolithic hunters must have possessed some sort of rafts and canoes. Mesolithic Europeans could succeed in crossing the stormy seas between Ulster and Kintyre; their neolithic successors made still more adventurous journeys. The Polynesians, of Oceania, though equipped only with stone tools, could build boats over one hundred feet long, capable of accommodating more than a hundred persons and provisions, in which they made journeys of a thousand miles or more. The Polynesian boats were equipped with sails, and sailing boats are frequently represented in the Mediterranean and Egypt during the third millennium. But the oldest evidence for the sail is provided by a model from an al 'Ubaid grave at Eridu and then by late Egyptian vases. The boats depicted on the latter are believed to be foreign to the Nile valley, but perhaps at home on the Persian Gulf. In any case they prove that the sail had reached Egypt before 3000 B.C. By this invention man for the first time harnessed an inorganic force to provide motive power. In this respect it remained unique till the invention of the water-wheel at the end of the first millennium B.C. The clumsy square sails depicted on the Egyptian vases needed much improvement before ships could be manoeuvred freely, but they must still rank as the direct precursors of those that propelled shipping till the nineteenth century. In any case, whether sailed, paddled, rowed, or merely hauled from the banks of rivers or canals, the boats of the fourth millennium could transport heavy and bulky loads far more economically than pack-asses or ox-carts. The commerce of antiquity, in so far as it handled cheap and popular goods in bulk, was mainly waterborne.

The new means of transport just described, by simplifying the distribution of goods, naturally furthered the emergence of the new class of artisans dependent on imported materials. They may themselves have evoked new specialists. The construction of wagons and boats calls for great skill in carpentry. Before the linguistic ancestors of the Hindus,

Greeks, and other Indo-European peoples split up, carpentry seems to have been already a specialized craft, since the carpenter is the only craftsman denoted by a word common to Sanskrit, Greek, and other branches of the linguistic family. Nevertheless, ethnography shows that farmers do construct carts and boats without calling in professionals. We cannot, therefore, deduce the specialization of boat-builders or wainwrights before the urban revolution. But one craftsman beside the smith is attested by archae-ology.

From a lump of plastic clay thrown on the centre of a wheel spinning fast on a vertical pivot, an expert hand can elicit in a couple of minutes a vessel that it might take several days to build up by hand. And the vessel thus made will be perfectly symmetrical. On the other hand, its production requires extreme dexterity that must be labori-ously acquired through long apprenticeship. Ethnography shows that potters who use the wheel are normally male specialists, no longer women for whom potting is just a household task like cooking and spinning. In antiquity, too, it may be assumed that the use of the wheel indicates the industrialization of ceramic production, the emergence of a new specialized craft.

Since his equipment is very simple and his raw material is available everywhere, the expert potter may be a per-ambulating craftsman as easily as the smith. In Crete and the Aegean today potters, with their 'families' and their wheel, travel from village to village and from island to island, turning out in each what local taste demands. We have a little direct evidence for such itinerants in the second millennium from Crete and Aegina. Perhaps, indeed, the earliest wheel-made pots were everywhere produced by such travelling workers. In any case, potters did exhibit the same mobility as characterizes other early craftsmen. They, too, might be emancipated from the restrictions of territorial society; potters' lore could become intertribal, if not international.

Hence the wheel early invaded the ceramic industry

throughout Hither Asia. We have met it in phase III of
the Copper Age of Assyria, at Sialk III in Iran, and by
2500 B.C. it was firmly established in India. In Egypt, on
the contrary, the potters' wheel arrived only after the
urban revolution under Dynasty III, and in a less efficient
form than in Asia, but still a thousand years before wheeled
vehicles were known beside the Nile. In Europe, the relations between these two applications of the wheel were
reversed. North of the Alps wheeled vehicles were known
by the second millennium, the potter's wheel not till the
end of the first.

In contrast to the predominantly female contributions
described in Chapter 3, the discoveries and inventions just
considered seem all due to the men, and certainly strength-
ened their economic position. By relieving women of a lot
of heavy but essential tasks in the way of hoeing, carrying
burdens, and making pots, they cut away the economic
foundations of mother-right. Moreover, the new specialists
will not really fit in to the old kinship organization. Even
if the potter settles permanently in a village, he is obviously
not a clansman in any physiological sense. His membership
of the local group and his duties therein are determined by
residence and function. A new basis is needed for a social
order that embraces such strangers. Moreover, their number
may have been augmented by the conquests and mixtures of
populations deduced from the change of cultures in the
archaeological record.

Now, among barbarians where some of the innovations
here discussed have been adopted, sociologists expect to
find the patriarchal 'family', and even that form of it in
which the household comprises married sons, their wives
and children, and perhaps even slaves, as well as the
patriarch. In such a society personal property may extend
from ornaments and clothes, implements and weapons, to
flocks and herds – and slaves – capital goods which can
increase. And now a man who has distinguished himself
as a 'war-chief' (in matriarchal society often a temporary
and elective office) has a chance of consolidating his

authority on an economic basis by wealth in cattle or servants. As this wealth will pass to his sons, so the authority it gives may become hereditary. But to become royal power it must be consecrated, perhaps in some such way as that suggested on page 72. But another institution may ease the transition.

Among barbarians on this sort of level of technical and economic development some of the fertility and other rituals that had been performed communally by all clansmen in savagery are often found to have been monopolized by 'secret societies', initiation into which must be purchased by feasts and presents. Within such a society there are generally grades; advancement up this ladder of rank is, like initiation, a sacramental rite, but it must be none the less purchased. The members of such a society normally remain fishers or hunters or herdsmen or farmers. If they became specialists and were exempted like craftsmen from these productive avocations, they would become professional priests. And if rank be hierarchical, the richest and highest will be very like kings. The archaeological material just described gives some hints that this sort of development had been going on in the Copper Age in Syria.

Seals, such as we met already in Halafian villages (p. 81), no doubt start as amulets that confer *mana* on their lucky wearers. But as well as, or instead of, being carved into the shape of a totem or a 'thing of power', they are engraved with magic patterns or representations of the totem. This pattern with its magic could be transferred to a lump of clay. By pressing his seal-amulet on such a lump affixed to the stopper of a jar, an individual could put a 'taboo' on it, transfer part of his personality to it, and mark it as his property. Even Halafians used amulet-seals in this way, presumably indicating a recognition of proprietary rights. Incidentally, the standardized symbols engraved on the seal for this purpose will help to provide the characters for a conventional script when the urban revolution has made writing necessary.

The repeated reconstruction on the same spot of the

shrines at Gawra through all the abrupt changes of other aspects of material and spiritual culture (pp. 81–2) can best be explained by assuming that, despite all changes of population, some society of votaries maintained its corporate personality. The hypothetical corporations may correspond to the 'secret societies' of modern barbarians or to the priesthoods into which these develop. By the fourth phase at Gawra the shrines had already assumed the distinctive form that farther south is attested as the house of a god where stands his cult image and the altar for sacrifices. The colours with which they are painted are those prescribed as symbolic and magical in later theological literature. The shrines are, then, the lineal precursors of temples that will symbolize the world order, and give some justification for assuming the worship or cult of personalized deities.

Now, the abrupt changes in secular architecture, pottery, and burial rites, noted at Gawra and other Syrian tells, must reflect substantial changes in population. It is difficult to believe such changes were peaceable. Just as much as in temperate Europe (p. 74), and, indeed, even sooner, growing populations had to find an outlet for surplus families by stealing other people's land. Presumably the Halafians had supplanted older 'neolithic' communities, to be replaced in their turn by the al 'Ubaid people. In that case the changes of archaeological 'cultures' must be the results of wars of conquest that would afford the chief the opportunity of winning secular power. But the vanquished need not have been exterminated. If some survived as guardians of the ritual tradition of a local god, others may have been left alive as serfs or slaves. Men would have been 'domesticated', like oxen and asses. Conquests would have produced stratified societies, divided into masters and slaves, embryos of the class division revealed in the oldest historical cities.

5

THE URBAN REVOLUTION
IN MESOPOTAMIA

METALLURGY, the wheel, the ox-cart, the pack-ass, and the sailing ship provided the foundations for a new economic organization. Without it the new materials would remain luxuries, the new crafts would not function, the new devices would be just conveniences. The societies living, albeit precariously, on the Syrian steppes or the plateaux of Iran, like those inhabiting the Mediterranean coasts and temperate Europe, could still scrape along without feeling the imperious need to face the formidable task of reconstructing the whole fabric of neolithic barbarism. The alluvial valleys of the great rivers offered a more exacting environment, but also greater material rewards for its exploitation. In them Copper Age villages turned into Bronze Age cities by processes more fully described in *Man Makes Himself*.

In a small tract no larger than Denmark, on the Tigris–Euphrates delta, the ancient Sumer (Shinar in the Bible), the transformation can be followed step by step in the archaeological record. Sumer was new land only recently raised above the waters of the Persian Gulf by the silt carried down by the two rivers. It was still covered with vast swamps, full of towering reeds, interrupted by arid banks of mud and sand, and periodically inundated by floods. Through tortuous channels among the reeds the muddy waters flowed sluggishly to the sea. But the waters teemed with fish, the reed brakes were alive with wild fowl, wild pig, and other game, and on every emergent patch of soil grew date palms offering every year a reliable crop of nutritive fruit.

By contrast to the arid desert on either side, this jungle must have seemed a paradise. If once the flood waters could be controlled and canalized, the swamps drained, and the arid banks watered, it could be made a Garden of Eden. The soil was so fertile that a hundred-fold return was not impossible. Actually, documents dating from 2500 B.C. indicate that the average yield on a field of barley was eighty-six times the sowing. Here, then, farmers could easily produce a surplus above their domestic needs.

They would have to; raw materials requisite for equipment were not so bountifully provided. From alluvial mud you cannot pick up stones or flints suitable for even the simplest cutting tools. Even such substances, as well as timber and stone for building, had to be imported from outside the delta. But the river channels not only unite the whole plain but provide moving roads on which boats can easily transport the essential materials from the mountainous lands upstream or from across the Persian Gulf. Trade was necessary, but also relatively easy. Incidentally, if material for axes and knives had to be imported in any case, copper would be found more economical than the less durable stones and flints.

The first pioneers arrived in Sumer with an equipment similar to that found in countless Copper Age settlement mounds in Iran and no less closely resembling that of Halafian villages in Syria and Assyria (p. 81). The oldest settlement yet recognized is marked by a tiny shrine at Eridu. Successive reconstructions and enlargements of the shrine converted its site into a tell surmounted by the historical temple of the god, Ea. The sixth reconstruction of the primeval shrine formed the centre of a village of reed huts of the al 'Ubaid culture described on p. 81. Remains of similar al 'Ubaid villages have been found on the sites of most historical cities – Erech, Eridu, Lagash, Ur – in Sumer, but not yet farther upstream in what became Akkad.

At all these sites the barbarian villages of the first al 'Ubaid colonists are separated from the oldest 'historical' cities (in which legible written documents occur) by fifty or more feet of debris, accumulated as in Syrian and Iranian tells from successive reconstructions of the nuclear settlements. Though cult was celebrated at all levels on the same hallowed spot, e.g., at Eridu, changes in ceramic styles, the introduction of the potter's wheel, the gradual substitution of cylinder seals for stamps, and so on must reflect an influx of fresh settlers with new traditions, who amalgamated with the pioneers to form a stratified society with composite traditions. Between the *al 'Ubaid* culture and the first historical or *Early Dynastic* civilization, archaeologists distinguish at least two phases, designated respectively *Uruk* and *Jemdet Nasr*, both of which are represented not only in Sumer but also in the later Akkad, as far north as the junction of the Diyala and Tigris near Baghdad, and up the Euphrates to Mari, opposite the mouth of the Khabur. So, too, from later written records, philologists deduce the presence of three linguistic groups – '*Japhetites*' (known only inferentially from a few place-names); *Semites* (speaking a language akin to Hebrew and Arabic); and the dominant *Sumerians*. (It is not yet possible to attach these linguistic labels to the archaeologists' cultures, but it is known that Sumerian was being written in Sumer before the close of the Uruk phase, and the Sumerian script was being used to transcribe Semitic names at Mari near the beginning of the Early Dynastic phase.)

Before the end of the Uruk phase at Erech, the ruins of successive settlements had already formed a tell some sixty feet high. At the top one is no longer standing in a village green but in the square of a cathedral city. In the foreground lie the ruins of a gigantic temple measuring over all 245 ft by 100 ft (cf. the Assyrian shrines mentioned on page 81) later dedicated to the goddess Inanna. Behind, attached to the temple of Anu, rises an artificial mountain or *Ziggurat*, 35 ft high. It is built of mud and sun-dried bricks, but its steeply-sloping walls have been consolidated by hammering into the brickwork while still wet thousands of pottery goblets. A flight of steps leads up to the summit – a platform covered with asphalt. On it stands a miniature temple measuring over all 73 ft by 57 ft

6 ins., containing a long cult room with narrow chambers on either side and an altar or an idol at one end. The walls, of white-washed brick and imported timbers, were embellished with niches and buttresses and pierced with clerestory windows; the doors were framed with imported pinewood and closed with mats.

The erection of these monumental temples and artificial mountains, the manufacture of the bricks and pottery goblets, the importation of pinewood (from Syria or the Iranian mountains), and of lapis lazuli, silver, lead, and copper to adorn the shrines presuppose a substantial labour force – a large population. In point of view of size the community has expanded from a village to a city. It has grown rich too.

The artisans, labourers, and transport workers may have been 'volunteers' inspired by religious enthusiasm. But if they were not paid for their labour, they must at least have been nourished while at work. A surplus of foodstuffs must, therefore, have been available for their support. The fertility of the soil that enabled the farmer to produce far more than he could consume supplied this. But its expenditure on temples suggests what later records confirm, that 'gods' concentrated it and made it available for distribution among their working servants. Perhaps these gods were projections of ancestral society and were regarded as the creators, and therefore the eminent owners, of the soil that society itself had reclaimed from desert and marsh by the collective labour of ancestral generations.

But the gods, being fictions, must have had real representatives, nominally their specialized servants, who must have done much to give concrete form to the imaginary beings, and by interpreting must have invented their desires. Temples presuppose priesthoods. Did these begin in 'secret societies', such as among some modern barbarian tribes have monopolized once communal rituals (p. 95)? By the beginning of historical records the Sumerian priests formed corporations as eternal as the gods they served and maintained; individual priests might die, but the vacant seats would find new occupants. Presumably these had already in the fourth millennium undertaken the not unprofitable task of administering the gods' estates and directing the works on which their surplus wealth was expended.

The construction of a temple was a cooperative task. The labour of the hundreds of participants must be co-ordinated and directed. The whole must be planned accurately in advance. The outlines of the temple were in fact laid out with strings before the walls were begun. The ground plan of a temple, marked out on the bitumen floor by the thin red lines left by a coloured string, has actually been found on the summit of the artificial mountain at Erech rather earlier than the one described above. From other cities and later times we have temple plans drawn to scale on clay tablets. The Sumerians believed that such plans were designed by the gods themselves and revealed in dreams. But the real architects were presumably the priests.

In a later temple, still belonging to the Uruk phase at Erech, and in the next phase in Akkad too, clay tablets turn up scratched with shorthand pictures and numerals. They are accounts, the direct precursors of the oldest tablets that we can read today. As administrators of the temple estates, the priests must give account of their stewardship to a jealous master and their colleagues in the perpetual corporation. So they have agreed upon a con-ventional method of recording receipts and expenditures in written signs that shall be intelligible to all their colleagues and successors; they have invented *writing*. Soon after 3000 B.C. the writing becomes fully intelligible to modern philologists too, and the documents speak to us across the millennia. With their aid let us examine the Sumerian cities of the Early Dynastic period, the first half of the third millennium B.C.

The city itself is girt with a brick wall and a fosse, within the shelter of which man found for the first time a world of his own, relatively secure from the immediate pressure of raw external nature. It stands in an artificial landscape of gardens, fields, and pastures created out of reed swamp and desert by the collective activity of preceding generations in building dykes and digging canals. The canals that drain the land and make it fruitful also provide the citizens with water and fish and bring to the quays merchandise from afar.

Even in physical size the city is contrasted with the older village. Though insignificant in comparison with London or New York, it represents a new magnitude in human settlement. The built-up area of Ur occupied 150 acres; on the analogy of contemporary Near Eastern cities that would accommodate 24,000 souls. A governor of Lagash, one of the smaller cities of Sumer about which we happen to be exceptionally well informed, claims to rule over ten shars of men – a round number, literally thirty-six thousand, and perhaps applying only to adult males. The populations of Lagash, Umma, and Khafajah are reliably estimated to have been 19,000, 16,000, and 12,000 respectively during the third millennium.

The spiritual and economic unity of the new aggregate was expressed most obviously in the temples of the gods, raised on an artificial platform and dominated by the towering ziggurat, but comprising also granaries, magazines, and workshops. The gods, as representatives of the tribe and clans, own the farm land created by social labour; town land is apparently individually owned already, while pasture remains common. The tribal territory of Lagash, for example, appears divided into the estates of some twenty deities, eminent domain over them all being perhaps retained by the chief god of the city or tribe. His consort, Baü (whose temple accounts alone have been preserved almost intact), thus owned seventeen square miles. As with the arable land of a barbarian clan, the use of three-quarters of this area was allotted to individual families in plots of varying size. The rest Baü retained as a 'personal estate', worked for her by wage-earners, by tenants paying the equivalent of a seventh or an eighth of the produce as rent, or by the customary labour of the remaining 'clansmen'.

Then in her temple worked twenty-one bakers, receiving 'wages' in barley, and assisted by twenty-seven female slaves, twenty-five brewers with six slave assistants, forty women engaged in preparing wool from the goddess's flocks, female spinners, female weavers, a male smith, and other artisans, as well as officials, clerks, and priests. The temple also owned and provided its employees with equipment – metal tools, ploughs, plough animals, wagons, and boats. Baü possessed further breeding stock, including a stud bull imported from Elam. (Stock was liable to deteriorate on the sultry plains if not crossed periodically with mountain breeds.)

So the temple appears as a sort of divine *household*, an enormously enlarged version of the patriarchal household of barbarism. But in this household the several tasks which were performed collectively by the members of a neolithic household (p. 67) have been differentiated and divided between specialists, each of whom concentrates on performing one of the functions which in a neolithic economy would be only one item in the daily toil. So the several operations of the textile industry, all of which would have been completed by the barbarian housewife, have been allotted to three distinct groups of craftswomen. The specialists thus withdrawn from direct food production are nourished by the surplus produced by the god's tenants and concentrated in his granaries.

The new class of specialist craftsmen which was arising before the revolution is provided for in the same way and fits easily into the temple organization. But, if thereby assured of food and shelter, the smith, for instance, loses the freedom and prestige earned by his skill under barbarism (p. 86). He must sell his skill and his products to the head of the household and will be dependent upon the household store for his raw materials. The same fate threatens other craftsmen who arise about this time – glaziers, jewellers, seal-cutters.

The system of divine households ensured the rational exploitation of the land, the maintenance of essential canals,

and the production of a surplus on a scale large enough to
support a substantially increased population. But the divine
households were not self-contained units, though all united
under the overlordship of Ningirsu. The urban population
was hardly exhausted in the foregoing enumeration based
upon early temple wage-lists. It included professional
merchants or traders, who would not all belong to any
particular divine household and so seldom figure in the
lists of temple employees that are our principal source for
knowledge of professions in Early Dynastic times. The archaeological record in any case gives abundant evidence for
the activity of traders.

Imports, as remarked on page 98, were essential for life on
an alluvial plain. By 3000 B.C. copper or bronze, timber for
building stone, at least for querns and door-sockets (in the
ancient East wooden doors were not hinged, but pi.   'd on
a hollowed stone set at the base of the jamb) had become
necessities to the urban population. For the gods, at least,
gold, silver, lead, lapis lazuli and other precious substances
were regarded as necessities, too. These and other materials
were, in fact, imported, and that fairly regularly, judging by
the quantities found in ruins, and still more in graves from
the Jemdet phase on. Copper came chiefly from Oman
(Magan) on the Persian Gulf, but probably also from the
eastern mountains; tin may have been obtained from
Drangiana in eastern Iran, from Syria, from Asia Minor,
or even from Europe. The Taurus mountains were a main
source of silver and lead. Timber came from the mountains
to the north-east, and perhaps also from the coastal ranges
of Syria, the best stone from Oman, lapis lazuli from Badak-
shan in north-eastern Afghanistan, mother-of-pearl from
the Persian Gulf, sank shells from peninsular India. Trade
was, indeed, so extensive and so active that it brought
from cities in the Indus valley manufactured articles – seal-
amulets, beads and, perhaps, even pottery bases.

The personnel engaged in this traffic must have been
heterogeneous. For reasons adduced on page 69 it may well
have been partly recruited from savages surviving on the

desert fringe, or at least from nomadic tribes devoted
mainly to pastoralism. These may well have been Semites
who in later historical times were everywhere conspicuous
as traders. The conditions of commerce must have been
exacting. Caravans must cross swamps, deserts, and mountain ranges; flotillas had not only to thread their ways
along the canals and tortuous river channels between
shoals and marshes, but also to brave the open waters of
the Persian Gulf and perhaps also of the Arabian Sea.
Both must traverse the territories of foreign tribes, who
had to be either induced by bribes or forced by arms to
permit passage and to supply water and other necessities.
So transport was expensive. The merchants needed, besides
trading stock, supplies and equipment for the journey, and
means of bribery and defence.

Semi-permanent agencies must be established at the
termini for the collection of freight and cargo, just as
European business houses have established 'factories' and
colonies on the coasts of Africa and China or in the cities
of the Levant and Istanbul. Many business documents and
letters have survived that belonged to such a merchant
colony established at the beginning of the second millennium at Kanes, on the plateau of Asia Minor, and engaged
in the export of copper, silver, and lead from the Turkish
mines. References in later epics imply that this colony
existed already about 2500 B.C.

Owing to these conditions 'trade' in the Orient was a
more potent agency in the diffusion of culture than it is
today. Free craftsmen might travel with the caravans
seeking a market for their skill, while slaves would form
part of the merchandise. These, together with the whole
caravan or ship's company, must be accommodated in the
home city. Foreigners in a strange land would demand the
comforts of their own religion just as much as English
colonies in a Catholic or Mohammedan country expect an
Anglican service every Sunday. So a scene carved by a
local Sumerian artist on a vase, recovered from a ruined
city on the Diyala, depicts an Indian cult being celebrated

apparently in a local shrine in Akkad. If cults were thus
transmitted, useful arts and crafts could be diffused just as
easily. Trade promoted the pooling of human experience.

Under such conditions the commerce essential to their
maintenance would increase the heterogeneity of the cities'
populations. The latter already consisted, according to the
testimony of philology and archaeology, of disparate linguistic and cultural stocks. The indispensable merchants,
compelled by their profession to travel, could not well be
obliged to trade with one city alone, and craftsmen, too,
could still sell their skills abroad; in the early accounts from
Lagash we read of a man from the neighbouring city of
Umma working in Baü's brewery. As a social order for
uniting such disparate elements, the barbarian principle
of kinship was becoming a threadbare fiction.

Now, traces of totemism can in fact be detected in the
symbols of the deities and in representations of cult scenes
in which the participants are dressed as animals. The
divine estates, plots on which were allotted – perhaps periodically – to the deity's 'people', may well be derived
from the communally owned clan lands distributed annually
for cultivation by the clansmen in many barbarian societies.
But any approximation to equality of lots in such common
farmland has disappeared by the time of the earliest
Lagash accounts. While many of Baü's 'people' seem to
have held only 0.8 to 2.5 acres, a high temple official held
35.5 acres. Moreover, though all members of a divine
household may have been in theory servants of the god,
the conditions of service were very different for the priestly
administrators on the one hand and the tenants, wage-
earners, and slaves on the other. The share farmers and agricultural labourers received only a fraction of the produce of
their labour. From the surplus collected by the temple the
bakers and brewers and other artisans were paid only a
modest wage in barley; the slaves who helped them presumably got little beyond their bare keep.

Indeed, before 2500 B.C. the divine households had ceased
to be anything like happy families. The abuses that

disturbed the households' harmony are quaintly set forth by Urukagina of Lagash in a decree aimed at restoring the old order 'as it had existed from the beginning'. Favoured priests practised various forms of extortion (overcharging for burials, for instance), and treated the god's (i.e. the community's) land, cattle, equipment, and servants as their own private property or personal slaves. Then 'the High Priest came into the garden of the poor ... and took wood therefrom.' 'If a great man's house adjoined that of an ordinary citizen', the former might annex the humble dwelling without paying any proper compensation to its owner. 'If a fair ass be born to a subject and his overlord say, "I will buy it,"' the privileged purchaser seldom paid 'as much as satisfied the owner's heart.' For all its clumsy language, this archaic text gives us unmistakable glimpses of a real conflict of classes.

The surplus produced by the new economy was, in fact, concentrated in the hands of a relatively small class. Such concentration was doubtless necessary for the accumulation of absolutely small individual contributions into reserves sufficient for the great tasks imposed on civilized society. But it split society into classes and produced a further contradiction in the new economy. For it limited the expansion of industry and consequently the absorption of the surplus rural population.

In so far as only 'gods' and their favourite servants were in a position to purchase the products of the new industries, the effective demand for such products would remain small. Only a few craftsmen could be sure of a livelihood in supplying them. For the rest, as in a neolithic economy, the offspring of a prolific peasantry must find new lands to till. So while reclamation works, the warfare against desert and swamp, might satisfy this need, warfare against neighbouring cities to seize the land their citizens had already reclaimed might be made to seem an easier outlet for the overflow, as in a barbarian community.

Be that as it may, though all the cities of Sumer and Akkad enjoyed a uniform culture and though, or because, all were dependent on the waters of the same rivers, each was politically independent and ready to fight its neighbours. Almost the oldest legible documents, other than account tablets, describe wars between the adjacent cities of Lagash and Umma for the possession of a strip of frontier territory. Metal war gear forms a prominent item in the furniture of all early graves. Even in the Uruk phase some seals were engraved with battle scenes. Of course citizens might also have to repel onslaughts by starveling barbarians from the desert fringe who cast envious eyes on urban wealth and on the cities' lands, created by centuries of toil.

A new institution was needed to restrain these conflicts. By the beginning of historical times the State had emerged, but it was embodied in the single person of the *city-governor* or king, who may be just 'corn-king' and war-chief amalgamated and writ large. The later Sumerian clerks pretended that 'kingship had descended from the heavens' thousands of years before the mythical Deluge, Noah's Flood of Hebrew tradition. In the archaeological record palaces and royal insignia are entirely overshadowed by temples and their furniture during the Uruk and Jemdet Nasr phases. But the symbols on some early seals may be pictographic representations of royal titles. And as soon as decipherable inscriptions begin, perhaps about 2750 B.C., 'royal' names occur.

The earliest city governors generally style themselves 'tenant-farmer' (of the god) – *ishakku* – only rarely *lugal* or 'king'. But as representative of the State a governor of Lagash, Urukagina, intervenes in the reform decree on page 107 to check the exaction of the rich; he appears in fact 'as a power apparently standing above society, but necessary to moderate the conflict of classes and keep it within the bounds of order'.

The city governor may have owed his authority on the one hand to a magical identification with the chief god of the city; he may, that is, have been the actor who played the role of the deity in some such fertility drama as was described on page 72. It is certain that in later times the king did impersonate the god in this way at great annual festivals. On the other hand, the magical authority of the ishakku was at least reinforced by the temporal power earned by leadership in war. The king as victor, smiting his enemies, is a favourite theme in Early Dynastic art.

As vicegerent on earth of the head of the local pantheon the city governor united the several 'divine households' into a sort of vaster family, albeit this time purely metaphorically. At Lagash the several deities worshipped by the citizens were imagined as related like the members of a patriarchal household. So under Urukagina the ishakku was high priest of the chief god, Ningirsu; his wife was high-priestess of Ningirsu's consort, Baü, and so on. As war-chief the ishakku commanded the citizen army. Nevertheless in the earliest historical documents it is the gods of the cities who go to war and win victories; the prize at stake is not described as a strip of the territory of, say, Lagash, but as the field of Ningirsu; when a peace treaty is concluded it is drawn up in the names of the belligerents' deities.

As representative of the 'tribal' god the ishakku receives the largest plot of the clan lands – at Lagash he enjoyed the use of 608 acres of Baü's estate alone – and 'taxes', the civilized counterparts of the gifts customarily offered to a barbarian chief. On behalf of the god too he receives a major share of the booty won by the victorious deity. The city governor thus came to concentrate a considerable portion of the land's surplus produce. The gods themselves might be indebted to the governor's munificence. In early inscriptions these dwell with special pride on the building or adornment of temples. But they also recall the expenditure of the accumulated surplus on reproductive works – the digging of canals and the building of granaries. They record also expeditions sent to Oman and other foreign countries for metal, stone, timber, and other war materials, needed by the crafts. The artisans were to this extent indebted to the ishakku for the requisite supplies. 'The industrial population were dependent on the city governor for their raw materials.' Indeed after 2500 B.C. trade in metals, vital for the armament industry, became at least at times and in theory a royal monopoly. In any case the king, as the State, must have been the principal purchaser of metal and similar commodities and so dominated the market.

Nevertheless the city state in Mesopotamia did not (as Heichelheim alleges) attain the exclusive position of a modern totalitarian State; the ishakku was never quite a Führer. The temple corporations could always maintain a certain freedom, both economic and intellectual; however much they might depend on the city governor's munificence, the perpetual corporations of priests were more permanent than any temporal dynasties. Rulers might be deposed by internal revolutions or subjugated by foreign rivals. The priesthood maintained its continuity in spite of dynastic changes; conquerors generally respected the temples and often embellished them as generously as native governors. At the same time always down to 2400 B.C. and often thereafter till 1800 the small area of Sumer and Akkad was divided among a multitude of independent city states, which offered alternative markets for exotic merchandise, industrial products, and the skill of artisans.

Naturally, ambitious city governors sought in the contradiction mentioned on page 107 an excuse for eliminating such competition by establishing hegemonies for themselves, their gods, and their cities. By 2000 B.C. the clerical historians of Sumer believed that one city or another had always enjoyed such a supreme sovereignty over the whole land. Some moderns too have seen in the universal worship of deities like Enlil, whose chief temple was at Nippur, the reflection of political union in prehistoric times. But such contemporary documents as survive give no definite evidence of the supremacy of one city over all the rest until about 2400 B.C. Lugalzaggizi of Umma conquered a number of cities. Even his 'empire' was transient. It was first a little later that a Semite, Sargon, the upstart ruler of a new city, Agade (tradition says he was the son of a gardener) achieved a real unification which endured for about a century. His achievement was repeated by the Sumerian kings of Ur, by Hammurabi of Babylon and others. But with Sargon the Early Dynastic period ends.

The new economic order not only invested barbaric chieftainship with the sanctity of kingship and bestowed upon its holders the authority of a territorial State. It also by its very nature called forth a novel method of transmitting human experience – accurate and impersonal – and generated sciences of a new kind – exact and capable of predicting results precisely. The invention of writing, the creation of a script, during the Uruk phase in Sumer has already been mentioned in passing on page 107. It deserves more than a passing reference, not only because the step was fraught with portentous consequences for the subsequent history of mankind, but also because nowhere else in the world is the whole process of building up a system of writing – a written language in fact – illustrated by a series of contemporary documents from the first experiments to the final adoption of an agreed orthography; for, very luckily for us, the Sumerians employed from the start as writing materials tablets of clay which by baking were made imperishable.

As explained already, perpetual corporations of priests found themselves charged with the heavy task of administering the unprecedented accumulations of wealth belonging to the Sumerian deities. The administration by such corporations of the temples' revenues on behalf of a divine master required the keeping of accurate records of all receipts and expenditures; a god's servants must be able to give account of their stewardship. The record must be intelligible not only to the official who made it, but to his successor and all the partners in the joint undertaking. No private system of reminders like the knot in the handkerchief was any use. The head of the brewery must note down what quantities of barley he received and how much beer and of what strength he delivered and note it in symbols that not only reminded him of something, i.e., meant something to him, but meant the same thing to his successor, to the controller of the granaries, and to other colleagues.

The invention of a system of writing was just the agreement on the meanings to be attached to the symbols by the society using them for its common ends. The symbols (characters) on the oldest tablets are mostly pictures which are often self-explanatory. They may be called *pictograms* (and a script composed of them *pictographic*). But even the simplest pictogram is more or less conventional. To denote an ass it is not necessary to draw painfully on the tablet a photographic portrait of an individual ass: a simplified and abbreviated shorthand sketch will suffice. The abbreviations used on the oldest tablets still show a certain variety; but they rapidly become standardized. This means that a particular shorthand version of an ass was gradually agreed upon and sanctioned by the consensus of the corporation.

The idea was just a development of that underlying the designs on seals from al 'Ubaid times, for these had been imprinted on clay and already bore symbolic meaning (p. 81). Even the particular abbreviations used as characters had sometimes been suggested by seal engravings.

Now many things to be recorded could not conveniently be represented by pictures at all. The difficulty was overcome by agreeing to attach a quite arbitrary meaning to a picture. For instance, a spouted jar was taken to stand for a given measure of volume, say a *gur*. By drawing strokes on the body of the jar a *gur* of barley (two strokes) might be distinguished from a *gur* of beer (three strokes). This was being done already in the fourth millennium B.C. The signs stood not only for things but for ideas or words (names). In technical language the script was no longer purely pictographic, but also *ideographic*. It would have been possible by adopting new pictures and agreeing upon further arbitrary modifications and combinations to expand the system to express most of the ideas to be recorded. Later on the Chinese actually took this course.

The Sumerians adopted a different line. Most of the

common Sumerian names were words of one syllable; the word for mouth, for instance, is *ka*. So the picture of the human head which stood for the word *ka* and the idea 'mouth', also stood for the sound *ka*. It thus got a phonetic value and could be used as a phonetic symbol or phonogram. By combinations of such phonograms it was now possible to spell out names and compound words instead of inventing new signs (ideograms) for them. The Sumerians worked out this idea in Early Dynastic times. They preserved a number of their conventional pictures and still used them as ideograms. But they also used them phonetically to spell out words. Very often they spelt a word and also added an ideogram (in this context termed a *determinative*) to suggest what sort of a word it was. Hence the number of current signs was not increased with the development of the script (as it was in China), but was actually reduced; in the earliest tablets of the Uruk phase some 2,000 signs may have been used; soon after 3000 B.C. the number current had been reduced to 800, by 2500 B.C. to about 600.

At the same time the signs themselves were simplified. For convenience and speed of writing the pictures were made so cursory that they often bear no recognizable similarity to the object denoted by the ideogram. Ultimately they were no longer traced but formed by the impressions of a wedge-shaped stylus that was stamped into the clay. The Mesopotamian script is therefore called *cuneiform* (wedge-shaped). The script was apparently devised by Sumerians for writing the Sumerian language in the manner just described. But the urban populations were cosmopolitan and comprised in Akkad at least a large Semitic element. Just after 2500 B.C. at latest Sumerian characters were being used phonetically to transcribe the names of Semitic kings. Soon Semites came to employ the script for official and business documents in the (Semitic) Akkadian tongue, spelling out the Semitic words as well as using ideograms.

A numeral notation was as necessary as a script. For

recording the reindeer slain in a communal hunt or the sheep in a village flock notches on a tally stick would meet all the requirements of savages and barbarians. For enumerating the vast herds of a civilized temple or the contents of a city granary such a notation would be intolerably clumsy. A convention must be agreed upon to save the trouble of making hundreds of notches on the tally or hundreds of dots on the tablet that replaced it. Numbers below ten were simply indicated in the old way by groups of from one to nine semi-circular impressions made with a reed held obliquely. But ten was denoted by a new symbol, the circle made by stamping the reed vertically into the clay, 20 by two such, and so on. In measuring volumes of beer a new symbol, a large semi-circle made with a larger reed, was introduced to denote 60, but in measuring grain this stood for 100 in the oldest tablets. So a decimal (1, 10, 100 ...) and a sexagesimal (1, 10, 60, 3600 ...) notation were once used concurrently. In Sumer the decimal system was abandoned and the so-called sexagesimal reckoning alone used after 2500 B.C.

Fractions other than two-thirds were always expressed as *aliquot parts*, i.e. fractions with the numerator unity: fractions with a numerator more than one would have to be resolved into a sum of aliquot parts, e.g., $\frac{3}{4}$ would become $\frac{1}{2} + \frac{1}{4}$. Of course, in the practical arithmetic of the fourth and third millennia it was hardly ever necessary to use these clumsy sums, for it dealt with concrete measures and weights. Five-sixths of a mina would be written 50 shekels and so on.

Owing to its conventional character the system of writing and ciphering had to be perpetuated by education. To fulfil their duties as administrators priests had to learn to read and write; that is to say they had to be taught the meanings and the phonetic values arbitrarily assigned to the characters by their colleagues, just as every child has to be taught the meanings attached by its society to the sounds of its spoken language (p. 17). Schools became a necessary adjunct to the temple. Of course they helped to standardize and maintain the approved conventions. Since in every temple and in every city from Jemdet Nasr times the same signs and the same conventions were accepted and employed, the priestly corporations must have cooperated at least in their educational work on an 'international' scale.

The oldest surviving collections of tablets include, beside accounts, lists of signs. The latter may have begun as simple records of the conventions agreed upon; some such record would be essential from the start to fix and maintain the standards approved. They were doubtless copied for use in schools where they would be no less necessary. By Early Dynastic times they had grown into regular dictionaries. Of course, as the first lists were collections of ideograms and they fixed the form, an alphabetical arrangement, such as seems both natural and convenient to us, was impracticable. Instead, words denoted by similar picture-signs were grouped together – for instance all words denoted by an abbreviated picture of a vase (phonetic value *duk*) and modifications thereof form a group. As a result not only various kinds of vases, but also contents of vases, such as beer and milk, and even measures would be classed together. The same principle was generally followed when dictionaries of spelt words came to be compiled in addition to the lists of ideograms. These lists, moreover, are confined to nouns – names; verbs and adjectives are not included. Later the lists of ideograms and of words were expanded by the addition of a column giving the Semitic (Akkadian) equivalent.

Both the monumental works carried out by States and temples with cooperative labour and the business activities of the priestly corporations and private merchants required the standardization of weights and measures, agreements by society for the use of common units. Measurement is of course necessary even for savages and barbarians. But for their simple needs the concrete standards of comparison supplied ready-made by nature suffice – the length of a finger, a palm, or a forearm, the weight of a grain or a jarful. If, for instance, a farmer were cutting rafters to span his barn he could measure the space to be bridged as so many times his forearm (so many cubits) and use his forearm to measure off the requisite lengths on his timbers. But if a hundred or more labourers were cutting rafters for a Sumerian temple, serious trouble might occur if each man used his own arm as a measuring rod. Men's arms are not all of the same length, and some beams measured by their aid might fail to span the temple, while others would project beyond its walls. The personal or natural cubit (forearm) must therefore be replaced by a social or conventional cubit, accepted by all co-workers as a stand-ard of comparison. The agreed standard must then be in-scribed on measuring rods of wood or metal that replaced individual limbs. Naturally it was found convenient to make the conventional cubit a simple multiple (in practice five times) of the 'finger', the next unit of measurement below it, and an aliquot part (one-sixth) of the next highest unit, the reed, and so on.

In the same way conventional standard 'grains' or 'loads' replaced the varying natural grains and actual loads in measuring cereals and other materials for social purposes. The new conventional units of weight were related nu-merically in the same simple way as units of length, and were represented by carved weights of haematite such as are often found by excavators. Incidentally a balance must have been invented before such standards could be estab-lished and used.

Finally the organized cooperation of an urban popula-tion requires more accurate divisions of time than are needed in a rural village. The Sumerians agreed to divide day and night into twelve double-hours (hence our twenty-four-hour day) and devised instruments – a sort of sundial and a water-clock worked on the principle of the hour-glass – for measuring these intervals. But for the year they were content to keep a lunar calendar, though learned clerks, by observation of the heavens, knew the length of the sidereal year and at least in later times corrected discrepan-cies between the calendar and the seasons by intercalating an extra month when astronomical observations indicated the need for correction.

Exact sciences were the direct outcome of the foregoing social agreements. The complicated economy that had evoked these demanded also arithmetic and geometry that could foretell quantitative results. The Sumerian clerks were not interested in the properties of numbers as such, nor in the measurement of abstract empty space (they probably could not conceive anything of the sort), or even of uncultivable desert and unharvested sea. They did need to know – at least approximately – how much seed should be laid aside for sowing the god's fields, how many brick should be ordered for a temple wall, how much earth must be dug for a ziggurat or a dyke and how many men would be needed to finish the job in the appointed time; the unit for area was a measure of grain, the word for 'volume' means literally 'mass of earth'. The chequer patterns so easily made on mats of coloured reeds and particularly popular on painted vases of the Jemdet Nasr phase gave visual demonstrations of our rule that the area of a rectangle can be obtained by multiplying length by breadth. A brickstack gave the corresponding 'formula' for volume.

The very form of the numerical notation would have graphically illustrated the simplest rules of reckoning had they not already been familiar from counting on the fingers. Multiplication is just repeated addition; '24 by 4' means 'add four twenty-fours together'. Before 1500 B.C. the Sumerians had noted the results of such additions and drawn up multiplication tables such as we learn at school. Even on pictographic tablets of the fourth millennium the areas of fields are calculated as length by breadth. Very soon the ratio of the circumference of a circle to its diameter, what we call π, had been approximately worked out by actual measurement. The Sumerians accepted the rough approximation 3. This was accurate enough for estimating the contents of a cylindrical granary which would of course be checked by weighing or gauging the number of bricks required for a column drum where a few spares would not matter and irregularities in shape could easily be amended.

The arithmetical and geometrical rules that the Sumerian clerks applied are the true prototypes of the quantitative 'laws' of modern science. They reduced to a generalized numerical form relations that had been actually observed and measured between classes of objects in the external world. They told men what to do in order to obtain a desired result. Obviously we need not bother to ask the names of the laws' discoverers. They are too patently social products called forth by the needs of a society affected by the urban revolution and discovered with the aid of the spiritual equipment produced by the revolution.

Observations on the stars proved so successful in fore-telling when to begin agricultural operations that the Sumerians were induced to hope by the same means to predict the unpredictable. In other words astronomy led to astrology, in pursuit of which the motions of heavenly bodies were studied not unprofitably by the Sumerians' cultural heirs.

The urban revolution provoked or at least re-enforced another convention that likewise led to standardization, generalizations, and quantization. The exchange of goods and services had been increased so greatly by the new economy as to demand a common standard in terms of which the several kinds of goods could be measured and 'valued'. This conventional standard of value would at the same time serve as a medium of exchange with which all services could be rewarded (i.e., wages paid) and every commodity purchased. The first standard socially approved was apparently barley, the staff of life that everyone needed and to obtain which they must work and produce goods; even in Early Dynastic times wages and rents were still most frequently paid in barley.

But already metal – silver and, for small sums, copper – had been generally accepted as the most convenient medium and standard, and so it remained in Mesopotamia for two millennia. The units, however, were not coins, guaranteed as to quality and weight by a State, but quantities weighed out for each transaction in accordance with the approved standards of weight. Nevertheless the adoption of a conventional metallic standard is equivalent to the transition to a *money economy* from what is termed a natural economy. In the latter, individual objects were bartered one against the other; now all can be priced at so many shekels of silver or gurs of barley and thus compared quantitatively.

Wealth can now be estimated not in foodstuffs, slaves, and commodities, which can themselves be consumed, used, and enjoyed, but in terms of the 'commodity of commodities', the general abstract medium which cannot itself be consumed but can be exchanged for any consumable commodity or useful service. As a consequence 'production for the market' of objects to be sold for silver can begin to replace production for use of commodities desired by the maker himself or ordered by somebody who desires them and promises the maker an immediate and chosen recompense.

Moreover, the new generalized wealth is regarded as possessing the property naturally inherent in the primary form of wealth – corn and cattle – of multiplying and reproducing itself. Like grain and livestock it may be treated as capital and used to secure an increase – profit. Consequently interest will be charged on any loans. In Mesopotamian society the – largely Semitic – merchant class that became increasingly prominent and prosperous from the days of Sargon developed and exploited these ideas brilliantly. They were destined to have revolutionary effects completing the breakdown of gentile organization, begetting a new middle class, and oiling the machinery of production. In Sumerian society of the Early Dynastic age the solvent process was only beginning.

In Elam, east of Mesopotamia, the lower valley of the Kerkha, that even in 700 B.C. still flowed directly into the Persian Gulf east of the Tigris–Euphrates delta, offered an environment very similar to that of Sumer, but on a smaller scale. Here the excavations at Susa reveal, albeit less clearly than at Ur or Erech, the successive stages of the urban revolution. The several steps seem strictly parallel to those described above down to the end of the Uruk phase. Till that point the similarities in ceramics and seal designs are striking. Even the pictographic script (termed proto-Elamite), traced on clay tablets, that marks the culmination of the revolution, shares many conventions with the Sumerian writing of the Uruk and Jemdet Nasr tablets, though the numeral notation seems exclusively decimal. No doubt Elamite civilization was not only based on the same elements as Sumerian but also organized in much the same way.

In the sequel Elam and Sumer developed along divergent lines, or rather Elam did not share in the progress of the Early Dynastic age. So the proto-Elamite pictographic writing does not spontaneously develop into a script that we can read. At the end of the third millennium it was simply superseded by developed cuneiform that was adapted to transcribe the local language. Our knowledge of Elam in the interval is indirect and fragmentary.

Susa had remained an influential military power and commercial centre. The Elamites successfully raided Sumer and Akkad and extended their domains inland to Sialk in Iran (p. 80). Their trade reached India as well as Mesopotamia. But in the end Elam became a province of the Mesopotamian economic system and culture just as from about 2100 to 2000 B.C. she was even politically incorporated as a tributary in the Empire of the Sumerian Third Dynasty of Ur.

Author's note. While it will not affect the over-all picture and need not worry the general reader, students should note that since this book was written it has become the fashion to deflate Mesopotamian dates prior to 2350 B.C. (Sargon of Agade). So they might replace 3000. B.C. by 2500 and make corresponding reductions throughout Chapters 4 and 5. (*June 1957*).

6

EARLY BRONZE AGE CIVILIZATION IN EGYPT AND INDIA

IN the Nile Valley the urban revolution that we have traced as a process in Mesopotamia can be studied only after its culmination. This coincided with the union of the whole of Egypt under the absolute rule of a sovereign king who was also a god – an event comparable to Sargon's unification of Mesopotamia, but more than five centuries earlier. The preparatory stages can be inferred only precariously from later legends and from indirect indications in the archaeological record. Only the wide marshy Delta offered the challenge and reward that had evoked the artificial environment of Sumerian cities. But archaeologically man's response is not directly known; the early settlements are buried deep in Nile silt under modern towns and cultivated fields. Indirect evidence comes from Upper Egypt.

South of Cairo the narrow valley through the barren desert plateaux has analogies, real but remote, with Sumer. It too was occupied by a chain of swamps covered with a jungle of papyrus that sheltered waterfowl and game and dangerous hippopotami. Through the swamps the Nile provides a perfect highway for transport. Its annual inundation, more regular and better timed for agricultural operations than the Tigris and Euphrates floods, will automatically irrigate such land as human labour has reclaimed. Within the valley neither timber for building nor metal is available.

On the other hand the desert on both sides offers supplies of good flint for knives and axes. Between the valley's precipitous sides there are strips of desert still raised above the floods from which the swampy valley-bottom could be exploited. On these settled the so-called Predynastic Egyptians in much the same stage of culture as the societies

described at Merimde and the Fayum on page 60. Within
the valley these settlers, by combining for a resolute assault
on swamps and wild beasts, succeeded in creating an
artificial environment in which they prospered and
multiplied.

They appear grouped in apparently autonomous villages,
each perhaps occupied by a totemic clan. Later the totems,
the animals, plants, or natural objects from which the
villagers may have believed themselves descended, became
the emblems and standards of the counties or *nomes* into
which Egypt was divided in historical times. In the earliest
stages, termed Badarian and Amratian, the villagers still
relied largely on hunting and fishing. But they did grow
grains by natural irrigation and breed stock on the meadows.
They could build large boats of bundles of papyrus for navigation on the river. For painting their eyes, malachite was
obtained regularly from Sinai, perhaps by barter with
desert hunters. The villagers were acquainted with gold and
copper (perhaps derived from the reduction of malachite, a
carbonate of copper), but they treated metal as a superior
sort of stone without appreciating the advantages conferred
by its fusibility.

The remarkable preservation of bodies buried in the dry
desert sand seems already to have suggested particularly
lively speculations about the future life and started a quest
for 'immortality'. The need for 'a good burial' certainly
provided a motive for the accumulation of surplus wealth
and magic jewels. Our knowledge of the Predynastic people
is derived mainly from their graves, which are richly furnished with jars of food and drink, hunting tackle and
fishing gear and toilet articles – particularly an almost
ceremonial set of slate palettes, rubbers, and decorated
pouches for eye-paint.

Next in the *Gerzean* stage the importance of hunting
waned; the villagers devoted themselves to farming and
fishing. Implements and weapons of cast copper and new
imported materials, many, such as lapis lazuli, of Asiatic
origin, began to reach Upper Egypt. Ships, flying standards

that in historical times belonged to counties in the Delta and on the Mediterranean coast, visited the southern villages; they are depicted there on vases from Gerzean graves that may themselves have been made in the north. The new materials certainly denote the influx of new ideas and new techniques emerge; the chemistry of glazing was discovered and faience was made.

The Asiatic substances and products of the Delta found in Upper Egypt may denote an infiltration of Semites and even a political domination of the valley by the Delta, of Upper Egypt by Lower; later legends tell of a conquest of the south by 'Followers of Horus' from the north and of the subsequent formation of two kingdoms of Upper and Lower Egypt respectively. But the archaeological record attests neither kings nor specialized craftsmen nor the use of writing.

Finally in the Late Gerzean phase sailing boats of the type reputedly native to the Persian Gulf (p.92) reached Upper Egypt. They are depicted on the rocky walls of dry wadis between the Nile and the Red Sea and on a tomb at Falcontown (Hierakonpolis, in historical times the county town of the Falcon nome and presumably the capital of the Falcon clan). On the tomb walls they are seen in battle with native papyrus boats. The same scene of a naval battle is carved on an ivory knife-handle found at Gebel-el-Arak, significantly near the Nile end of a cross desert route to the Red Sea. Its other side depicts a figure whose costume is quite alien to Egypt but agrees precisely with that shown on a basalt stele from the Jemdet Nasr city at Erech in Sumer. Moreover, in contemporary Egyptian art we find motives, at no other time popular on the Nile, but familiar on the Tigris–Euphrates from the Uruk period on. However indirectly, Sumerian ideas were surely influencing Upper Egypt; Nilotic barbarism was being fertilized by contact with Mesopotamian civilization.

To the same phase belong a series of ivories and slate palettes carved with pictures of animals in combat, mythological versions of struggles between totemic clans and in particular of the victories of the Falcon clan. This clan may already have occupied the walled town covering twelve and a half acres, the ruins of which mark its capital.

Meanwhile some tombs become increasingly elaborate and richly furnished; one at Falcon-town is lined with bricks and adorned with painted scenes. A growing contrast between rich and poor tombs marks a division of society into classes, if not the emergence of chiefs. It culminates in the so-called Royal Tombs of Abydos in Upper Egypt. The simple trench in the sand that held the Pre-dynastic dead has now grown into a huge excavation, at the bottom of which is a miniature palace – it measured 26 ft long by 15 ft wide by 10½ ft high in B10 – built of bricks and imported timber, surrounded with storerooms and a range of small tombs for court officials who must serve their lord even in death.

The Royal Tombs are crowded with jars of grain, fruits and liquors, superb vases of stone and precious metal, ornaments of gold, turquoise, lapis lazuli and other gems, arms, and toilet articles of copper. These attest the concentration of unheard-of wealth, the existence of a multitude of specialized and expert craftsmen, extensive foreign trade. And in the Royal Tombs the first written documents appear; a system of writing, the *hieroglyphic* script, has been invented. The archaeological record merges in the literary record. The latter explains what has happened.

'Menes', chief of the Falcon clan and himself magically identified with its totem, the divine Falcon (Horus), has conquered the rest of the Valley and the Delta and welded the independent villages and clans into a single State – we might almost say a single household. The head of this State is not the tenant-farmer of a god, but himself a god, made immortal by magic rites and guaranteeing by his own magic the fertility of flocks and crops. By right of conquest he has absorbed – in the cannibalistic terminology appropriate to barbarism the texts say 'devoured' – the local totems that personified the ancestral generations who created the land out of swamp and desert. Therefore, like the Sumerian city god, he holds eminent domain over the whole land of Egypt and is entitled to a tribute of offerings and services from its cultivators.

Thus the pharaoh instead of the temple concentrates in his treasures the surplus products of the land – a surplus that dwarfs into insignificance the revenue of any Sumerian temple or city-governor. The symbol of this concentration is not a temple – temples to local and national gods exist but by favour of and with endowments from the king – but a monumental tomb. It is designed to preserve the physical remains of the god-king and so to ensure the continuance of his magic work on behalf of his land. As the land's population and wealth increased, the tombs were made ever grander and stronger, until the maximum was reached under Cheops (Khufu) of Dynasty IV. His Great Pyramid measures 755 ft on a side and rises to a height of 481 ft. It contains some 2,300,000 blocks each weighing on an average 2½ tons. The blocks were quarried on the east side of the valley, floated across during the inundation, and then dragged up an enormous stone ramp to a plateau, 100 ft above the river, on which the pyramids stand. A tradition preserved by the Greek historian Herodotus and accepted by Petrie reports that the pyramid demanded the labour of 100,000 men for twenty years.

But the pharaohs used part of the vast surplus they controlled in ways that even modern sceptics will admit as practical. Menes himself girt with the 'White Wall' Memphis, a new city at the apex of the Delta. A king of Dynasty I had himself depicted 'cutting the first sod' of a new canal. The pharaohs sent expeditions supported by the royal army to Sinai to mine copper. The State equipped and manned ships to sail to Byblos for the Cedars of Lebanon; by the end of the Third Dynasty these sea-going ships might attain a length of 170 ft, though 70 to 100 ft was more normal. As military chiefs the early pharaohs organized a system of frontier defences that kept out raiding Asiatics, Libyans, and Nubians. Finally they enforced internal peace, suppressing the wasteful feuds between neighbouring villages that have always plagued the Nile valley whenever the central government is weak.

A civil service appointed by the real god fulfilled the functions of the self-appointed servants of a Sumerian deity. As a perpetual corporation engaged in collecting and administering the enormous revenues of Egypt it too required a script to record receipts and expenditures. In Egypt as in Sumer pictures were assigned conventional meanings, and in the *hieroglyphic* script the characters preserved their pictorial form for over 3,000 years.

The earliest hieroglyphs are better pictures than the Sumerian ideograms of the Uruk phase and show no less variability. Nevertheless, they hardly represent the beginnings of Egyptian writing; for they co-exist from the first with simplified cursive forms, precursors of the *hieratic* script that throughout historical times was used concurrently with the hieroglyphic without ever replacing it. The cursive signs are written in ink on pottery or wood in the Royal Tombs, later on papyrus. The hieroglyphs and their cursive forms presumably are pure ideograms, but as in Sumer many soon acquired phonetic values too; some indeed came to stand not for syllables as in Sumer but for single consonants. The Egyptians had in fact all the elements of an alphabet. But they continued, like the Sumerians and Babylonians, to use ideographic, syllabic, and consonantal signs side by side.

Writing accordingly must remain a mystery, a specialized profession too abstruse to be combined with manual avocations. The initiates, the clerks, formed a class apart to whom alone was open the coveted career of a government official or the steward of a great estate. But the clergy did not form a caste; for the recruitment of officials schools were maintained by the Treasury and later literature seems to imply that a lad has a choice between going to school, apprenticeship to a craft, or agricultural work.

Though the principles of Egyptian writing were essentially the same as those followed by the Sumerians, even the pictographic forms are quite different in the two areas. So too the Egyptians devised a numeral notation constructed on the same principle as the Sumerian, but on a purely decimal basis with different signs for units, tens, and powers of ten. Again for the same reasons as the Sumerians the Egyptians had to standardize weights and measures, but they gave different values to the units. Even for the conventional division of time they adopted the principle of 'seasonal hours' – daylight and dark were each equally divided into hours, the lengths of which would vary with the season.

Writing, being a mystery, was not used to transmit craft lore, and its adepts being 'exempt from all manual tasks' were divorced from the practical science applied in the workshop. But as in Sumer the urban revolution had generated learned sciences and pseudo-sciences transmitted in writing – arithmetic, geometry, astronomy, medicine, theology. Treatises on these survive only from the second millennium. But it is plain from the results achieved and attested in the monuments that the Egyptians under the early dynasties were already successfully applying the simple arithmetical and geometrical rules illustrated by examples in the later 'mathematical papyri'.

From these we see that in arithmetic the Egyptian clerks were behind their Sumerian colleagues. In fractions they too were tied to aliquot parts (p. 114), but they had not tabulated the results of additions to form multiplication tables beyond the first – 'twice one is two, etc.' Multiplication therefore was laboriously performed by the tedious process termed duplation, a combination of multiplication by two and addition. In geometry on the contrary they used more accurate formulae, owing presumably to better observation. Owing to the importance of pyramids in funerary cult, the Egyptian clerks were expert in calculating the 'batter' of a pyramid so as to enable the mason to cut the facing blocks of such a monument accurately. They had discovered, moreover, the curious formula for the volume of a truncated pyramid: $1/3 \, h \, (a^2+ab+b^2)$, where a stands for length of base and b length at top – which was never used in Mesopotamia. Even this formula could be obtained by measurement. But the Egyptian approximation to π,

$(16/9)^2$, much more accurate than the Sumerians' 3, is not easily explained.

The greatest achievement of Egyptian science and one unmistakably inspired by the conditions of the urban revolution in the Nile valley was the creation of a solar calendar that is the immediate ancestor of our own. Pharaoh's officials from the days of the first kings measured and recorded each year the height of the Nile flood on which the Egyptian harvest depends and on which taxes can accordingly be assessed before the harvest. By collating these records they found that in fifty years or more the average interval between floods is to the nearest day 365 days. On this basis they established an official calendar which for a century or more must have really helped Egyptian agriculture by indicating to the farmers when to start agricultural operations; in Egypt the whole cycle of agriculture is pivoted round the inundation.

When the accumulated effect of the six hours' error had produced a manifest discrepancy between the calendar year and the natural phenomena it should predict, it was too late – or too soon – for calendar reform. But by the Third Dynasty observations on the stars disclosed in the heliacal rising of Sirius in the latitude of Cairo a herald of the flood. The bureaucracy used the sidereal year based on this observation to correct the abortive official calendar, to instruct their peasants when to start work on the fields.

So, about 3000 B.C., an economic revolution not only provided Egyptian craftsmen with a livelihood and raw materials, but also called forth writing and learned sciences and produced a State. But the social and economic organization conferred upon Egypt by Menes and his successors as agents of the revolution was centralized and totalitarian in harmony, with the homogeneity of a land watered by a single river and isolated by deserts.

In theory, at least, the whole land belonged to the Pharaoh, and its surplus produce was concentrated in royal granaries and treasuries. In practice a substantial share was assigned to a nobility of office – the ministers of state and governors of counties (nomarchs). At first, at least, these were appointed by Pharaoh and held office at his pleasure. Indeed, to the king they owed literally their immortal souls; for had not the king devoured and digested the totem souls of the clans, and by his own magic won immortality? On favourite officials the king might graciously bestow souls and immortality by granting them individually, as their tombstones proclaim, the right to build, and facilities for building and endowing, the monumental tombs essential for the future life.

In practice, ministers and governors were recruited from a limited circle – perhaps royal children, the companions of the first conquerors and the families of such local chiefs as had made timely submission. They enjoyed the use and revenue of landed estates or whole counties which were organized as self-contained 'households', miniatures of the royal 'household' of which they formed parts. Later such estates came to be inherited by the holders' children, and eventually disposable by will. After the Pyramid Age governorships too became hereditary, and the governors treated their counties as their own estates or principalities, though owing dues and services to Pharaoh.

Even local and national gods depended for their temples and offerings upon the king who was also a god; in theory he alone worshipped the gods on behalf of the nation. In practice he appointed priests who actually presented the offerings 'for the life, prosperity, and health of the Pharaoh'. These offices, too, may have been filled in some cases by descendants of the local priesthoods or 'secret societies' who had served the totems of Predynastic clans. They too might become hereditary. Permanent endowments in land were consecrated to the service of the temples and the maintenance of their priests. So too from the First Dynasty parts of the royal domain had been dedicated to the service of the departed kings whose tombs were combined with mortuary temples, and to the support of chantry priests. Later, nobles' tombs too were similarly endowed – at first by the king, later by their future occupants.

Thus priests and clerks started out as officials of the totalitarian State, members of the Pharaoh's 'household', supported by the royal revenue. In time the former gained 'households' of their own; clerks might find an alternative livelihood in the 'households' of the nobles and the temples.

The specialist craftsmen and industrial workers, placed in Pharaoh's great 'household', were guaranteed sustenance from the surplus collected in the royal granaries, and were supplied with metal tools and raw materials from the king's stock. By the Pyramid Age we find smiths, carpenters, jewellers, masons, boat-builders, potters, and other artisans permanently attached also to the mortuary foundations and the nobles' estates; for such were largely self-contained economic units aiming at supplying their own needs in industrial products as well as foodstuffs. In each case the craftsmen can have enjoyed very little economic freedom; probably indeed they, like the cultivators, changed hands with the estate on which they worked. The crafts plied were the same as in Mesopotamia, but their individual products were quite different. So even the simplest Egyptian copper tools can be readily distinguished from the Sumerian. The potter's wheel was adopted only under the Third Dynasty, and then in a less efficient form than the Asiatic. Tin bronze seems to have been unknown. For textiles flax, but not wool, was used.

The requisite foreign materials – copper from Sinai, gold from Nubia, ebony, perfumes, and spices from Arabia or Somaliland, lapis lazuli and other magic gems from Asia – were secured largely by expeditions dispatched by the State, manned by royal servants and led by government officials. There was thus much less scope for merchants in Egypt than in Mesopotamia.

Within the 'households' a natural economy reigned; paintings in tombs illustrate market scenes where a pot is bartered for a fish, a bundle of onions for a fan, a wooden box for a jar of ointment. Nevertheless, metals (gold and copper) were socially recognized as standards of value and rings served as currency in certain transactions.

The great peasant masses – the farmers and fishers who supplied the foodstuffs to maintain themselves and the whole economy as well as collecting the raw materials (hides, fibres, papyrus) for industry – multiplied exceedingly. The union of Egypt had put an end to deadly feuds between villages; the Pharaohs' frontier policy protected the cultivator from the depredations of raiding nomads; public works had added to the arable land; the calendar permitted rural operations to be rationally planned; the surplus grain stored in the royal granaries might provide relief in time of famine.

On the other hand, these reserves had been collected by force. Their producers had little left for the purchase of industrial products. Save when directly employed by a king or a noble they could not afford metal tools, but made shift with a neolithic equipment of stone hoes and wooden ploughs and mattocks. By gift and by dedications, later even by testament, peasants were disposed of together with the land they cultivated as if they had been part of its livestock. They were liable to compulsory labour, digging canals, towing barges upstream, quarrying and transporting stone, building pyramids, and the like. When thus removed from agricultural production they were presumably fed and clothed by the State or the noble employer – perhaps better than a free neolithic cultivator. In any case, in the second millennium King Seti I records that he provided each of the thousand labourers employed on building his temple with '4 lb. bread, 2 bundles of vegetables and a roast of meat daily, and a clean linen garment twice a month'!

Under this régime the enormous wealth produced by the new economy in Egypt was more highly concentrated than in Mesopotamia. Industry was cramped within narrow bounds. Export trade absorbed relatively few industrial products; for imports were either taken as tribute without payment, or paid for in gold and foodstuffs. Internally the market for industrial products and craftsmanship was limited to the State and the dependent nobility. To these

preparations for the future life constituted the main object
for the accumulation and expenditure of wealth. An extravagant proportion of the surplus they collected was buried
in tombs. (To the chagrin of the scientific robbers of the
twentieth century, a flourishing industry of tomb-robbery
rapidly restored a not inconsiderable fraction of the buried
treasure to circulation; the avarice of nobles and officials
in time diverted to mundane use the produce of mortuary
estates dedicated to feed and cheer the corpses in their
tombs!)

'Ancient Egypt,' writes Keynes satirically, 'was doubly
fortunate, and doubtless owed to this its fabled wealth, in
that it possessed two activities, namely, pyramid building
and the search for precious metals, the fruits of which, since
they could not serve the needs of men by being consumed,
did not stale with abundance. Two pyramids, two masses
for the dead, are twice as good as one; not so two railways
from London to York.' In the event the bounds of these
activities were reached with the pyramids of the Fourth
Dynasty Pharaohs. Not even the fabulous reserves of fertile
Egypt could support indefinitely such unproductive expenditure. The economic system began to shrink. The nobles'
great estates became increasingly self-contained 'households', a relapse towards neolithic self-sufficiency. After the
Fourth Dynasty they could aim at political autonomy, too.
The Old Kingdom dissolved in political and economic
anarchy about 2475 B.C.

*

Before 2500 B.C. a third Bronze Age civilization, symbolized by populous cities, highly skilled industries, far-flung
commerce, and a pictographic script, had emerged in India.
On the flood-plains of the Indus and its five tributaries (the
Punjab) peoples of mixed origin and diverse racial types
had combined to create artificial islands of culture in a
desert jungle. The natural environment differed from the
Mesopotamian and Egyptian in its vaster expanse, in the
régime of the flood, in its scrub of ugly useless trees and in

the animals sheltered by these trees. It agreed in the low rainfall and the lack of building timber, good stone, and metal. The Indus and its tributaries provided moving roads for the transport even of heavy goods over long distances; foodstuffs could be collected from a wide area to support large urban populations.

Over a huge triangle, four times the area of Sumer, bounded on the west by the mountains of Baluchistan and Waziristan, on the north by the Himalayas and on the east by the Thar desert, reigned a civilization as uniform as that of Mesopotamia or Egypt. The physical remains of the artificial world in which it flourished are equally imposing. The cities, as large as those of Sumer, are built almost entirely of kiln-fired bricks, the manufacture of which must have consumed stupendous quantities of laboriously gathered fuel (presumably the ugly trees that disfigure the desert). The ruins of Mohenjo-daro, in Sind, cover at least a square mile; at Harappā, 400 miles farther north, the walled area visible in 1853 had a perimeter of 2½ miles, but buildings once extended farther. Since then bricks from its ruins have provided ballast for a hundred miles of railway line and material for the modern village of five thousand souls. Yet the mounds are still impressive.

The cities were devastated by several severe floods. After each inundation the lower floors of the houses were filled up with bricks so that the whole quarters of a city now rest on an artificial platform, 20 feet or so high. We can, therefore, infer populations at least as large as those of contemporary Mesopotamian cities supported by the surplus produced by a rural peasantry. The latter cultivated the same grains and bred the same beasts as their Sumerian colleagues, but perhaps grew rice also and certainly kept zebu cattle, domestic fowls, and probably elephants, but apparently no asses or camels.

The same variety of specialized crafts as in Mesopotamia is attested in the archaeological record, and often the processes are identical in both countries. For example, the potters used (as they still do) the same sort of fast spinning wheel, and the smiths alloyed copper with tin to make bronze. On the other hand the craftsmen's products are quite different. Even the simplest metal tools made in India – axes, saws, daggers, and spearheads – can be distinguished at a glance from Sumerian or Egyptian products. Weavers worked cotton, not wool or flax. The chemistry of glazes was understood; vases and ornaments were made of faience, and even pottery vessels were occasionally glazed.

Carts with solid wheels, such as are used in Sind today, as well as boats, were available to transport produce to the cities. The raw materials for industry had to be imported from long distances; deodara wood was obtained from the Himalayas, copper from Rajputana and perhaps Baluchistan, sank shell from southern India. Tin, gold, and various precious stones, including lapis lazuli (which was, however, rare), were brought from countries outside India altogether.

Regular supplies of these materials can have been obtained only as the result of extensive trade. Indeed, as remarked on page 104, manufactures from the Indus cities reached even the markets on the Tigris and Euphrates. Conversely, a few Sumerian devices in art, Mesopotamian toilet sets and a cylinder seal were copied on the Indus. Trade was not confined to raw materials and luxury articles; fish, regularly imported from the Arabian Sea coasts, augmented the food-supplies of Mohenjo-daro.

The stalls of water-sellers and other retailers have been recognized among the cities' ruins, giving quite the impression of a modern Indian bazaar and implying an interchange of goods by small-scale transactions such as takes place there. The floor of the water-stall at Mohenjo-daro was found strewn with the shattered fragments of rough clay cups. Presumably these were turned out on such a scale that each client of the stall, after drinking, threw away his cup as is done in India still, or – with papiermâché cups – in American trains and restaurants.

It would seem to follow that the craftsmen of the Indus cities were, to a large extent, producing 'for the market'.

What, if any, form of currency and standard of value had been accepted by society to facilitate the exchange of commodities is, however, uncertain. Magazines attached to many spacious and commodious private houses mark their owners as merchants. Their number and size indicate a strong and prosperous merchant community.

In India, too, extreme concentration of the social surplus by a divine monarch, or a small priestly caste, may be deduced from a strongly walled citadel unearthed in the heart of Harappā during 1944. In its shadow stood symbolically a vast granary measuring 150 ft by 56 ft. At Mohenjo-daro a similar citadel actually enclosed the granary in which the rulers' real wealth was accumulated. Commodious two-storeyed houses of baked brick, provided with bathrooms and a porter's lodge and covering as much as 97 ft by 83 ft, may be contrasted with monotonous rows of mud brick tenements, each consisting of only two rooms and a court, and not exceeding 56 ft by 30 ft in over-all area. The contrast doubtless reflects a division of society into classes, but it would seem only into merchants or 'business men', and labourers or artisans. A surprising wealth of ornaments of gold, silver, precious stones, and faience, of vessels of beaten copper and of metal implements and weapons, has been collected from the ruins. Most appear to come from the houses ascribed to 'rich merchants'. But a hoard of copper tools and gold bangles turned up in the 'workmen's quarters' at Harappā.

Many well-planned streets and a magnificent system of drains, regularly cleared out, reflects the vigilance of some regular municipal government. Its authority was strong enough to secure the observance of town-planning by-laws and the maintenance of the approved lines for streets and lanes over several reconstructions rendered necessary by floods.

In any case, society in the Indus valley could agree upon a conventional script and numeral notation (on a decimal basis), and on standards of weights and measures (different from the Sumerian and Egyptian). The script was current throughout the huge province of Indus civilization. Its characters are conventionalized pictograms like the hiero-glyphic, early Sumerian, and proto-Elamite writings, though quite distinct from these. The values of the characters, whether ideographic or phonetic, and the meanings of the words they transcribe are alike unknown. Only brief in-scriptions, too short for decipherment without a bilingual but most probably incantations, survive, mostly on 'seals' which were never used for sealing anything and were per-haps just carried as amulets. Of course the letters were not invented for this purpose, but the documents for which they were primarily devised (on Sumerian and Cretan analogies, accounts) have perished with the unknown material on which they were written.

With this equipment the Bronze Age citizens of the Indus valley, as well as Sumerians and Egyptians, could have – and, indeed, must have – developed exact science, and for the same imperious reasons. For instance, a free use in decorative art of squares inscribed in compass-drawn inter-secting circles suggests a study of geometry. But the results of such sciences are not directly known.

Small clay figures of women, scenes on 'seals' and ritual objects, notably large stone *lingas* and *yonis* (phalli and vulvae), give glimpses of totemic survivals, of magic fertility rites and of personal deities arising out of them. Some of the rites thus disclosed unmistakably foreshadow practices dis-tinctive of later Hinduism; the latter represents certain deities under the same forms as the Indus art. Indus art itself used patterns, and was inspired by principles, quite different from those accepted in Egypt and Mesopotamia. Representations of the human form are unusually natural-istic; a small bronze figure of a dancing girl breathes an air of movement and vitality that cannot be matched elsewhere till the classical period of Greece.

This imposing civilization perished utterly as a result of internal decay accelerated by the shock of barbarian raids (p. 176). Only since 1920 have its dumb outlines been rescued from complete oblivion by archaeologists.

Its antiquity can be determined solely by the importation of Indus products into Mesopotamia during the third millennium.

Nevertheless, since Indus manufactures were imported into Sumer and Akkad, and Indus cults were actually celebrated there (p. 105), the forgotten civilization must have made direct if indefinable contributions to the cultural tradition we inherit through Mesopotamia. Moreover, the technical traditions of the Bronze Age craftsmen, at least of potters and wainwrights, persist locally until today. Fashions of dress, established in the Indus cities, are still observed in contemporary India. Hindu rituals and deities have roots in the cults depicted in the prehistoric art. So classical Hindu science too, and through it occidental science, may be indebted to the prehistoric to an unexpected degree. From this standpoint the Bronze Age civilization of India has not utterly perished; 'for its work continueth, far beyond our knowing'.

7

THE EXPANSION OF CIVILIZATION

BY 3000 B.C. economic revolutions had integrated the discoveries of the preceding thousand years into civilizations in three tiny patches of the earth's surface. The new social organisms, contemporary and interrelated, were all distinct, and differ from one another in the details of their composition and structure. Yet all exhibit certain features in common, notably dependence for industrial equipment on relatively uncommon and socially expensive metals or alloys of metals. The label Bronze Age may sum up their distinctive peculiarities, but it needs expansion.

In the great alluvial valleys of the Nile, the Tigris-Euphrates, and the Indus system collective effort had created artificial environments. Societies dwelling therein had emancipated themselves from immediate dependence on the caprices of raw nature and had discovered uniformities that permitted rational planning. The organized exploitation of lands reclaimed from swamp and desert was yielding unprecedented supplies of corn, fish, and other foodstuffs. A local failure of crops need no longer mean starvation; for thanks to improved and artificial waterways food supplies could be collected for storage in the city granaries and distributed all over the valleys. State organizations, based on residence instead of kinship, abolished blood-feuds between clans, mitigated the violence of other internal conflicts, and probably reduced the frequency of wars.

The biological consequence had been an immense numerical increase in the species *Homo sapiens* within the valleys. The vast areas of the new cities as compared with any barbarian village, the immense cemeteries attached to them, and the stupendous works executed by the citizens, place this conclusion beyond question. The standard of life had risen, too. The rulers and the new middle classes certainly enjoyed a variety of food and drink, and comfort in accommodation and clothing that no barbarian chieftain could imagine. Even the masses secured a more varied edit and more salubrious housing. The sea-fish, for instance, brought to Lagash from the Persian Gulf and to Mohenjo-daro from the Arabian Sea were probably articles of popular consumption that a Stone Age peasant could never enjoy. The workmen's quarters at Harappā are more commodious than neolithic huts.

The new economy, furthermore, permitted the effective utilization of the discoveries described in Chapter 4 for the improvement of man's equipment for living, the reduction of drudgery, and the enrichment of enjoyment. It secured in particular adequate supplies of metal, and guaranteed a livelihood to the specialists who could alone work it. It engendered exact and predictive sciences that could really lift at least a tiny corner of the veil that shrouded the menacing future. At the same time the new order encouraged and consolidated old but, as we think, delusive hopes of predicting the unpredictable and controlling the future. Finally it opened new possibilities to architects, sculptors, painters, and musicians, and new values in art.

On the other hand, the enjoyment of these benefits was restricted at once by the scarcity of the industrial metal and by the form the revolution had assumed. In the first place copper or bronze remained too costly to replace stone in industrial equipment. For deposits of copper ore, large enough to be worked economically, are far from common and always remote from alluvial valleys; tin is absolutely rare. With the technical equipment at first available and under the conditions of transport outside the river valleys and coastal tracts, the extraction, working, and distribution of metal must have absorbed a lot of social labour – that is to say, consumed the time of agents who had to be supported out of the surplus of food-stuffs available to society.

Secondly, this surplus – at first absolutely small – had been concentrated in the hands of a few kings, temples, and nobles. So the peasant masses from whom it was gathered could hardly afford the new equipment. In practice the cultivators and quarrymen of Egypt had to be content with neolithic tools through the third millennium. Wool in Sumer was still plucked, not shorn, Even in the Indus cities chert knives are common enough to suggest a shortage of metal tools. In general it was only the divine and royal households as such, the army and navy, craftsmen employed by the State, by temples and, in Egypt, by the noble and mortuary estates, the tenants and serfs of gods and territorial magnates that were regularly equipped with metal tools or weapons.

Both the cost of metal equipment and its superiority reacted to consolidate the authority of those who could alone command its use. An actual or virtual monopoly of metal armament placed the pharaoh, the king, and the city-governor – the personifications of the Egyptian and Sumerian States – in an almost impregnable position. On the other hand, the craftsmen, for their part, had lost the independence they enjoyed under barbarism. They were dependent on the city-governor or pharaoh for their raw materials, and could in practice hardly dispose of their products or their skill save to great households.

The merchant class was similarly, if less severely, handicapped. Under the totalitarian régime of Old Kingdom Egypt merchants had little scope. In Mesopotamia the market for the rare goods of small bulk that could alone be profitably transported over long distances, at least by land, must have been to a large extent restricted to the city-governors' courts and the gods' temples. In India alone the archaeological record suggests a wider market and larger profits, but it is unsupported by written documents. A corollary was the slow and incomplete replacement of a 'natural' by a 'money' economy.

The distinctive achievements of civilizations that differentiate them from barbarism are the invention of writing and the elaboration of exact sciences. In Sumer, Egypt, and India the new economy had required and elicited conventional systems of writing and numeral notation, of weights and measures and of time-keeping. It had thus revolutionized the methods of accumulating knowledge and transmitting experience, and produced sciences of a new kind.

By the written word a man can accurately transmit his experiences to correspondents in another city and to generations yet unborn – provided, of course, they use the same conventional symbolism. Written tradition is more impersonal and more abstract than oral. An artisan shows an apprentice concretely how to make a given article or to perform a specific operation. Craftsmanship is therefore imitative and so conservative, as explained on page 87. A prescription on the contrary, just because it is expressed in words, deals with general classes of objects and actions. More scope is given to originality when a verbal rule or abstract formula is translated into action and applied to individual cases.

But the cuneiform and hieroglyphic scripts and doubtless the similarly constructed Indus script too were so cumbersome and complicated that their mastery demanded a long and specialized apprenticeship or education. On purely practical grounds a peasant or an artisan had no chance of learning to read and write. Literacy was confined to a special class of initiates, comparable to the Mandarins in China. Like the latter, the adepts enjoyed a privileged status in Egypt and Mesopotamia. A late Egyptian papyrus in the form of a father's advice to his son contrasts the prospects of a clerk who may 'become an official of high rank' and will be 'exempt from all manual tasks' with the position of a metal-worker 'with fingers like a crocodile's', of a mason, and of other craftsmen.

Consequently, craft traditions were not committed to writing, craftsmanship and literacy were divorced. To the practical sciences, successfully applied in the workshops, were opposed a body of 'higher learning' and literary or learned sciences – mathematics, astronomy, and medicine – and pseudo-sciences – theology, astrology, hepatoscopy, and other vain methods of foretelling the future.

Owing to its specialization and remoteness from the

successful activities of the workshop, the written tradition
tended to be as conservative as craftsmanship. What was
painfully expressed with the symbols of the abstruse Bronze
Age scripts acquired a sanctity and magic prestige. As a
class, the clerks tended to attach more value to the products
of their craft than to the experiences of daily life. A scholastic attitude is engendered in the cloisters. The development of theoretical science was in fact entrusted to a leisured
class, relieved by society of the active labour whereby the
opposition between mind and matter is overcome, and thus
cut off from the sources of empirical knowledge. On the Nile,
in the second millennium, clerks were busily copying down
medical prescriptions and arithmetical problems that, they
claim, had been composed in the Third. A medical text is
advertised as having been 'found in ancient writing at the
feet of Anubis [a god] in the days of King Usaphaïs' (of the
First Dynasty). A certain Ahmes boasts, in the fifteenth
century, that his arithmetic book is 'in the likeness of a
writing of antiquity made in the time of King Nemare'
(1880–50 B.C.). In Babylonia and Assyria clerks still diligently collected and copied texts in the long extinct
Sumerian tongue as late as the first millennium.

Moreover, judged by the extant texts, teaching in the
schools may have been almost as concrete and imitative as
in an artisan's workshop. The so-called mathematical
tablets and papyri are just collections of concrete examples
worked out – in fact, specially constructed so that they
will work out with the means available to their composers.
No general rule is ever stated, nor written explanation of
the reasons for any step added. Egyptian and Babylonian
medical texts describe symptoms of particular maladies and
prescribe remedies – drugs and spells – again without a
word of explanation.

The compilation of sign-lists or dictionaries, the arrangement of accounts or tax-assessments required more rigorously systematic classifications than did the craft or ritual
lore of barbarians. The rules applied, if never formulated, by
the temple-administrators of Sumer and the architects of

Egypt to obtain the areas of fields and the volumes of pyramids served the same purpose as the mathematical laws of physics and mechanics; they did enable the officials to foretell the quantities of grain needed for sowing the fields and of stone required for the monuments. The Egyptian calendar and its correction by Sirius were truly applications of quantitative astronomical laws.

Nevertheless, the scope of science was circumscribed by the nature of the Bronze Age civilization. The limitations of Mesopotamian and Egyptian sciences were not, of course, due to any hereditary deficiencies in the Sumerian, Semitic, or Hamitic races, but to the social background from which the sciences sprang. The charge is commonly levelled against ancient Oriental science that it was inspired by purely practical aims and not by a 'divine curiosity' as to the 'essence' of things. But the aim of science is surely to amass and systematize knowledge that society can use to control events in the external world, in fact to operate more efficiently on nature; the best test of the 'truth' of scientific laws would seem to be their success in so doing.

Now Egyptian and Sumerian societies – and apparently that of the Indus valleys too – were firmly convinced, as are barbarian societies today, that the most reliable way of operating on nature was by means of sympathetic magic or by religious ceremonies that were themselves largely magical. Their clerks and officials naturally accepted this assumption without question. Their whole view of the world was inevitably based on the philosophy – or lack of philosophy – behind it. They had perforce to use its language for the new scientific terminology they were creating.

It is an accepted principle of magic among modern barbarians as among the literate peoples of antiquity that the name of a thing is mystically equivalent to the thing itself; in Sumerian mythology the gods 'create' a thing when they pronounce its name. Hence to the magician to know a thing's name is to have power over it, is – in other words – 'to know its nature'. (The silly questions with which a scientist is plagued: 'What do you call that?' 'Who built this?' show a popular survival of this attitude today.) The Sumerian lists of names may then have not only served a useful and necessary function as dictionaries, but also have been regarded as constituting in themselves instruments for mastering their contents. The fuller a list was, the more of nature could be mastered by its knowledge and use. This may explain the extraordinary fullness of the lists, and the care with which they were preserved and copied.

A Nazi has indeed argued that the aims of Sumerian science were confined to the compilation of exhaustive lists of such magical names and their arrangement in an order which should correspond to the order of the real world. The latter would naturally be conceived in terms of the hier-archical order of Sumerian society. As that society was still dominated in the last resort by tribal custom to which even city-governors were subject, so the world order would be ruled by an impersonal Fate, older than gods and superior to them. Of course, this concept was never very sharply formulated, and later had to contend with that of a high god whose personal legislation constituted Fate when a con-quering king, like Sargon, attained such power that he could override Custom and create Law by his fiat.

Again, architectural forms – like the Sumerian ziggurat and the Egyptian pyramid – came to be regarded as symbols of the divine order of nature, and the contrast between symbol and meaning was not yet sharply defined. But Babylonian and Egyptian geometry had been partly developed by – and for – the construction of these symbolic monuments (hence the accurate knowledge of pyramids displayed in Egyptian arithmetic books). As successful instruments for the construction of symbols of the natural order, geometrical propositions were liable to be regarded also as instruments for the knowledge of that order, for controlling the external world.

Finally, the terminology for the new sciences might be borrowed from the language of liturgy and magic; the Akkadian word for 'working out a sum' is the same as that for 'performing a ritual act'.

Accordingly, it was not the business of Egyptian and Sumerian clerks to test experimentally or criticize the magico-theological view of the world held unquestioningly by their societies; were they not themselves servants of gods and divine kings, owing their existence and prestige to superstitions? Their task was rather to systematize the incoherent beliefs of barbarism that they had inherited. So they created not what we call philosophy, but a theology or mythology. Thereby they gave to the nebulous and fluid superstitions of the barbarism from which Sumer and Egypt were just emerging the more rigid forms of theological dogmas, backed up by organized 'churches' and supporting the vested interests of priesthoods, their royal patrons and divine kings.

As the converse of this inevitable confusion between theology and science, the aims of Oriental religion seem to us materialistic. The cult of the gods was, in fact, designed to secure not what we call holiness, purity, and the peace of God, but good harvests, rain in due season, victory in war, success in love and business, children, wealth, health, and an indefinitely long life. Immortality was conceived by the Egyptians (the Sumerians and Akkadians had only the vaguest notions of anything of the sort) as essentially a prolongation of earthly life. That is why the noble dead have to be provided continually with food, drink, and other offerings, supplies of which were to be secured by the perpetual dedication of mortuary estates and chantry priests. The recognized passports to their 'heaven' were magic rituals – particularly embalmment.

It is true that even in the Pyramid Age a judgement of souls had been conceived. In securing a favourable verdict the appropriate spells and ritual purity were supposedly the essential factors, but what modern, like barbarian, societies consider moral virtues were admittedly helpful. So nobles plead in their sepulchral inscriptions: 'Never have I taken a thing belonging to any person ... Never have I done aught of violence towards any person.' And a county governor: 'I gave bread to the hungry [of my district]; I clothed him who was naked therein ... I never oppressed anyone in possession of his property.' Even so the attainment of immortality was not presented as a motive for moral virtue. Still less did an Egyptian or a Sumerian pray to his god, as Christians do, to help him to be honest, just, or charitable.

In the same way, the Bronze Age artist did not aim at expressing an abstract ideal of beauty, or even primarily at delighting his fellow men. The Sumerian architect must design a temple worthy of the gods, symbolical of the divine order, and yet modelled substantially on the barbarian shrine of reeds in which gods had been worshipped from time immemorial. The result, judged by contemporary representations and modern reconstructions (the actual buildings of mud-brick and timber have lost all pretence at beauty), must have possessed the severe beauty of an American sky-scraper. The Egyptian architect had to translate into imperishable stone and so immortalize a palace of reeds, planks, and mats. Incidentally he created the colonnade of fluted columns (copying the papyrus bundles that had been the first pillars). But it was an illiterate barbarian who discovered how to compensate for the perspective foreshortening that would spoil the effect of the Stonehenge lintels when viewed from the ground.

The Egyptian sculptor had to carve in the hardest and most durable stone a portrait statue of the deceased that contributed magically to his immortality. The statue was not intended for display to mortal eyes, but was walled up in the funerary chapel. None the less, the statues of Mycerinus in Boston, for example, are today hailed as masterpieces of the sculptor's art. His Sumerian colleague was charged with expressing the divine presence as an idol in human form, and with carving statues of city-governors and high priests that, by standing perpetually before the idol, should magically keep the originals ever before the deity's eyes. His efforts fail to arouse enthusiasm among art critics today. They, at least, illustrate a connexion between the urban revolution and an art that seeks to portray the human form realistically. That, at least, can be said of a couple of statuettes from Mohenjo-daro in the Indus valley too.

In Egypt, lively representations of life on the mortuary estate – seed-time and harvest, boat-building, pot-making, even the sports of the peasantry – painted on the tomb walls would ensure to its dead owner the enjoyment of its produce. To depict them the painter had consciously to face the problem of representing the three-dimensional in two dimensions, solids on a flat surface. A selection from his solutions has passed at length into the aesthetic tradition of Atlantic civilization.

The music of drums, pipes, or stringed instruments excites exaltation even in savages. It is no less efficacious on civilized worshippers, and therefore on their gods. With the technical aids of civilization the Sumerians could gather in the temple a regular orchestra of drums, rattles, flutes, horns, trumpets, and harps. They doubtless gave form to barbaric melodies. They certainly used, if they did not invent, the heptatonic scale that has been characteristic of civilized music ever since.

In architecture, sculpture, painting, and music Oriental societies established canons of art, not 'for art's sake', but for supposedly practical ends. Once the requirements of society had been met, the canons became rigid conventions. The artist inevitably turned copyist, so that his products lost the individuality that had made the models truly artistic. But in the sequel the dead conventions, adopted, adapted, and blended by fresh societies with new requirements, could – and did – provide the materials and scaffolding for a living art.

*

If the economy of the Early Bronze Age cities could not expand internally owing to the over-concentration of purchasing power, if its ideological expression were doomed to fossilization, the fossils were at least preserved to serve as models and building materials for the future, the urban economy must – and did – expand externally, as explained in *Man Makes Himself*.

The alluvial cradles of civilization were dependent on

imports for many of the raw materials required by the urban industries, and for luxuries that became necessities. It is not surprising that products of urban workshops are found in barbarian lands from – or through – which the requisite imports must come. In the ruins of villages in Baluchistan Stein found metal-ware and even pottery exported from the cities of the Indus valley. Seals such as were fashionable in Mesopotamia in the Jemdet Nasr phase just before 3000 B.C. have turned up as far afield as central Asia Minor and the Isles of Greece. Egyptian manufactures were carried to the North Syrian coasts and to Crete, and imitated there.

In fact not only the products of urban industry, but the new economy that produced them spread and were bound to spread. To persuade their possessors to exchange the needed raw materials for manufacturers, they must be induced not only to demand the latter, but also to adjust their economy to absorb them. In practice the manufactures that could be exported over long distances under the conditions of Bronze Age land transport were mainly luxury goods of modest bulk that would appeal to a small class enjoying a concentrated surplus of wealth. To market them the chiefs or gods of barbarian tribes must be induced to extort from their followers and worshippers a surplus of foodstuffs to support woodsmen and miners as well as courts and temples. And this is apparently what happened.

Byblos, the best port for the Lebanon lumber trade, had even before the unification of Egypt been occupied by a Copper Age community of fishers and farmers who cultivated olive trees as well as barley and bred chiefly goats and sheep. After the revolution in Egypt a stone temple to the local deity, Ba'alat Gebal, was built in the village, covering about 80 by 50 ft. It was soon replaced by a quite monumental temple measuring over 90 by 63 ft of handsome and richly adorned masonry.

The pharaohs sent to the shrine stone vases inscribed with their names and other offerings. Egyptian ambassadors, officials, clerks, and merchants frequented the temple and the local chieftain's court, and even settled at the port.

Native Giblite clerks were apparently trained in Egyptian hieroglyphic writing. In exchange for the cedars of Lebanon and perhaps olives and dyes, the Giblites received and adopted elements of Egyptian civilization, including writing and all that that implied, as well as manufactured articles and corn. They remained a friendly but independent civilized community.

The same sort of thing must have been going on round Mesopotamia. Just after 2000 B.C. we find a regular colony of Semitic (Assyrian) merchants established round the court of the local prince of Kanes in the Halys basin in Central Asia Minor. They were engaged in trading metals in exchange for Mesopotamian textiles and other manufactures. Their business letters which happen to have survived give a lively picture of caravans of pack-asses regularly crossing the Syrian steppes and the Taurus Mountains on the way to and from Mesopotamia. Legends imply that such colonies were already established in the Halys basin in the days of Sargon about 2400 B.C. The seal, mentioned on page 148 and contemporary copies of Sumerian devices may mean that such commerce went back to 3000 B.C.

An alternative way of securing the necessary raw materials was to turn the new metal weapons against the societies controlling the supplies and to extort the requisites as tribute. The Egyptians, who traded amicably with the Giblites as with Arabians and Ethiopians, 'smote the wretched nomads' who dwelt round the copper mines of Sinai. The pharaohs sent armed expeditions to extract the ores and left warlike inscriptions on the mountain's rocks. They conquered the gold-bearing region of Nubia and compelled the natives to send them gold as tribute. But beyond this the Egyptians avoided imperialist ventures outside the Nile valley till about 1600 B.C.

It was otherwise with the Semitic kings of Mesopotamia. The Sumerians too may have tried conquests outside the delta as well as over one another. The alluvial plain of Sumer and Akkad was no more a self-sufficing unit than was the individual city state within it. As imperial hegemony was the accepted recipe for overcoming conflicts between the cities, so military and political domination over the sources of indispensable raw materials – metals, stone, timber – would be the dream of an ambitious city-governor. The expeditions these sent to get stone and timber may have been ventures in economic imperialism. The earliest temple of Ishtar at Assur (the capital of Assyria) looks like the foundation of a Sumerian conqueror. The annexation of Sialk by 'Elamites' (p. 80) was apparently a military conquest designed to secure routes to the north. But on the whole the stalwart inhabitants of stony, well-wooded and metalliferous mountains were able to defend their independence till the rise of the Dynasty of Akkad about 2350 B.C.

Sargon, his sons, Rimush and Manishtusu, and his grandson, Narâm-Sin, extended their conquests 'from the Lower Sea [the Persian Gulf] to the Upper Sea [the Mediterranean]'. Sargon not only imposed his sway upon the rival cities of Mesopotamia. He was the first to create a vast military empire, the prototype of all the conquerors who have captured popular imagination from Alexander to Napoleon. Like Alexander, Sargon became a hero of romance. Nearly a thousand years after his empire had crumbled, his deeds were being celebrated in epics, fragments of which have turned up in the Egyptian archives at Tell-el-Amarna and in the Hittite library at Boghaz Keui in central Asia Minor.

Both the poetic tradition and the actual inscriptions of Sargon and his successors reveal economic objectives in their conquests. An epic fragment depicts Mesopotamian merchants in the Halys basin inviting his aid against local princes and not asking in vain. Sargon himself explicitly boasts of reaching 'the Cedar Forest' (Lebanon?) and the 'Mountain of Silver' (Taurus). He 'caused the ships of Melukha [Arabia?], the ships of Magan [Oman, source of copper] and the ships of Dilmun [the Bahrein Islands?] to anchor at the quay in front of Agadé'. His son, Manishtusu, again 'took possession as far as the Silver Mines, and from the Mountains of the Lower Sea he carried off their stones'.

The kings of Akkad brought back vast booty. Therewith they endowed and adorned temples, not only in the capital, but also in the subjugated Mesopotamian cities. Their victorious soldiers shared in the spoils. Thus the forcible distribution of the wealth, hoarded in conquered treasuries, spread purchasing power in Mesopotamia. Production was thereby stimulated. At the same time war captives swelled the supply of service producers. In disposing of loot and tribute merchants could make profits. So the middle-class, now comprising victorious veterans as well as merchants, and independent of the old 'divine households', profited from inperialism. Money economy spread till land was now bought and sold like any other commodity.

Nevertheless, trade in metals was made an imperial monopoly. To consolidate his position Narâm-Sin took a leaf out of the pharaoh's book and became a god of empire; he styles himself no longer 'tenant-farmer' nor even 'king', but 'the divine Narâm-Sin, the mighty, god of Agadé'. Thereby he set a precedent that later imitators of his imperialism, the kings of Ur, of Babylon, and of Hatti, and at last the Roman emperors, did not fail to follow. Nevertheless, the Empire of Akkad was ephemeral and collapsed in chaos after a century.

But it had more permanent results than the forcible extraction of raw materials for Mesopotamian industry. At Nineveh (opposite Mosul in Assyria), previously at best a country town, Rimush, Sargon's son, built a monumental temple to Ishtar. Still further west, Narâm-Sin founded an imposing palace at Tell Brak on the Khabur. As in Sumer, such monumental buildings are outward symbols of the establishment of the new urban economy with all its consequences; written documents have actually been found in both buildings. Literate city life persisted here even after the disruption of the empire and the recovery of independence by the new cities.

Even where full city life was not thus established by the

conquest, successful resistance or revolt involved an adoption of part at least of the urban economy. The success of the Akkadian, as of the Egyptian, armies was due to their superior copper weapons and armour against which sling pellets, flint daggers, and stone axes were of little avail. To resist them similar armaments must be manufactured; smiths must be trained and supplied with raw materials; copper and tin must be collected; trade must be organized; a sufficient surplus must be available to support the artisans. Even resistance to imperialism generates a 'Bronze Age economy', dependent on trade at least for armaments to supersede neolithic self-sufficiency.

So, like peaceful trade, economic imperialism did extend the area of civilization. As a result of one activity or another on the part of the original nuclei, new cities, new centres of civilization arose around the original foci and beyond them barbarians abandoned neolithic self-sufficiency at least far enough to secure the new metal armament. And of course each Bronze Age city or township became itself a new centre of demand, irradiating, if only by reflected light, an ever-widening hinterland.

Now the new centres were not just copies of the old. Urban arts and crafts were superimposed upon neolithic cultures, but did not obliterate them. These cultures were adaptations to varied environments, different from those of the great alluvial valleys. They offered opportunities for novel developments in industry and organization. The sea, for instance, now offered new means of livelihood to the peoples of the Mediterranean, and doubtless of the Persian Gulf too.

On the Syrian coast we have seen how Byblos quickly rose to urban status as a result of maritime commerce with Egypt. In Cyprus villages with burials under house floors disclose a vigorous neolithic population. No cities of the early Bronze Age have yet been identified, but large cemeteries of collective tombs bear witness to larger aggregations that must be nearly urban. In one cemetery at Vounous no fewer than forty-eight family vaults, each used over many

generations, have been explored. The island's exceptional
wealth in copper – the metal takes its name from Cyprus –
must have contributed to the support of the increased
population.

A wealth of metal tools in the tombs shows that the local
ores were exploited, that specialist miners and smiths were
working on the island. But neither pottery nor any other
craft had demonstrably been industrialized. Nor do foreign
imports in the tombs show where the surplus metal was
marketed. Indeed, though the Cypriots cast for their own
use a very distinctive kit of metal tools and weapons, the
Cypriot forms are hardly ever found outside the island, even
when the exportation of Cypriot copper, on a large scale is
proved by written documents. As then, so even in the early
Bronze Age, the metal must have been exported in the form
of crude ingots or ore and not worked on the island.

The neolithic farmers and fishers of Crete were joined
about 3000 B.C. by refugees from the Nile Delta and fresh
colonists from Syria, bringing with them some of the technical and artistic traditions of Egypt and Asia. The cultivation of vines and olives, and the exploitation of the island's
natural resources in timber, copper, and murex shell (used
for dyes), could now profitably yield an exportable surplus.
Above all, the island's geographical position between
Egypt, Asia, and mainland Greece, its endowment with
timber for ship-building and a happy conjuncture of winds
and currents offered prospects of wealth in the carrying
trade.

Little townships arose, even on tiny islets utterly destitute
of arable land wherever there was a good harbour. A surplus
was available to support smiths, carpenters, goldsmiths,
jewellers, and seal-cutters. Craftsmen, traders, and sea captains became rich enough to need seals on which are carved
the tools of their craft or their high-prowed rowing-boats.
Otherwise there is no evidence for concentration of wealth.
Large collective tombs, often constructed with considerable
labour, perhaps in imitation of the houses of the living,
crowded with skeletons and quite richly furnished, may well

be the communal burying-places of clans and not just of chieftains' families. Stone axes and obsidian knives were still used side by side with metal tools and weapons. But self-sufficiency had been left behind. Gold, silver, lead, obsidian, and marble were imported; even Egyptian and Asiatic manufactures in the shape of stone vases and faience beads reached the island.

Farther north the little islands scattered in a belt across the Aegean (the Cyclades) had no attractions for self-sufficient farmers. But they possessed marketable resources – copper, emery, obsidian, marble – which, if not edible, could be exchanged for foodstuffs. So in the third millennium they were thickly populated by people who worked metals, quarried obsidian and carved marble vases and traded the products to Egypt, Crete, the coasts of the Dardanelles, and mainland Greece. Their graves are aggressively furnished with metal weapons. So it may be suspected that these insular communities combined piracy with peaceful trade, adding loot to profits, a practice normal in the Mediterranean at many subsequent periods. They would then have discovered the secret of making a living off the urban surplus by simply stealing it!

The plateau of Asia Minor is dotted with settlement tells, so small that they look like villages rather than townships. Their inhabitants were able to secure perhaps from travelling merchant artificers and migratory smiths some copper weapons and trinkets, but on the whole retained a barbaric self-sufficiency. For their agriculture (probably based on irrigation) they still relied entirely on a neolithic equipment. But on the western coast piratical commerce under the leadership of militarist chiefs led to the accumulation of wealth. The 'city' of Troy, made famous by the epics ascribed to Homer, began as a fortified hamlet or citadel, not much more than one and a half acres in area, dominated by the chief's palace. In time it expanded till as 'Troy II' it covered nearly two acres. Accumulated loot and profits now attracted to the chieftain's court goldsmiths trained in Asiatic schools and skilled in filigree work, and at length even professional potters using the wheel. Trade and plunder secured supplies of copper, tin, lead, silver, gold, and obsidian and manufactured luxuries like vases of island marble.

This wealth was concentrated in the personal treasury of a petty war-chief. For its administration neither writing nor even seals were needed. Nor did it support any substantial industrial population. The chief's subjects or followers continued to use stone axes and hoes, picks and mattocks of stags' antlers and sickles armed with flint or obsidian blades. There were apparently enough demand and reserves to justify a quest for further supplies for the armament industry in Europe; ornaments, fashionable in Troy II, were scattered about in the Lower and Middle Danube basins as a result.

Industry on the scale attested at Troy and at other less warlike villages could not absorb an expanding population, which must accordingly seek fresh land. With barren mountains and an already populous plateau behind it, the surplus could only overflow westward in overseas colonization. And so in Macedonia and mainland Greece communities of neolithic peasants, already established in the narrow valleys and coastal plains, were joined by Asiatics and islanders, already accustomed to metal tools and weapons and practising the culture of vines and fruit trees in addition to mixed farming and fishing. The resultant *Early Helladic* settlements show already an urban character; for the culture of vines and olives, metallurgy and a few other specialized crafts, small-scale but fairly regular trade in metal and luxury articles and perhaps some piracy were superadded to the subsistence farming of the neolithic population. There is no more evidence for a concentration of wealth than in Crete. Though jars or bales of merchandise duly sealed in Crete reached Helladic ports, no need was felt locally for seals, and writing was of course unknown.

So all round the eastern Mediterranean maritime cultures arose in which the subsistence economy of barbarism was tinctured with civilized industrial specialization and commerce. They built up new traditions of seamanship and geographical lore and transmitted to the Oriental pool knowledge of new lands, materials, and techniques.

These partially urbanized communities then served in their turn as new centres from which civilized ideas were diffused westward and northward. East Mediterranean manufactures were transported as far west as Sicily and Malta. In Sicily they are found in collective tombs or family vaults, each containing fifty to two hundred skeletons. These are grouped in cemeteries of from ten to thirty which must belong to small villages whose inhabitants, while relying mainly on home-made tools, did import a few ornaments or amulets from further east. It is thought by many that they imported spiritual goods too; for the tombs and the ritual observed in them are suspiciously like those of Crete, Cyprus, and Syria.

Now all civilized peoples are troubled to know how to appeal to barbarian tastes and how to induce 'natives' to work for them. The most acceptable inducements today are arms, showy trinkets, and spirits. Perhaps in antiquity spirituous inducements to labour were replaced by spiritual incitements – hopes of immortality. That might be one explanation for the Copper Age of Sicily.

In that case the same enticements must have been held out to induce the natives of Sardinia, south-eastern Spain (Almeria), and southern Portugal (Algarve) to mine and smelt the local ores of copper, silver, and lead. They certainly did extract these metals and did build tombs more or less on the same general plan as those used farther east. But they supplied the dead at least with a predominantly neolithic equipment, very few copper tools and daggers, and no east Mediterranean manufactures.

Still farther afield the great family vaults built of huge undressed stones and termed megalithic tombs (in Britain long barrows or chambered cairns) that are scattered along the Atlantic coasts of Portugal, France, and the British Isles and across the North Sea to Denmark and southern Sweden are regarded by one school as clumsy and barbaric attempts to copy Spanish, Sicilian, and Cretan funerary architecture and as inspired by the same beliefs. If the megalith-builders were thereby induced to produce a surplus above domestic needs, they certainly did not expend it on obtaining metal tools, still less Oriental manufactures. The megalith-builders of Britain and Denmark are, in fact, classical examples of neolithic self-sufficiency.

In central and north-western Europe the competition for land, described on page 74, had prepared societies to desire superior weapons and in places had produced ruling classes, extracting from a vanquished peasantry a surplus which they were prepared to expend in gratifying that desire. The necessary technical knowledge reached central Europe from Syria, Britain, probably from Spain. Hungary and Bohemia, Ireland and Cornwall could provide the requisite copper and tin. So soon after 2000 B.C. a Bronze Age could and did begin in central Europe and Britain – a few centuries later also in Denmark, northern Germany, and southern Sweden.

A regular trade in metal linked up the whole of central Europe from Upper Italy to the Harz Mountains and from the Vistula to the Rhine into one economic system which joined on to a second in the British Isles and was subsequently extended to embrace Denmark where metal was bartered for amber. It was conducted by itinerant artificers who manufactured or at least 'finished' metal goods to order and may, like the pedlar in Derbyshire during the eighteenth century, have practised petty brigandage as a side-line. But metal remained rare and very costly for centuries and was used almost exclusively for weapons and ornaments. The only specialized metal tools current were those of the metal-workers themselves. For tree-felling, reaping, and other rural pursuits, the peasantry had still to rely on stone axes, flint sickles, and a general Stone Age equipment. Bronze did not open forest lands to the hoe or the plough as iron later would.

So the new bronze industry neither absorbed any

appreciable proportion of the surplus rural population nor equipped it to conquer virgin lands. Pressure on the land was thus unrelieved. Moreover, at least in Denmark and southern England, the costly bronze armament merely consolidated the authority of ruling groups as did the knight's armour in the Middle Ages. Here Bronze Age burials reveal 'an aristocratic world with richly developed upper class life based on organized luxury trade and the labour of the lower classes'.

But the petty chieftains were now equipped with weapons not only to enforce obedience on their followers, but also to lead them to conquer the new lands that their still neolithic rural economy demanded – even to plunder the rich civilizations that had unwittingly armed them. In the sequel civilization is repeatedly threatened by onslaughts from barbarian war-bands impelled as much by the failure of their own economy to support a growing population as by envy of civilization's wealth. The war-bands from Europe, whose arming archaeology allows us to observe so clearly, had not perhaps yet reached the frontiers of the tiny civilized world. But the process revealed in Europe may have been repeated in Asia. There Sargon's tottering Empire was finally overthrown by the barbarians from Gutium who fell upon Mesopotamia.

8

THE CULMINATION OF BRONZE AGE CIVILIZATION

SOON after 2300 B.C. the imposing State organizations just described and the economic systems they dominated disintegrated. In Egypt, Mesopotamia, and India, eras of prosperity that have left a vivid impression in the archaeological record were succeeded by Dark Ages from which few buildings and inscriptions survive. In India civilization itself seems to have been extinguished. In Egypt and Mesopotamia it soon re-emerges, and re-emerges liberated from some of the shackles of ancestral barbarism and deepened so as to benefit more fully new classes in society. In the interval in the newly urbanized areas like Assyria the germs of civilization have had time to develop on original lines.

In Mesopotamia the clouds of darkness are represented by the barbarians from Gutium, armed, as we have seen, against imperialism to attack their civilized attackers. In the devastation they wrought, imperial monopolies were violently overthrown, the hoarded wealth collected in treasures was brutally restored to circulation, or simply annihilated, great households were broken up.

But by no means all temples were sacked; invaders generally feared the gods of conquered lands too much to violate their sanctuaries. Perpetual corporations of priests survived to preserve their deities and their traditions. Most temple libraries remained intact; their schools still functioned. The conquerors may have been illiterates; still they would want clerks and their sciences.

Similarly craftsmen survived, even though they had to work for barbarian masters and may have been hampered by some shortage of raw materials. Above all, trade was never completely paralysed, however many merchants may have been killed or robbed. Even the barbarians would want metal for armaments and some civilized luxuries, and these, in default of a State system of distribution, private traders could supply. Indeed, as the merchant class had made profits out of the plunder of conquered provinces (p. 151), so it could out of the loot of palaces and estates at home. Moreover, as the urban economy spread, traders found ever wider scope.

Hence, when after about a century Sumerian kings of Ur reunited once more the rival cities of Sumer and Akkad, establishing internal peace and security for foreign trade, civilization started to expand again from the level attained under the Empire of Akkad. By 2100 B.C. the Sumerian monarchs had recovered at least so much of Sargon's Empire as to be able to dominate Elam and Assyria and to found cities as far west as Qatna between Homs and Damascus. They began the organization of a professional imperial administration and the codification of customary laws. But their empire too collapsed just before 2000 B.C., and with it the Sumerian ruling class became extinct.

In the second Dark Age that followed semi-barbarous Amorites, Semites from the West, filtered into Mesopotamia. About 1800 B.C. an Amorite dynasty, ruling from Babylon in Akkad, welded Sumer and Akkad into a kingdom that may henceforth be termed *Babylonia*. King Hammurabi consolidated the new kingdom, not only by becoming himself a god of empire, but by giving it a civil service of governors and judges appointed by the king and a unified code of laws to supersede independent traditional codes hitherto observed in each city. Improvements in the old Sumerian war-chariot had enhanced the military power of the Babylonian monarchy and accelerated communications within its domains; for the heavy solid wheels were about this time replaced by spoked wheels and swift horses were replacing asses as tractive power.

Still the machine thus created was not strong enough to prevent infiltrations by barbarian Kassites and invasions by Hittites and Elamites. The Amorite Dynasty of Babylon was replaced by a Kassite Dynasty. But the Kassite monarchs took over the administrative machinery Hammurabi had created and the whole apparatus of Sumerian–Babylonian civilization. Babylonia survived as a civilized State, albeit impoverished and cramped by new States in Elam, Assyria, and Syria.

In Egypt it was the great landlords, county governors who had become hereditary counts, who were the agents in the destruction of the Old Kingdom (p. 129); they made themselves independent of the pharaoh, or rather each tried to make himself a pharaoh on his own. The result was not only political anarchy, but also economic chaos; for it was the centralized State that had secured and distributed supplies of raw material and had accumulated the surplus needed for the support of artisans. Later clerks have left vivid glimpses of the chaos of the resultant Dark Age. One writes: 'Men take up arms for battle, because the land lives on disorder; they make them spears of copper to beg their bread with blood.' And another: 'All the materials for the crafts are lacking; no worker works any more; enemies have despoiled the workshops.'

But on the Nile, as on the Tigris and Euphrates, craftsmen and craftsmanship survived, even if rendered idle for lack of materials. If there were no promising careers for clerks as State officials, they could be county officials and were as necessary as ever on nobles' estates. So learned sciences too could survive. From the very depths of the Dark Age designs painted on coffin lids illustrate a development of astronomical lore in the direction of stellar clocks, dividing the watches of the night month by month by the appropriate rising constellations, with the aid of which the dead man could tell the time.

Local temples and their gods were generously endowed by county magnates. The latter and their priests were as anxious as ever for 'immortality'. But they no longer looked to the god-king to bestow it; instead priestly specialists and embalmers provided – for a fee – the needful spells and rites.

Finally private merchants could do what the State had

done, in importing raw materials. The various independent courts might compete with one another for merchandise as well as for craftsmen's skill. This multiplicity of competing buyers enlarged the opportunities for a middle class of artisans, priests, and merchants to sell their skill, their magic, and their wares. So in Egypt, too, the techniques of civilization and many of its superstitions were preserved intact.

The political framework requisite for their full revival was provided by what is termed the *Middle Kingdom*. The counts of Thebes by war and diplomacy reunited the whole of Egypt into a feudal monarchy. Those rival counts who made timely submission were continued in their provinces; recalcitrants were replaced by royal children and supporters; all were made vassals owing tribute and allegiance to the royal house of Thebes. So about 2000 B.C. Egypt recovered a political unity commensurate with the land's unity as symbolized by the Nile.

After a couple of centuries this unity was again destroyed by the insubordination of the vassal counts. In the ensuing anarchy barbarians, usually known as the Hyksôs or Shepherd Kings, and armed with new engines of war, burst in from Asia and established from the Delta a temporary barbarian empire that drew tribute not only from the Nile valley but also from adjacent parts of Asia. In 1580 B.C. the barbarians were expelled by the military power of a count of Thebes, Ahmose, founder of the *New Kingdom*. He had adopted the new Asiatic war engine, the light horse-drawn chariot. With it the wheeled vehicle appeared for the first time on the Nile, albeit as a piece of armament.

As military conquerors the new pharaohs made Egypt a centralized military monarchy, as Sargon had made Sumer and Akkad. Like Sargon, too, they set out on a career of imperial expansion and won Egypt an Asiatic empire which extended over Palestine and Syria to the Euphrates and the Amanus Mountains and across the sea to Cyprus. Conquest brought to the New Kingdom of Egypt as it had to the empires of Akkad, Ur, and Babylon an immense access of wealth. But this new wealth arrived as loot and tribute concentrated in the treasuries of the new royal war-lords. The New Kingdom became a totalitarian State as the Old had been.

The rejuvenated civilizations of Mesopotamia and Egypt in the second millennium differ from their parents of the third most significantly in the greater prominence of a middle class of merchants, professional soldiers, clerks, priests, and skilled artisans, no longer embedded in 'great households' but subsisting independently alongside these.

The partial disruption of great estates and the pillaging of the countryside had emphasized the value of conventional, incorruptible metal wealth as against the real but perishable wealth produced by the land. In periods of invasion and anarchy the impoverishment or destruction of 'great households' within which a natural economy reigned had encouraged the spread of a money economy. Of course, gold or silver gained by usury, trade, plunder or even manual labour smells as good as that earned by the ownership of land or agriculture. In Mesopotamia, indeed, land had become a commodity, salable and disposable by will since the days of the Empire of Akkad. Even in Egypt under the New Kingdom parcels of land, though held on lease from pharaoh and generally carrying obligations to military service, could be transferred by testament or sale.

With the spread of the money economy production for the market became commoner. The speculative importation of miscellaneous cargoes for sale in the market might yield greater, if less reliable, profits than the collection on commission of specific articles ordered by great households or States. Merchants could in this and other ways (p. 161) make money and find uses for it as purchasers. Soldiers brought back from the war gold, silver, or saleable commodities like slaves, and must use the proceeds to buy in the bazaars satisfactions for their needs.

Both in Egypt and Mesopotamia an army of literate officials appointed by the State, and ranging from junior clerks to judges, now enjoyed assured incomes in money and a secure status. They were no longer attached to 'households' that supplied all their needs, nor could many possess such households of their own. So they too must appear as buyers in the bazaar. In Egypt professional priests had multiplied as a result of the generous temple endowments by victorious pharaohs and the credulity of their fellow-citizens. These and their Mesopotamian colleagues found needs to satisfy by 'shopping'.

Hence craftsmen need no longer be attached to great households, but had an open market for their products. Whether they produced for stock or only worked to order, craftsmen could earn enough to purchase the products of other crafts. Even peasants found a market for produce outside great households, and could so obtain a larger share in the technical benefits conferred by civilization. In Egypt the rural population remained indeed legally 'royal serfs', liable as before to compulsory labour and practically attached to the estate on which they worked, even when it was held by a noble or small tenant. Still, even the Egyptian fellah was sometimes left with a surplus of rural produce for sale when dues and taxes had been paid.

Under this régime the circulation of commodities certainly increased, industrial production expanded, and imports were multiplied. New luxury manufactures – in Egypt, for instance, glass vessels and new imports – appeared on the market and soon became necessities for the middle class. The use of metal at last spread effectively to the countryside. In Egypt bronze first became known under the Middle Kingdom, and almost plentiful under the New. Even the peasantry were equipped with metal tools.

The growth of the middle class was reflected ideologically in law and religion. Universally valid codes of law and judges appointed by the king replaced local and customary laws administered by elders or nobles. Indeed the reign of law began to limit even the absolutism of monarchs. A king of Babylon or a pharaoh of the Middle and New Kingdoms prided himself on being the 'guardian of just laws' rather than the unfettered creator of law by the fiat of his divine will.

Now in Egypt rights for the masses meant rites for the masses. So after the first Dark Age immortality, originally the prerogative of the divine king and of nobles on whom he had conferred it, was made open to all – in practice to all who could pay the embalmers' fees and buy the magic passports to heaven. This was equivalent to a popular revolution, but for the benefit only of the middle class. An inevitable corollary of opening the gates of heaven was to enlarge the maws of hell too. Even in the Pyramid Age the divine king and his nobles had to submit to a judgement of souls (p. 145). Naturally in the case of such august personages little was said of the punishments in store for a transgressor. In the second millennium for the encouragement of a more vulgar clientele the pains of hell were vividly depicted; the most powerful instrument for domination over men's unruly wills was forged!

In practice hell was not made a sanction for morality. The lucky Egyptian could buy a magic passport through the dread tribunal. Rolls containing the welcome verdict of acquittal were sold by the priests' clerks. The fortunate purchaser's name was inserted in blanks left for the purpose, thus securing by itself a verdict before it was known whose name should be inserted. Charms were even purveyed to still the voice of conscience. Breasted describes an amulet inscribed, 'O my heart, rise not up against me as a witness'.

So the 'popular revolution' in Egypt did not promote a higher morality, but reinforced the powers of the new professional priesthood. In the same way the Babylonian business men provided credulous clients for the soothsayers and fortune-tellers of the old temples.

Yet even under the new economic régime the use of civilized equipment was still relatively restricted, and the possibilities of industrial expansion were limited in like degree. In the alluvial valleys that expansion had been made possible in the first instance by the collection of a surplus from a peasantry practising subsistence agriculture in the great households of kings or gods. The system not only secured the accumulation of an adequate surplus and the maintenance of irrigation works, it proved very convenient to the tax-collectors of the new military States. Contributions were more easily collected and converted into money from the real wealth stored in the granaries of great landlords than from the tiny stores of individual farmers. Great landed estates, so organized as to be as far as possible self-sufficing, therefore remained common economic units, though now often in possession of the captains and veterans of war-lords. They may have been extended at the expense of tribal lands farmed communally, since we read of Sumerian cities buying these up.

Then the new money economy became itself an instrument for concentrating wealth. Neither artisans and primary producers, not even travelling merchants and retailers, were the principal beneficiaries of the new metal currency. Insolvent debtors were added to war-captives in replenishing the slave market and so degrading the status and reducing the emoluments of manual labour. The free craftsman was often dependent on the merchant both for raw materials and for the sale of his products, and such dependence might easily lead to indebtedness. The peasant, too, after a bad harvest or a hostile raid might find interest added to the burden of taxes and rent. The small merchant who travelled abroad often borrowed trade goods or capital from a temple or a private capitalist who became a sleeping partner in the venture, entitled to a share in the proceeds.

Babylonian law as codified by Hammurabi might be said ' to secure the creditor against the debtor and consecrate the exploitation of the small producer by the possessor of money'. The debtor might not only mortgage his land, but pledge his children, his wife, or his own person. Enslavement for debt was legalized. Trading partnerships were regulated in the interest of the capitalist, and fraud by the working partner was severely punished. Interest rates on loans in barley ranged from 20 to 33 per cent, from 10 to 25 per cent on silver. The concentration of wealth in the hands of financiers would in the end react to restrict the market for industrial products and so industry itself.

At the same time producers in their capacity of consumers must have suffered from the price fluctuations that followed the introduction of metallic money. In Mesopotamia the price of the staple food, barley, rose steadily throughout the Bronze Age. A gur of barley cost a shekel of silver under the Empires of Akkad and of Ur, two shekels by the time of Hammurabi, three and a third perhaps under the Kassites.

Such price increases may just as well be regarded as effects of inflation. The new wealth with which imperialism enriched Babylonia and Egypt was really just loot, and represented no addition to the total supply of real wealth available to humanity; quite the contrary. The destruction of houses or the ravaging of gardens is the reverse of wealth-production. 'An army is a body of pure consumers, nay negative producers, producers of illth.' But money veils any discrepancy between real wealth, the available supply of commodities, and its consumption. Its possessors did not suffer from any shortage and could indeed make more money by loans to those who needed it to meet the rising prices.

At the same time professional soldiers are hostile to production, in that their trade is robbery on a grand scale, and robbery has been described as 'the oldest labour-saving device'. They were even liable to plunder their fellow-citizens, as fragments of Egyptian legislation make painfully clear.

The new judges and officials did not scruple to enrich themselves by extortion and bribes from rich litigants. Hammurabi's letters contain instructions for the suppression of such abuses. Harmhab, a pharaoh of the fourteenth century, found it necessary to prescribe the cutting off of the nose and exile as a punishment to check extortion by tax-collectors against the poor. An earlier papyrus describes the plight of the poor man 'who stands alone before the court when his opponent is rich while the court oppresses him [demanding] "silver and gold for the clerks, clothing for the servants".'

Finally the money economy spread and the middle class grew under the shadow of absolute theocratic monarchy. No private accumulation of silver and gold could possibly compete with the hoards in imperial treasuries. Even in Mesopotamia the kings took care to keep private capitalists in their proper place. The seal of an Assyrian merchant in Asia Minor is perhaps symptomatic of the position of commerce in Mesopotamia; it is inscribed 'N., servant of the King of Ur'. There was no question of states borrowing from private capitalists as they do in Europe and did in Hellenistic Greece. The metal trade remained a royal monopoly, or at least strictly regulated. The comparative scarcity of copper and tin made this none too difficult.

By decree Hammurabi of Babylon and later Hittite and Assyrian kings fixed maximum prices and maximum – not minimum – wages. The great estates of kings, temples, and nobles, internally independent of money, further limited production for the market. So throughout the Bronze Age the middle class remained completely subordinate to the monarchy and the priesthood.

To the peasant and the small man, on the contrary, the divine king appeared as a saviour from the rapacity of usurers, the extortions of officials, oppression by the nobles, and abuse by the soldiery. Hammurabi published his law code 'to make manifest justice in the land, to destroy the wicked and evil-doer and to prevent the strong oppressing the weak'. A pharaoh warns his vizier (chancellor): 'It is an abomination of the god to show partiality'. Egyptian popular tales repeatedly introduce an oppressed peasant turning confidently to pharaoh for redress.

Mythologically the absolutism of the ruler was reflected not only in his own deification. The whole world of gods was increasingly conceived as an empire presided over by a supreme god. So under the Amorite dynasty Marduk, god of Babylon, usurped the place of the Sumerian Enlil as creator. In Egypt, Amon, a local deity of Thebes, had absorbed attributes of Ra, the sun-god, under the Middle Kingdom and under the New was on his way to becoming a veritable god of gods. Nevertheless, even the high gods retain their tribal character. Marduk is primarily lord of the Babylonians, Amon of the Egyptians. Amon can be lord of Cyprus or Syria only in so far as his 'son', Pharaoh, conquers the land for him. So no Egyptian or Babylonian would have felt the least scruple in saying:

> A thousand Frenchmen sent below,
> Praise God from whom all blessings flow.

Thus till nearly 1200 B.C. Bronze Age civilization survived in the alluvial valleys of the Near East, preserving its essential structure throughout political vicissitudes and economic changes.

Meanwhile new centres of civilization had arisen and grown to maturity. In the Far East a literate civilization emerged in the alluvial valley of the Yellow River soon after the middle of the second millennium. The neolithic revolution had affected China, where cereals were cultivated and pigs and cattle bred at a still uncertain date. Out of this vague barbaric background emerged the great city of Anyang, capital of the Shang dynasty, soon after 1400 B.C. Its setting in the flood plain of a great river is essentially like that of Egyptian and Sumerian cities. The urban economy it symbolized agrees in general outlines with those of earliest Sumer, Egypt, and India as described in Chapters 5 and 6. A surplus derived from breeding pigs, cattle, sheep, and goats, as further west, together with water buffaloes and chickens, and the cultivation of wheat and millet, but also of rice, was concentrated in the hands of a divine monarch who would be buried with extravagant pomp in a wooden chamber at the bottom of a pit 65 ft square and 43 ft deep. The surplus supported bronze-smiths using the same alloys and techniques as their western colleagues, potters using the wheel and other civilized craftsmen, together with clerks who had already devised an ideographic script based on conventional pictures. Horse-drawn chariots were used in war.

In its concrete details Far Eastern civilization differed conspicuously from Near Eastern, but the differences are no more pronounced than those distinguishing the three civilizations of the early third millennium from one another. Some are obviously due to the utilization of local resources – rice instead of barley, silk instead of cotton or flax, for instance. The general agreement can hardly be accidental. Only the lack of excavations in the intervening areas precludes the demonstration that impulses from the Near and Middle East had been fertilizing Far Eastern barbarism. China must have been receiving Western traditions even before 2000 B.C. Conversely, after 1400 she must have reacted on the West as a full partner in civilization.

In the Near East in any case the seeds, dispersed from the original centres, as described in Chapter 7, now sprouted into full-blown civilizations. The Assyrians had learned well from Sargon of Akkad and started a civilized state on the Akkadian model. After a further lesson from the kings of Ur, Assyrian kings tried an empire on their own. The Assyrians had taken over from the Sumerians and Akkadians the whole equipment of civilization – not only their techniques and armaments, but also their script, their learning, and their ideology. So they embarked upon imperialist ventures, conquering an empire west of the Tigris and organizing it on the approved lines. In the nineteenth century the city of Tilsha-annim (now Chagar Bazar), on the Khabur in North Syria, appears as the 'great household' of Prince Iasman-adad, son of Shamsi-adad I of Assyria. In the household accounts even clerks seem to occupy the same dependent position as the smith or the brewer in Baü's household at Lagash (p. 103). But the breeding and training of horses to draw war-chariots was an important activity on this estate.

But about 1450 B.C. this western province of the Assyrian Empire fell into the hands of Aryan (p. 176) chiefs, who made it the centre of a new state, Mitanni. These, too, adopted the old equipment and organization of Sumero-Akkadian-Babylonian civilization, using not only the cuneiform script, but for diplomatic correspondence even the Akkadian language.

On the plateau of Asia Minor, since water for irrigation was derived from many different springs and torrents, and supplies of raw material were generally near at hand, the urban revolution could be postponed as long as the primary producers could make shift with a neolithic equipment (p. 154). At best local gods or divine kings may have accumulated small surpluses in a number of independent 'households' on a tiny scale. But soon after 2000 B.C. Indo-European Hittite chiefs (p. 176) began to unite these small units into a feudal empire. By 1595 they were strong enough to invade Babylonia and later still ousted the Aryan dynasts from Mitanni, and even challenged the Egyptians in Syria.

Naturally the mortal princes who attained such power attained divinity too, but only as leaders in a federation of local gods. In his treaty with pharaoh 'the sun-god of Hatti' still signs also on behalf of 'the goddess of Arinna', 'the god of Kizzwadana', and so on. But Sargon of Akkad, who had invaded their future domain in the third millennium, was their pattern, and the Assyrian merchants established there even longer sold them the material and spiritual equipment of their civilization. The Hittites borrowed theology, law, poetry, and science as well as writing materials and characters from Mesopotamia. Still they modified what they borrowed to suit their own traditions and local needs.

On the coasts of Syria many Phoenician settlements as far north as Ugarit (Ras Shamra opposite Cyprus) now became cities in the same way as Byblos had early in the third millennium (p. 148). The Phoenicians profited from both Egyptian and Sumero-Akkadian experience, adopted Mesopotamian and Nilotic techniques and traditions and copied the products of both centres. Situated on a narrow coastal plain, better adapted for fruit trees and vines than to corn-growing, they could only find on the sea an outlet for their overflowing populations. Byblos offered a standing example of the possibilities of maritime trade with the rich markets on the Nile. Owing to the relatively low cost of transport by sea – by rowing a ship could reach the Nile in eight days, and the return journey, with a favouring wind, might be accomplished in four – even low-priced goods for popular consumption could be profitably sold there. Paintings in New Kingdom tombs show the Phoenicians from their barges bartering trinkets with the peasants of villages along the Nile. A much larger proportion of the Phoenician population must have been engaged in industry and commerce than in the predominantly agricultural States of Egypt, Babylonia, Assyria, and Hatti.

At the same time, if the local gods (Baals) and their royal representatives accumulated wealth derived from the soil in great households, these accumulations were so modest as not to overshadow the wealth amassed by private trade and industry so completely as in the other civilizations. In Phoenician society the middle classes had a chance to make their demands effective.

In Crete what is termed the *Minoan civilization* emerges into literacy about 2000 B.C. Even in the third millennium specialist farming, the exploitation of insular resources like timber and the carrying trade had offered a livelihood to classes which a neolithic economy could not support (p. 153). Now the wealth thus gathered was partly concentrated in the hands of merchant princes who were also priest-kings. At Knossos, Mallia, Tylissos, Phaestos, and Hagia Triadha in central Crete, they built themselves palaces that were also factories and warehouses like an Oriental temple or court.

Specialist craftsmen – potters from Asia using the wheel, glaziers, and fresco painters – flocked to the palaces to share this wealth. For its administration the Minoans invented and simplified a pictographic script. Like the oldest written documents from Sumer, the surviving remains of Minoan writing are almost exclusively account tablets, also traced on clay. Unfortunately they are still undeciphered. Like a city-governor in Sumer, the Minoan princes financed public works, but the most conspicuous are harbours and bridges to facilitate trade – the wheeled cart had been introduced soon after 2000 B.C.

The Minoan palace is no doubt the symbol of a great household like the divine households of Sumer described on p. 103. But magazines and workshops are proportionately more conspicuous and occupy a relatively larger area at Knossos or Phaestos than in the temples of Erech or Lagash. A smaller proportion of their contents and products must have been absorbed in supplying the household's needs; the balance must have been used for trade. In other words the priest-king's economic power must to a quite high degree have depended on secondary industry and commerce as contrasted with agricultural production.

Nor was the royal wealth so overwhelming as to overshadow altogether that earned by private traders and craftsmen. Provincial towns and cemeteries, particularly in eastern Crete, give an impression of modest prosperity, even though they are not dominated by any palace. Gurnia in the fourteenth century covered six and a half acres and comprised sixty houses, each probably two-storeyed and occupying a block about forty by thirty feet. As merchant, the priest king was only one among many, although, thanks to his subjects' piety, the best endowed. Even so, each 'divine merchant' had peers in adjacent palaces. Only during the century 1500 to 1400 B.C. does the lord of Knossos, the Minos of Greek legend, seem to have succeeded in eliminating his competitors by the methods of Akkadian imperialism; the horse-drawn war chariot appears in Crete at this time and figures conspicuously in the Knossian accounts.

These peculiarities of the urban economy in Crete reacted in an interesting manner on Minoan industry and commerce. In Crete the specialist potter was not one of the craftsmen already differentiated before the local urban revolution and degraded socially thereby. He arrived in the island as the honoured exponent of a new technique while the revolution was still in progress; he was welcomed to island courts whose rulers were not yet rich enough to adorn their tables exclusively with vessels of gold and silver. So, while in the Orient the aesthetic quality of pottery almost everywhere declined after the revolution, in Crete the new specialists in the palace workshops turned vessels, delicate and beautiful and worthy to adorn the tables of princes. The same good fortune may have rewarded other craftsmen. The painters who adorned the Minoan palaces with lovely frescoes had probably been trained in Egyptian technique and conventions. But by their originality they may have earned such a reputation that they could find patrons even among Mesopotamian monarchs. The frescoes in a great palace built by a powerful king of Mari on the middle Euphrates in the nineteenth century betray so strong a Minoan inspiration in design and technique that they seem to be the works of actual Cretan artists.

The area of Minoan trade is defined by the distribution of Minoan pottery. By the eighteenth century at least this was already reaching mainland Greece, the Aegean islands, Cyprus, the Syrian coasts, and Egypt. At first no doubt the fine products of the palace potteries may fairly be classed as luxury articles for the conspicuous consumption of ruling classes. Such a vase was in fact found in the tomb of an Egyptian noble under the Middle Kingdom. On the other hand, pottery in general falls within the class of cheap popular goods. Judged by the shapes and decoration, even the products of the palace workshops were substitutes for more costly stone and metal vessels. Potentially at least the export of vases points to long-distance trade in cheap goods for popular consumption.

Moreover, the pots were hardly exported empty. Huge oil-jars found in the palace magazines give the impression that products of specialized farming, such as olive oil, formed staples of Cretan commerce with the Oriental civilizations. Popular goods, on the contrary, are not included among the surviving imports – Egyptian stone vases, rare Babylonian cylinder seals, ingots of Cypriot copper.

Piracy must always have threatened the security of Cretan commerce. Later Greek tradition credits Minos with its suppression. But if his 'empire' policed the paths of the sea as well as eliminating rivals from the island, the resultant centralization seems in the end to have weakened Minoan economy. After 1400 B.C. Crete became a province of the semi-barbarous Mycenaean culture that had arisen on the Greek mainland (p. 178).

Beyond and between the new and enlarged provinces of urban civilization the penumbra of Bronze Age barbarism likewise expanded. Eastward migrations of peoples as well as peaceful trade further diffused some arts of civilization. From Greece and Bulgaria across the plateaux of Asia Minor and northern Iran certain types of seals and pins (with double spiral heads) are scattered along the famous route that, until the railway age, has been followed by the caravans travelling across central Asia to China and to India. These trade goods hint how ideas and devices from the west may have been transmitted even to China to fertilize civilization on the Yellow River (p. 170).

In India the same sort of western objects have been unearthed in slummy, illiterate settlements built on the ruins of some old Indus cities such as Chanhu-daro in Sind. Later, perhaps about 1200 B.C., 'literary' documents that were not yet preserved in writing give vivid glimpses of the arrival in India of the Aryan Hindus and of their barbaric culture.

The hymns of the Rig-Veda, the oldest Hindu sacred book, describe the Aryan tribes scattered about the north-west from the Kabul and the Kurrum (western tributaries of the Indus) to the head-waters of the Ganges and the Jumna. They live predominantly by pastoralism, growing some grain, of course, but reckoning wealth in cows and horses. The tribes are frequently at war and are led by petty chiefs or rajas, fighting from chariots and delighting in racing, dicing, and strong drink. They worship natural forces personified in their own image and including deities worshipped also by the rulers of Mitanni (p. 170). The hymns themselves are really also charms sung to enhance the efficacy of sacrifices that were at the same time sympathetic magic rites to secure rain, wealth, and victory.

The priests who sang them and performed the rites enjoyed essentially the status of any highly-skilled craftsman under Bronze Age barbarism (p. 178); they were, that is to say, entirely dependent on the generosity of royal patrons, but not permanently attached to royal households, since rajas competed for their services. Yet they are the ancestors of the Brahmans who built up such a reputation as monopolists of magic and sole intermediaries between gods and men that they could at length claim to form the highest caste, superior even to kings. The rites on which their livelihood depended were memorized to the minutest detail and handed down as secrets in the priestly families. The words of efficacious hymns were similarly committed to memory and repeated from generation to generation long after their words were becoming unintelligible, and their language was more remote from current speech than Chaucer's English is from ours. So as craftsmen the Hindu priests devised a method of transmission by sheer retentive memory that made writing superfluous.

The language thus transmitted, (Vedic) Sanskrit, is allied to Persian, Greek, Latin, the Celtic and Slavonic tongues and our own in much the same way as Italian is related to Spanish, French, and Portuguese. As these 'Romance languages' are all derived from Latin, the language of the Romans, so, it is inferred, Sanskrit, Greek, and the other *Indo-European* languages are descended from an extinct 'parent tongue', spoken by some people or society now long dispersed. Because the early Hindus and Persians did really call themselves *Aryans*, this term was adopted by some nineteenth-century philologists to designate the speakers of the 'parent tongue'. It is now applied scientifically only to the Hindus, Iranian peoples, and the rulers of Mitanni, whose linguistic ancestors spoke closely related dialects and even worshipped common deities. As used by Nazis and anti-Semites generally, the term 'Aryan' means as little as the words 'Bolshie' and 'Red' in the mouths of crusted Tories.

The 'parent people' cannot be identified archaeologically,

still less by its physical racial type. Its linguistic offspring, i.e. peoples who accepted, even if they modified in divergent ways, the conventions of the 'parent tongue', have already been met in Mitanni and Hittite Asia Minor (p. 171); many of the European barbarians to be mentioned next also must have by this time adopted Indo-European linguistic conventions. When their societies are stratified, their rulers' habits display a family likeness to those of the Vedic rajas.

In any case European barbarism was being increasingly penetrated by radiations from Oriental civilization during the second millennium. To the north 'royal barrows' in the Kuban valley richly furnished with manufactures from Mesopotamia (axes, spears, cauldrons, gold-work, and jewellery) and materials (meerschaum) from Asia Minor prove intercourse across the Caucasus between Europe and Hither Asia, and the fertilization thereby of an illiterate Pontic Bronze Age in which wealth was concentrated by barbarian war chiefs.

In mainland Greece the Early Helladic farmers and navigators had been replaced or subjugated about 1800 B.C. by more war-like farmers, probably Greek-speaking Indo-Europeans. These barbarians added their own contributions without extinguishing the agricultural, industrial, and commercial traditions of their predecessors. The old townships were reconstructed; metallurgy and the other crafts were still plied, though directed more than heretofore to armament manufacture. Professional potters using the wheel immigrated from Crete, and perhaps also from Asia Minor, starting a new specialized industry.

Then from 1600 on Greece was inundated with Cretan products and techniques. The Helladic villages became the citadels of rich war-lords disposing of concentrated wealth. By barter or plunder these obtained first Minoan products – weapons, jewellery, pottery, and luxury articles. Then they persuaded or compelled Minoan craftsmen – smiths, armourers, goldsmiths, seal-engravers, fresco-painters, architects and, last of all, clerks – to settle at their courts and train native apprentices to turn out rather tasteless copies

of the imported models in Minoan techniques. Eventually
the mainlanders were equipped to annex Crete, too, and
the mainland *Mycenaean* civilization usurped the dominion
of the Minoan throughout the Aegean world.

It was a semi-barbarous, barely literate,* highly militarist
civilization. The Mycenaean 'cities', girt with tremendous
walls of great unhewn blocks in so-called Cyclopean
masonry, and dominated by the war-lord's palace, are,
like Troy, little better than glorified castles. At the capital,
Mycenae itself, the ramparts enclose only eleven acres: the
'great hall' of the palace was 38 ft long by 42 ft wide. Still,
large cemeteries of family vaults cut in the hillside outside
the cities' walls denote a substantially increased population.

The princes owed their power and wealth to a monopoly
of new implements of war – long rapiers of costly bronze,
huge shields and light horse-drawn war-chariots. The social
implications of this armament are disclosed by the Greek
epic poems ascribed to Homer, the *Iliad* and the *Odyssey*.
Battles resolve themselves into single combats between
richly-armed champions who arrive in chariots. These
decide the issue; the infantry are mere spectators. In fact,
only the few could afford the long blades of bronze, the
chariots – marvels of the wainwright's skill – and the
highly-trained steeds, so that the masses were militarily
worthless and accordingly politically impotent.

But in Mycenaean Greece the costly war gear was not supplied, as in Egypt and the Asiatic monarchies, by a centralized
State to a professional soldiery, but belonged to the princes
themselves. So the latter are sovereigns or at best owe a vague
allegiance to the king of Mycenae as overlord whom they
support as vassals in the 'Trojan war' according to the *Iliad*.

The surplus wealth thus won with the sword or extorted
from a subject tenantry was devoted to luxury display rather
than public works or even the endowment of temples and

*Although it is true that writing played only a restricted role in
Mycenaean society, it is interesting to recall that the recent decipher-
ment of linear B script has shown that the spoken language was Greek. –
J.G.D.C.

tombs. But craft products were in demand, and a skilled artisan enjoyed a position of freedom and prestige that is probably characteristic of Bronze Age barbarism. 'A sooth-sayer, a doctor, a singer, and a craftsman is sure of a welcome everywhere,' says 'Homer' in his *Odyssey*. Trade was essential to supplement piracy in supplying materials for armaments and ornaments. So merchants might earn sub-stantial profits and doubtless some social standing too, since even a war-lord's wealth in a poor valley could never reach overwhelming proportions.

Mycenaean trade is the continuation of Minoan after 1400 B.C., and was even more popular in character. My-cenaean pottery was exported in masses to Troy, the coasts of south-western Asia Minor, Syria, Palestine, and Egypt, and westward reached Sicily and southern Italy. Trade was followed or preceded by actual migrations of Mycenaean Greeks or Mycenaeanized Cretans seeking beyond the sea a livelihood that narrow valleys and Bronze Age citadels could not supply. Colonies established themselves on Cyprus and on the adjacent coasts of Asia. In the island the colonists may also have been conquerors. Just opposite on the Syrian coast at Ugarit the Mycenaeans appear as prosperous merchants, sojourning peaceably in a Phoenician city like British merchants in Istanbul.

But Mycenaean trade was orientated largely towards barbarian Europe, which thereby was enabled to make direct contributions to the main cultural pool. Actual Mycenaean vases were exported as far afield as Macedonia and Sicily (Map II). Indirectly Mycenaean trade extended much further. Beads of east Mediterranean faience such as were fashionable about 1400 B.C. reach southern Eng-land, and a dagger manufactured in Mycenaean Greece was dug up from a Bronze Age barrow in Cornwall. Un-doubtedly Cornish tin and Irish gold were brought to Greece in return. Indeed actual ornaments made in England were worn there. Amber from Jutland (Denmark) was cer-tainly traded to Greece and Crete along a well-marked route across central Europe, where the same sort of

Mediterranean faience beads were received in exchange. However indirectly, Ireland and Denmark were now contributing positively to the collective experience of humanity, pooled in the Near East.

The Bronze Age barbarisms of western and central Europe, described on p. 157, may quite possibly have been generated by the trade now first attested. In any case they remained unchanged late enough to be quickened by it. The barbarian aristocracies in whose graves in southern England the imported faience beads were deposited, and who in Denmark profited most from the far-flung luxury trade in amber, were sociologically and economically the counterparts of the Mycenaean chivalry just described, only poorer and more provincial. It might be as true to say that the 'heroic age' of Greece resulted from the transplantation of such a northern aristocracy to the fringe of the rich Minoan world.

Be that as it may, just before the second millennium ended improved methods of mining and smelting, allowing the exploitation of even deep ores in the Austrian Alps and perhaps on other minefields, superior processes of casting and hammering, and a reorganization of the metal trade to ensure the scrupulous collection and use of scrap had materially cheapened bronze, first within the central European economic system, later also in Britain, Denmark, Sicily, and Sardinia. Specialized metal tools for carpentry and a few other crafts became at last available, as well as weapons and ornaments. If the revolution in the metal industry did not produce an urban civilization to absorb the farmers' surplus sons, it supplied them with shields and swords for renewed onslaughts on the civilized world.

During the second millennium the continuous area of civilized life and literacy had extended from the alluvial valleys over the greater part of the Near East with an outpost far away in China. The tendrils of commerce reached out into the barbarian fringe right to the Atlantic and North Sea coasts and the steppes of central Asia and southern Russia. Obvious results were a vast increase in the human stock, a rising standard of living for part of it, and a commensurate enlargement of the pool of human experience.

In spite of wars and dark ages the cities and villages of the alluvial valleys were at least as populous in 1500 B.C. as they had been in 2500. The number of cities had been multiplied many times. The new cities in Assyria, Syria, Asia Minor, and Crete, to say nothing of China, were immensely larger than the villages that had preceded them. Assur, the Assyrian capital, now covered 120 acres, Qatna in North Syria perhaps more. Even Troy had grown from $2\frac{1}{2}$ to nearly 4 acres. If Mycenaean citadels do not exceed 11 to $7\frac{1}{2}$ (Asine) acres, the great cemeteries of family tombs round them all imply that a considerable population was housed also outside their walls.

Cemeteries in the barbarian fringe illustrate a like growth. In Sicily by the fifteenth century the Bronze Age cemeteries consisted of from 1,000 to 3,000 family vaults as against 10 to 30 in the Copper Age, though the Bronze Age tombs are less crowded with skeletons. On the Hungarian plain Early Bronze Age cemeteries may comprise as many as 180 graves as against a maximum of 50 in the Copper Age; in the Late Bronze Age the numbers rise to 300 or more.

At least for the middle classes the standard of living rose too. Of course in imitation of their royal and sacerdotal superiors much of their wealth went to purchase spiritual or material goods and services, such as good burial, magic rites, slaves, perfumes and jewellery, in which no progressive changes can be detected in subsequent ages. On the other hand, in some domains of consumption, such as housing, one can detect an advance over barbarism destined to be itself outstripped in the Iron Age. A middle-class house in Ur about 1800 B.C. boasted two storeys with several rooms in each, grouped about a central court, 16 ft square, and measured overall 40 ft by 33 ft. At the Egyptian capital of Tell el-Amarna in the fourteenth century an average house covered 73 ft by 68 ft.

The arrival of new peoples – Amorites, Hittites, Kassites, Aryans, Hurrians, Hyksôs – in the old centres had enriched them with spiritual and material equipment (such as new languages and the ways of thinking these make possible [p. 20]), that had been created to deal with other environments. With the conversion of barbarism to civilization ideas and devices evolved in Crete, mainland Greece, and Asia Minor flowed into the common pool. Indirectly at least a trickle of foreign materials filtered in from the outer barbarism of Britain, the Baltic coasts, Russia, central Asia, and East Africa.

Improvements in transport accelerated communications by sea and land. Under the Middle Kingdom Egyptians could already build ships up to 204 ft long with a beam of 68 ft and carrying 120 men. Contemporary Cretan ships probably did not exceed 70 ft in length, but reached 100 ft by the Mycenaean period. In the right season a voyage from the Delta ports to Byblos need take only four days' sail, but the return journey, propelled by oars, took a boat eight to ten days.

A caravan on the Syrian steppes travelled at some thirty miles a day (the trip from Tirqa on the Euphrates to Qatna via Palmyra, some 360 km., for example, took ten days in the nineteenth century B.C.). But the light horse-drawn chariot had vastly reduced journey-times for those who could afford it – in practice only the soldiers and officials of States or great war-chiefs like Homer's heroes. For the vehicles had to be constructed of costly imported woods by highly skilled wainwrights; the horses that drew them, since their harness, devised originally for broad-shouldered oxen, half-choked the wretched beasts, needed special breeding and long training. From the nineteenth century B.C. horse-training was an important, even literate, profession in north Syria and chariot-racing a practically useful sport. The chariot, in fact, being used mainly for war, consolidated the authority of the States and chiefs who could alone afford it, as did the knight's armour in the Middle Ages. But the relative stability of the Assyrian, Egyptian, and Hittite Empires in the second millennium as contrasted with earlier empires was due not only to the sole command

today, as among Homer's heroes in Bronze Age Greece, even chiefs have to work with their hands. The more exalted kings of the Orient were entirely exempt from manual tasks and could even do much of their fighting vicariously. Turning from Europe to Asia or Egypt any archaeologist is struck by the extent to which metal tools preserve the same form throughout the two thousand years of the Oriental Bronze Age. In military equipment there were a few more advances. But the most important, the light horse chariot, was developed in north Syria, first perhaps by the newly civilized Assyrians, later by the barbarian Aryan rulers of Mitanni, and was forced upon the Egyptians by the Hyksôs. Similarly the rapier was invented in Crete and exploited by the Mycenaeans. It looks as if the Oriental kings and generals, lacking all practical experience in the workshop, simply failed to appreciate what craftsmanship could do for them.

A genuine science of higher mathematics, from which modern mathematics, through Hellenistic and Arab, largely springs, was founded in the temple schools of Mesopotamia, apparently under the Dynasty of Hammurabi. Its rise would thus coincide with that little triumph of the middle class consecrated by Hammurabi's laws. Moreover, many of the examples that illustrate it are concerned with the division of inheritances, partnerships, and business operations. The new mathematics may therefore respond to the social demands of the middle class. But the fundamental discovery was a by-product of the simplification of the script imposed on the clerks much earlier by the sheer volume of sacred, governmental, and private business.

As a result of the simplification the signs for 1 and for 60 had come to coincide. During the same period clerks had come to accept *gin*, originally a weight equivalent to one-sixtieth of a mina, as standing for 1/60 in general, just as in Latin, *uncia*, an ounce, came to mean also one-twelfth. Moreover, in practice the clerks saved themselves trouble by omitting the sign for *gin*; one unit and eleven *gin* was written simply ❚❮❚: From this point the learned went on

to conventionalize a purely abstract system in which the
unit symbol, ▼, stood for any power of 60, positive or
negative, i.e., 1, 60, 3,600 . . . 1/60, 1/3,600, while a collection
of ten such signs, e.g. 10, 600, 1/6, was denoted by the
other cipher ◄. The Babylonian arithmetician thus found
himself in possession of a notation based on what we call
'*place value*'; the value of a sign is determined solely by its
position in relation to other signs. And this system was
applied not only to integers (whole numbers), but also to
fractions, precisely as in our own decimal fractions. Only the
absence of signs for zero and the decimal point introduced
an element of ambiguity that was not very serious in actual
practice.

So the Babylonian temple scholars had invented a system
that enabled them to operate with fractional quantities that
cannot be represented on the fingers or with counters, and
that without the tedious calculations entailed in the unit
fractions or aliquot parts that their forerunners had been,
and their Egyptian colleagues still were, forced to employ.
This purely technical improvement in the instrument used
in reckoning in fact gave man mastery over – almost – the
whole domain of real numbers.

Incidentally it eliminated all the difficulties that the
beginner even nowadays – let the reader recall his own
troubles at school – experiences with division. For division
is nothing but multiplication by the reciprocal of the
divisor (i.e. the number that, multiplied by the divisor,
gives one). As the Sumerians had drawn up multiplication
tables (p. 117), so now their Babylonian heirs compiled
tables of reciprocals expressed as sexagesimal fractions. In
order to divide by 12 you looked up the reciprocal of 12,
5 in the sexagesimal notation, and multiplied by that.

Of course the Babylonian system was imperfect. They
lacked any · and o till late in the first millennium. They
had not discovered anything to correspond to our recurring
decimals. Their base, 60, is divisible by a large number of
factors, 2, 3, 4, 5, 6 . . . so that most reciprocals can be
expressed as reasonably short sexagesimal fractions. But in

the reciprocal tables the spaces for $1/7$, $1/11$, and so on, are blank. With such divisors they must still have recourse to ordinary division and use clumsy unit fractions in the quotient.

Similarly they had no means of representing or dealing with surds such as $\sqrt{2}$ and $\sqrt{3}$. In problems that should lead to such quantities they replace the correct method of working by others involving processes which give approximations to the true result. The 'rule of signs' seems to have been beyond their comprehension altogether. The 'negative root' of a quadratic equation is simply ignored.

Moreover, the Babylonians had discovered empirically by actual reckoning some properties of numbers that we should express by algebraic formulae. So they were certainly aware of the result we express as $(a+b)^2 = a^2 + 2ab + b^2$, and used this result to solve quadratic equations by 'completing the square' very much as we do. Such properties of numbers, rules of arithmetical grammar as Hogben calls them, appeared to the clerks not as revelations of *a priori* 'laws', but as results and processes actually found to work. They are never expressed in the extant 'mathematical tablets' by general formulae. All that survive are 'examples' worked out and in fact constructed so that they will work out by the methods available; for instance the values for quadratics are chosen so that $ac + b^2/4$ is a perfect square.

Still the Babylonians lacked what we term an algebraic notation, using letters with indefinite numerical values instead of concrete numbers. In solving 'equations' they therefore had recourse to a procedure similar to the 'false position' used in medieval arithmetic.

Fragmentary tablets prove that the schools were experimenting with geometrical figures – inscribing squares in circles, and so on. What conclusions they drew the tablets do not say. But by 1800 B.C. the Babylonians had discovered, again presumably by actual observation and measurement, certain geometrical relations in addition to those rules for areas and volumes the application of which is attested much earlier. In particular they were perfectly well aware that in rectangles the sides of which are in the proportions of 3 to 4 and 5 to 12, the square on the diagonal is equal to the sum of the squares on two adjacent sides. A whole series of examples on a tablet in the British Museum has been built up to illustrate this truth. In fact, learned clerks knew for nineteen independent cases the result of what is now called the 'Theorem of Pythagoras'. Even if they 'knew' this theorem in general, they could not apply it in cases where the diagonal is not a rational whole number, in a square for example. In such cases the examples in the tablets are worked out by methods which we should use to obtain approximations to the correct result.

The Babylonian clerks had devised a system of mathematical symbols and methods of working that enabled them to solve with the requisite accuracy the actual problems in accountancy, surveying, architecture, and military engineering that their society had in practice to face. They drew up series of examples to illustrate the solution of precisely such problems. In so doing they had stumbled upon several important properties of numbers and of space. None of the tablets that survive suggests an interest in numbers as such or any conception of abstract empty space! (Some actual examples of Babylonian mathematical texts are quoted in *Man Makes Himself*.)

In the third millennium the Egyptian, Sumerian, and Indus citizens had known enough of the chemistry of glazing to be able to make faience – an opaque paste of sand coated with a glaze. The chemical discovery involved is that alkaline silicates fuse easily like metals, and that such silicates can be made by heating with silica (i.e. sand), potash (which is just a product of burning wood), or natron (which occurs as a mineral in the western desert of Egypt). Under the New Kingdom Egyptian craftsmen discovered a process for making clear glass that could be fused and cast like metal by heating sand and natron, and devised means for colouring the product. The glass was cast into rods and reeds which could be moulded while hot and even built up into vessels on a sand core. It was applied to the production of imitation precious stones, 'synthetic jewels' in fact, to be converted into bangles or vases and then sold at a modest price to the new middle class. The art was soon adopted in Phoenicia, where potash took the place of natron.

If glass manufacture were developed to suit the purses of the small middle-class buyer, a simple alphabetic script seems to have been devised to expedite the business of small merchants. As pointed out on page 172, the Phoenicians trafficked very largely in low-priced popular goods. Such traffic involved a number of small retail transactions, all of which ought to be recorded. At the same time it earned the craftsmen, or at least the merchants, sufficient wealth to make them independent of 'great households' that would of course include professional clerks (p. 164); the merchant would have to be his own bookkeeper. This was the social background of the Phoenician script.

Its philological background is also noteworthy. In Semitic languages like the Phoenician the words are built up out of triconsonantal roots (that is bases that can be expressed by three consonants); vowel changes denote only grammatical differences – tenses and cases. Hence for practical intercourse where the general context is clear meanings can be adequately conveyed by the consonants alone and the vowel sounds ignored.

By about 1500 B.C. the priests and merchants of Ugarit had selected twenty-nine of the cuneiform characters used by their Babylonian teachers and colleagues and agreed to assign to each of these a single phonetic value. They thus created a true alphabet, by means of which any word could be accurately spelled out without recourse to the cumbersome apparatus of ideograms and syllabic signs employed by earlier scripts.

Further south in a still nameless Phoenician city a different alphabet was agreed upon, suitable for writing on papyrus, the use of which had been introduced at Byblos by the Egyptians (hence the Greek word for 'book'; our Bible is *the* book). Twenty-two signs were chosen to denote simple consonants – vowels were not written. The signs may on one view be themselves versions of Egyptian hieroglyphs, or on another theory be derived from non-pictorial cattle-brands and ownership marks current among Semitic pastoralists or Mediterranean mariners. In any case the resultant alphabet is the parent of the Greek, Etruscan, Roman, Aramaic, and South Arabian scripts and their modern European, Hebrew, Arabic, and Indic derivatives.

Thanks to the reduction of the number of characters and the elimination of the complexities introduced by ideograms and determinatives, reading and writing became as simple as they are today. Literacy ceased to be the mysterious privilege of a highly-specialized class. The small shopkeeper or pedlar could easily learn enough at least to sign his name and keep accounts. The new idea caught on so fast that no one can say precisely where it started. It was in fact an international body of merchants who sanctioned by use the new conventions; it was their activity that diffused and popularized the system in the Iron Age.

It has been repeatedly shown how peculiarities of the civilizations and barbarian cultures described in the last four chapters were conditioned by the high cost of the sole metal used for tools and weapons. The cost in turn was due to the comparative rarity of the constituent elements, copper and tin. Iron on the other hand is one of the commonest elements in the earth's crust. It can be extracted from its ores by the same chemical process as copper and other metals – reduction by heating with charcoal. But at the temperatures obtainable in antiquity (without a mechanical blast) iron would not melt and reduction would leave only a spongy mass. This had to be purified from slag and compacted into a 'bloom' by prolonged hammering. Even then the metal could not be cast, as copper and bronze had been, but must be forged or wrought, i.e., shaped by hammering.

Even in the third millennium a few implements of wrought iron had been used occasionally both in Egypt and Mesopotamia, but neither Nilotic nor Mesopotamian smiths had devised, nor had any incentive to devise, effective and economic methods for producing in bulk iron of good quality. A suitable process was apparently first invented by a barbarian tribe living among the Armenian mountains in what the Hittites called Kizwadana. The Aryan rulers of Mitanni who incorporated the iron workers in their military monarchy appreciated the value of the new metal, but guarded the secret of its production and controlled the output in virtue of the normal State monopoly over the metal trade. The Hittites who succeeded the Aryans maintained the policy of secrecy. The Aryan kings had sent iron objects as presents to the pharaohs. But when a pharaoh writes to ask the Hittite king for a supply of iron towards the end of the fourteenth century, the latter puts 'his brother' off with excuses and sends only a single dagger. But iron weapons were supplied to the Hittite army, and barbarian mercenaries serving therein eventually learned and divulged the secret of their manufacture.

Efficient and economic methods of iron working made metal cheap at last. In Babylonia under Hammurabi during the eighteenth century B.C. a shekel of silver would buy 120 to 150 shekels of copper or perhaps $14\frac{1}{2}$ shekels of tin (in Asia Minor at this date it would purchase 40 shekels of iron). A thousand years later the silver shekel would bring in no less than 225 shekels of iron; the price of copper had also fallen from 150 to 180 to one of silver as a consequence of the saving due to the use of cheap iron tools in mining and the manufacture of vehicles and vessels.

Cheap iron democratized agriculture and industry and warfare too. Any peasant could afford an iron axe to clear fresh land for himself and iron ploughshares wherewith to break up stony ground. The common artisan could own a kit of metal tools that made him independent of the households of kings, gods, or nobles. With iron weapons a commoner could meet on more equal terms the Bronze Age knight. With them too poor and backward barbarians could challenge the armies of civilized States whose monopoly of bronze armaments had made them seem invulnerable.

The last result was the first to be made manifest. The

Bronze Age in the Near East ends in renewed barbarian inroads which threatened the whole civilized world with chaos and actually hurled the two latest outposts of civilization – Greece and Asia Minor – back into illiteracy.

9

THE EARLY IRON AGE

IMPERIALISM had not eliminated the contradictions of Bronze Age economy. On the contrary, if it had at first secured to the imperialist state the requisite supplies, it had led in the second millennium B.C. to conflicts of Empires, more destructive than the internal conflicts between Mesopotamian cities that imperialism claims credit for abolishing. The tribute collected by the empires did not mean the production of fresh wealth, but quite simply the theft of wealth from those who had produced it. Such wealth could not therefore support an indefinitely expanding population.

Already in the fourteenth century, when tribute was still pouring into imperial treasuries, symptoms of decay were becoming manifest. Both the protagonists of civilization, the Egyptian pharaoh and the Hittite great king, hired barbarian mercenaries for their contending armies. Presumably they were hired to replace a not inconsiderable proportion of the native populations – or at least of the military classes – that had either been killed off or completely debauched by plunder. By such employment barbarians received a new lesson in civilization. They were apt to learn at least 'civilized' methods of warfare, urban processes of armament manufacture, and the secret of iron working. Then they applied the fruits of their schooling to their masters with disastrous results to the Hittites and Egyptians. Imperialism could not even mask the contradictions so long in the newly-civilized provinces as it had in the older centres.

Mycenaean society, dominated economically as well as politically by the war-lords' rapiers, chariots, and great estates, became poorer and poorer during the late fourteenth and thirteenth centuries. The grave-goods became cheap and nasty. Art declined. Egyptian imports, so common in the early fourteenth century, are missing in the thirteenth. Mycenaean manufactures are proportionately rare in Egypt and Syria. Late Mycenaean pottery does indeed turn up in south-eastern Asia Minor at this date, but here it may have been brought by warlike colonists. It would mean that the Mycenaeans were adopting the late neolithic solution of their population problem (p. 75) and were trying to dump the surplus overseas on other people's land. The Trojan war described in 'Homer's' epics sounds like a venture in imperialism. But the Mycenaean princelets lacked the resources needed to imitate the kings of Akkad.

So the Bronze Age in the Near East ended round about 1200 B.C. in a dark age, blacker and more extensive than those that opened our last chapter. Not in a single State alone but over a large part of the civilized world history itself seems to be interrupted; the written sources dry up, the archaeological documents are poor and hard to date. Barbarians from the north wiped out the Mycenaean civilization in Greece. The Hittite Empire foundered. In Babylonia the Kassite dynasty came to an end; barbarian Aramaeans and Chaldaeans filtered in; for a time Babylonia became subject to Assyrian over-lords. The pharaohs Merneptah and Rameses repelled the invaders from the Nile. But soon Libyan mercenaries and Nubians seized the pharaoh's throne itself till the Assyrians annexed Egypt too to their military empire. About the same time in China the Shang capital was sacked, and the barbarian Chous began a new empire, organized on more feudal lines.

Nevertheless the continuity of civilization was not completely or universally interrupted. The Assyrian State and its component cities were flourishing. Sumerian and Akkadian texts were copied and collected for the Assyrian royal libraries. Astronomical studies were fruitfully pursued in the observatories attached to Assyrian, as to Babylonian, temples. In Babylonia itself, as in previous dark ages, economic and scientific life, like worship, continued in the cities and temples, albeit impaired by foreign rule and poverty. Neither the craft lore of artisans nor the business acumen of merchants, nor yet the traditional learning of the clerks was dissipated when their cities changed masters. The same is true of Egypt and of China. Finally the Phoenician cities weathered the storm, preserving at least the standard of civilization they had reached in the fourteenth century. They could even exploit and develop such Minoan traditions and techniques as had been added to their own by the merchant colonists at Ugarit (p. 179).

Even in Greece more came through than might have been expected. No doubt the Mycenaean chivalry, like the Minoan priest-kings, had been wiped out. Any clerks they had employed lost their employment. The luxury industries of the nobles' courts consequently became obsolete. Cheap iron swords replaced costly bronze rapiers. What were left of the Mycenaean cities relapsed into almost self-sufficing villages. But Greece did not revert quite to neolithic barbarism, nor even to the stage represented by the Helladic towns before 1600 B.C.

The standardized techniques of viticulture and olive-growing described by the poet Hesiod about 800 B.C. cannot be fresh discoveries but must be legacies from the Helladic pioneers of Greek farming. The same poet's rustic calendar embodies the astronomical observations and botanical lore accumulated by an Aegean peasantry during the Bronze Age. Throughout the dark age pottery, usually called Geometric, is made on the wheel, and its technique is Mycenaean; only the forms and designs are novel. So Mycenaean potters had escaped destruction and taught their craft to children and apprentices, handing on to classical Greece the appropriate pre-Indo-European names for their products. The same must have been true of other crafts. Certainly 'Crete had preserved the secret of the purple and had not forgotten metal-working'. The Phoenicians had indeed temporarily ousted the Greek mariners from supremacy even in Aegean waters; incidentally the Asiatics taught the Iron Age Greeks their alphabet somewhere between 1000 and 700 B.C. But the traditions of Minoan seamanship were never lost. The Greek ships depicted on the early Iron Age geometric vases seem to be

Bronze Age Mycenaean ships with a ram added for fighting. Finally, that sparks of Minoan art gleamed through the dark age is evident from Homer's poems.

So the Indo-European Greeks of the Iron Age did not have to create miraculously out of sheer barbarism the foundations for classical techniques, sciences, economy, and art. The barbarians had not demolished the whole Minoan-Mycenaean edifice. In fact, here as everywhere, the invasions merely gave the final push to fabrics already tottering through internal decay. In the most favourable instances, particularly in Greece itself, they just swept away top-heavy superstructures to make room for more progressive additions to a fundamentally healthy building. The substantial achievements of the Bronze Age were on the whole saved. By 1000 B.C. recovery was beginning. The losses were more than made up in the next five centuries.

In the first five centuries of the Iron Age the continuous area of civilization, after the temporary contraction at its start, expanded more than it had in the previous fifteen centuries of the Bronze Age. By 500 B.C. the zone of literate societies, accustomed to urban life and dependent on an urban economy, extended continuously from the Atlantic coasts of Spain to the Jaxartes in Central Asia and the Ganges in India, from southern Arabia to the north coasts of the Mediterranean and the Black Sea.

The several portions of this zone were integrated and interconnected to a degree never before attained. An educated Persian or Greek, however vague and inaccurate his knowledge of its extremities, could feel himself an inhabitant of a humanly populated world – an *oikoumene*, as the Greeks called it – four times as large as an Egyptian or Babylonian could have dreamed of a thousand years earlier. And in the barbarian fringe on either side, but most noticeably among the Celts of western Europe and the Scyths of the Eurasiatic steppes, new techniques and devices were penetrating rapidly and fruitfully.

The expansion had been effected on the one hand by the enlargement and consolidation of Asiatic military empires

on the Akkadian model, on the other by colonizing activities
of Phoenicians, Greeks, and Etruscans following Minoan–
Mycenaean traders along the Mediterranean seaways.

In the Near East the Bronze Age collapse had left, besides
the ruins of Egypt, an enfeebled Babylonia, the Phoenician
cities, and vigorous Assyria, only a debris of partially
barbarized communities that in time reorganized themselves into small and feeble imitations of the Bronze Age
theocratic states. Of these the Hebrew kingdom in Palestine,
the realm of the Phrygian Midas in western Asia Minor,
and the commercial kingdom of Lydia to the south-east
displayed significant originality. The first stage in the
reduction of these economically interdependent units was
effected with unparalleled brutality by the Assyrians. By
700 B.C. the Assyrian Empire extended from the Nile and
the Mediterranean coasts to the mountain countries north
and east of the Tigris.

In 610 this empire changed masters, and was divided
between a renascent Babylonia and the Aryan Medes, who
added to it their homeland in Iran. But after 540 both
domains fell into the hands of the equally Aryan Persians,
who subsequently added the rest of Iran, western India,
Egypt, Asia Minor, and the Eurasiatic steppe. By 500 B.C.
the Empire of Darius extended from the Nile and the
Aegean to the Indus and the Jaxartes.

This unification had doubtless been achieved at frightful
cost in human lives and real wealth. The Assyrian kings in
particular boast how they have massacred, flayed, and
impaled the inhabitants of cities that 'rebelled against
Assur' (their tribal god), and have destroyed fruit-trees,
gardens, and canals so that once populous lands are 'left
for the asses, the gazelles, and all manner of wild beasts to
people' (referring particularly to Elam). Nevertheless,
political unification had promoted intercourse on an unprecedented scale over a wider area than ever before and had
enormously accelerated the pooling of human knowledge.

Albeit primarily for the collection of tribute, the Assyrians, and still more the Persians, had organized

communications. From Sardis in Asia Minor through Babylon and Susa to Persepolis in southern Iran the Persians constructed the famous 'royal road', equipped with inns and relays of horses for the use of official messengers. The journey of 1,700 miles from Sardis to Susa could thus be accomplished in ninety days. Such facilities for travel enabled even intelligent Greeks of modest means, like the historian Herodotus, to visit distant Babylon. The Assyrians and their Neo-Babylonian heirs forcibly transported whole communities from one end of their empires to the other, thus incidentally effecting a very thorough pooling of experience and making their cities eminently cosmopolitan. The effects of this transplantation on the Jews are well known. Members of subject communities were recruited for service in the imperial armies. Under Darius and Xerxes Indian chariotry and nomad archers from Central Asiatic steppes fought side by side with Greek mercenaries and Syrian levies in Egypt and Greece itself. Moreover, when all the plundering was done, the imperial power did establish a régime of comparative security within its domain and check small wars.

The unification of Hither Asia and the civilization of its backward enclaves was thus effected by the forcible imposition of alien rule and of a modified version of the government and economy created in the Bronze Age monarchies. In the Mediterranean basin, on the contrary, civilization was diffused by the plantation of colonies on the coasts from which urban life spread inland.

The new cities founded by the Phoenicians, the Greeks, and the Etruscans were not established, as Sargon's foundations in Syria had been, to be provincial collecting posts for a surplus to be partly drawn off as tribute to the parent city.

The new cities were actual overseas settlements of emigrant farmers for whom there was no room in the narrow coastal plain of Phoenicia and the still narrower valleys of Greece. The colonists sought beyond the seas new lands to till, new fishing grounds and bases for piracy and commerce. They brought with them the economy and equipment of their homeland, though as pioneers they had at first to forgo some of its refinements. But migration by sea, owing to the slow, precarious, and irregular voyages of ancient ships, always involved a greater dislocation and disassociation of cultural elements than follows upon landwise migrations. By the voyage itself the component elements get jolted out of the rigid frame of custom in which they are embedded. They can be resorted and reintegrated in new wholes. The colonial cities in North Africa were far less replicas of the parent Phoenician states than the new foundations of Sargon or the kings of Ur in Syria (p. 150) had been. They did not reproduce in the West the centralized economy and theocratic polity of the Orient; even Carthage was a republic.

The colony was not dependent upon or tributary to the mother city. But it was connected with the latter by traditional sentimental ties and found there a natural market where any surplus of home-grown produce and raw materials obtained from the barbarian hinterland could be exchanged for the manufactures of the more highly skilled artisans who would remain at home in the metropolis. So the Phoenicians colonized particularly North Africa and, from Carthage, western Sicily, Sardinia, and the coasts of Spain. The Greeks for their part, having occupied all the coasts of the Aegean, spread round the Black Sea and westward to eastern Sicily, southern Italy and Campania, and thence to Marseille, thus securing a port in western Europe.

Finally the Etruscans or Turseni, a people from Asia Minor who had learned civilization through mercenary service in imperial armies, turned their backs on their eastern home and established themselves as a ruling class among Indo-European farmers on the western coasts of central Italy and across the Apennines as far north as the modern Bologna. They brutally imposed civilization on conquered barbarians, founding small cities as centres of an urban economy. But some of the conquered, notably the Romans, like Sargon's victims in the third millennium, were enabled to expel their alien masters and turn the weapons of civilization against their oppressors.

In the Iron Age civilization not only spread over a wider

area than in the Bronze Age, it also spread deeper; it was more popular. That was because it made use of two 'popular' inventions already mentioned – iron and the alphabet – to which was soon added a third – coined money. Iron, as already explained, first gave the masses, and especially the rural population, a real independent share in the benefits of civilization. Cheap iron tools abolished or at least reduced the dependence of the small producers on State monopolies and great household stores. With the new metal implements for breaking the ground, clearing it of trees and digging drainage channels, the small farmer might earn independence by reclaiming for himself a piece of waste; in any case, he could produce more. Similarly the efficiency of industry was enormously increased. As a result transport costs could be reduced; vessels and vehicles were improved or cheapened. Use of the new metal spread rapidly after 1200 in Hither Asia and Greece and thence westward with the Phoenicians and Etruscans. On the other hand, it did not become common in Egypt till after 650 B.C. How and when iron-working spread to India and China is still uncertain.

The alphabet, as explained on page 189–90, made literacy possible to all classes. By the seventh century common mercenary soldiers, both Greek and Phoenician, were educated enough to be able to scratch their names on Egyptian statues. The Phoenicians' invention had spread rapidly. In Mesopotamia, indeed, the old cuneiform script remained the normal medium even for private correspondence down to 500 B.C., and in the temple schools and observatories continued in regular use till 50 B.C. Even the Persians, like the Hittites a thousand years earlier, used cuneiform signs as the basis of a syllabary for transcribing their own Indo-European language. In Egypt, too, hieroglyphics and their simplified cursive derivatives were current till the beginning of our era. Nevertheless, the alphabetic writing, well established on the coast of Syria by 1100 B.C., was adopted by the new States in southern Arabia and was used in competition with cuneiform by Aramaic merchants in Mesopotamia even under the Assyrian Empire. Thence the idea spread to

Iran. Finally, before 300 B.C., it had inspired the creation of a suitable alphabet for expressing the sounds of the Aryan languages of India. Westward the Phoenicians took their alphabet to Carthage and thence to her colonies. Between 1000 and 700 B.C. the Greeks learnt to write it too. They converted some superfluous signs for peculiarly Semitic consonants and invented others to express the vowel sounds that the Semites had ignored (p. 189), but that are indispensable for the unambiguous expression of an Indo-European language. It was apparently from the Greek colonists in Italy that the Etruscans and Romans learned to read and write.

*

Two grave embarrassments to early trade were, firstly, that at every transaction the quantity of silver representing the price had to be weighed out – and it was all too easy to falsify the weights – and, secondly, that the metal paid out might be fraudulently debased. Soon after 800 B.C. Assyrian and Syrian kings began stamping bars of silver, guaranteeing the quality of the metal. The second defect of the old Bronze Age money was thus eliminated. Coins, pieces of metal of a fixed shape and a standard weight stamped and guaranteed by the State as to both quality and weight, eliminated the first too. Greek tradition attributes to Croesus of Lydia, a frontier kingdom owing its prosperity to transit trade, the initiation of this practice about 700 B.C. It immensely simplified all commercial operations, but was not in itself absolutely revolutionary.

The earliest Lydian coins were in electrum, a natural alloy of gold and silver, and of relatively high value. The first Greek silver coins and the gold coinage of Persia were also for high denominations. But shortly after 600 B.C. the Greek city states of Aegina, Athens, and Corinth began issuing small change, copper or small silver coins, with truly revolutionary consequences. Now it had doubtless been a nuisance for the wholesaler to have to travel about with scales and weights, bars of metal and sacks of grain; for the small retailer it was a crippling handicap. A big landowner when he sold his harvest or oxen may have grumbled at the bother of weighing out the silver and the sharp practices of the purchaser who tried adulterating his silver with lead. But how was the small farmer to pay for a new pot, an iron ploughshare, or a trinket for his wife? Under a natural economy such little men must have generally been done when haggling with a travelling pedlar. Again the workman paid in kind had little choice in the disposal of his wages.

Small change corrected these difficulties. The peasant can convert his small surplus of farm produce into an easily divisible medium of exchange which he can reconvert into manufactured goods of any kind and quantity. The workman is no longer condemned to eat his wages. The small producer or the retailer can exchange his goods for coins, which can be added together till substantial values are accumulated. So in the long run coinage made accessible to small primary producers and artisans an increasing variety of the refinements made possible by civilized technology. Conversely it made the manufacture of cheap goods for popular consumption profitable, and allowed even the small landholder to turn from subsistence agriculture to specialized farming – the production, for instance, of olives or oil for sale.

But if coined money emancipated the small producer from one set of masters, it threatened to hand him over to another just as money in general had done (p. 166). Usury, mortgages and enslaved debtors followed the new medium of exchange wherever it was introduced. In the early Jewish, Greek, and Italian communities that had only recently abandoned a natural economy the struggles of debtors against creditors dominated the first political conflicts, if they did not, as Engels argues, call forth the State itself among the Greeks and the Romans.

In continental Asia neither the barbarian invasions nor the use of iron changed permanently and radically the structure of society and the economic organization that had been established since 2000 B.C. The barbarian war chiefs generally usurped the sacred thrones of Bronze Age kinglets, taking over the existing administrative machinery, but restaffing the higher offices from their own retinue. Most tried to imitate Sargon's imperialism, and the Persians eventually succeeded brilliantly.

In primary production the organization of servile peasants practising subsistence agriculture as the household of a great landowner was found as convenient by the new tax-gatherers as by the old. The conquerors, notably the Persians, just replaced the old nobility as lords of such domains. They thus became an aristocracy ruling serfs and forgot altogether the communistic forms of land-ownership appropriate to their recent condition of barbarism. Owing to the cheapness of iron such estates could often attain to an almost neolithic self-sufficiency. To provide the tenantry with the metal tools that were now necessities, all that was needed was to purchase a smith in the slave-market and perhaps to buy him raw iron if no sort of ore were available on the estate. The surplus requisite was not large, and owing to the increased efficiency of agriculture could be collected from a smaller estate than formerly. The balance was available to purchase industrial products and imports on the market.

At the same time land transport was still extravagantly costly. It is true, of course, that the roads, built primarily for administrative and military purposes by the Assyrians and the Persians, did simplify travelling. Moreover, for caravan traffic across the deserts camels and dromedaries were now extensively used, though a camel-load is not very large. Still, only high-priced luxuries could be profitably carried far, or rather anything thus carried became a luxury.

With the rural economy and a transport industry thus constituted, the urban economy supported thereby must follow the familiar Bronze Age lines. As the number of large estates was greater, they could support more nobles, and therefore a larger middle class of merchants, craftsmen, clerks, artists, and even teachers to share in the surplus collected by the landowners by supplying their wants. At Nineveh the walls encompassed an area of 1,800 acres – including parks, gardens, and temples – in the seventh century. The middle class was also freer in that its members

had a wider market and a greater choice of patrons.
Accordingly it could live better. A merchant's two-storeyed
house in Babylonia covered 100 ft by 82 ft and boasted
eighteen rooms (including a bathroom) grouped round a
central court. Real wages, too, were doubled in Babylonia
under the Persian Empire.

Moreover, the variety of crafts plied, commodities manufactured, and materials imported and used had greatly
multiplied. In building his new palace at Susa, Darius got
his cedars from Lebanon via the Euphrates, oaks from
Gandhara (the upper Indus and Kabul valleys) and Car-
mania (Iran), gold from Sardis in Asia Minor, ivory from
India, Seistan, and Ethiopia, silver and copper (? bronze)
from Egypt (perhaps really via Egypt from Spain and
Britain, as there is neither copper nor silver in Egypt).
Though the Persian king goes farther afield, he was just
following the example of Sumerian city-governors in the
third millennium. So again it was in an equally ancient
tradition to employ on the work Egyptian, Greek, Lydian,
Babylonian, and Median craftsmen, as Darius says he did.
In fact, as in the Bronze Age, the craftsman went to the
market instead of sending his products thither.

In the Persian Empire of Darius the economic objective
of Sargon's Akkadian imperialism had been realized. All
the materials needed for the crafts and even the luxuries
demanded by nobles were obtainable within its bounds.
Trade and industry had in fact expanded as a result, though
the position of the peasantry was little if at all bettered. But
a disproportionate amount of the surplus produced was
absorbed by the imperial exchequer, and there not used to
support reproductive works, but stored as bullion or
squandered on war and futile display. So the absolute
increase of real wealth was not very great and purchasing
power was still unduly restricted. The centralized imperial
system of Persia began to break up as the smaller and still
more centralized empires of Mesopotamia and Egypt had
done. In the next period it was absorbed in a European
Empire embodying an economic system evolved in Greece.

The possibilities opened up by iron tools, alphabetic writing, and coined money were more fully realized in communities that could exploit the cheapness of maritime transport for commerce, or such as had emerged from barbarism directly into an Iron Age civilization unfettered by too many legacies from the Bronze Age. The Phoenicians and Etruscans enjoyed the first advantage, the Jews, the Romans, and the Phrygians the second. Only the Greeks benefited from both.

The geography of their poor and mountainous homeland drove the Greeks to the sea, and they inherited from the Bronze Age traditions of Minoan–Mycenaean seamanship. But Mycenaean civilization as an economy in which crafts functioned had been obliterated. The Dorians and other invading tribes were frankly barbarians with an appropriately communistic system of land tenure. The unconquered provinces had sunk into illiteracy. The Bronze Age hero's castle as a nucleus for accumulating surplus wealth had been dismantled. The city, in so far as it survived to become the *polis*, differed from a village only in the presence of professional potters, smiths, and perhaps a few other craftsmen. It was almost self-sufficing, for trade had virtually ceased. The multiplication of distinct styles of ceramic decoration in each district, in contrast to the uniformity prevailing all over the Aegean in the Mycenaean age, is symptomatic of parochial isolation, which led also to the multiplication of distinct dialects.

Most of the 'citizens' must have lived by subsistence agriculture and fishing. To find land for its growing population each city tried to steal from its neighbours in neolithic fashion. The Dorians of Sparta (who had already won their own Laconia by force and reduced its Mycenaean occupants to serfdom) thus found allotments for three thousand young men at the expense of their Messenian neighbours, but only after a prolonged contest and organizing their whole life for war in truly totalitarian fashion.

It was better to emigrate. Land-hungry peasants followed piratical raids by permanent settlements on the coasts first in Asia Minor, then round the Black Sea and in Thrace and Macedonia, in Italy, Eastern Sicily, and even in Cyrenaica in North Africa. But trade and industry soon began to offer alternatives to piracy, emigration, and mercenary service in Oriental armies to the farmers' superfluous younger sons. For the traditions of Minoan craftsmanship and navigation were not dead, and Phoenician visitors gave ocular demonstrations of the possibilities of commerce. The new overseas colonies, with their barbarian and agricultural hinterlands, guaranteed a market (p. 199).

Even in the eighth century B.C. industry was getting so crowded that the poet Hesiod sings of 'potter competing with potter and carpenter with carpenter'. Early in the seventh century the mass production of cheap but remarkably good commodities for the export market was started, first apparently in Aegina, which as an island was soon congested, and at Corinth, commanding seaways to east and west alike, shortly thereafter in other coastal cities, including Athens, and overseas in Ionia (Asia Minor), and later in the western and northern colonies. The best evidence for the extent and intensity of Greek trade is supplied, as in the Mycenaean age, by the distribution of pottery vases. These cheap articles of universal use, exported from various Greek cities – Aegina, Corinth, Athens, Rhodes – begin to turn up in quantities in graves and city ruins all round the Mediterranean and the Black Sea and far into the hinterland in Asia Minor, Syria, and Egypt from 700 B.C. till, before 400, Greek (mainly Attic) vases reach right to the edge of the forest belt north of the South Russian steppes and to the Celts of south-western Germany and the Marne Valley in north-eastern France.

Of course these ceramic exports are only indices of the manufacture of and trade in other articles that may have been equally popular. And the vases contained the products of specialized agriculture, too. By the sixth century even the small peasants of Attica (the territory of Athens) could switch over from subsistence farming to the specialized cultivation of vines and olive trees; thanks to coined small

change, not only the surplus collected on large estates, but
the exclusive produce of small gardens and vineyards went
to swell the volume of export trade.

As a consequence the Greek cities became increasingly
dependent on overseas trade for foodstuffs – not only for
luxuries and supplements to the daily cereal diet, but even
for the basic necessity, corn itself; the latter was brought
from or through the colonial cities in Macedonia and
Thrace and, above all, round the Black Sea. By 450 B.C.
Athens provides perhaps the first example of a political
unit risking dependence for the staff of life upon distant lands
across the sea in order to concentrate on the production of
goods for which the country and its inhabitants were peculiarly fitted. By the fourth century it is estimated that the cereals
imported into Attica were four times the home production.

The venture was successful. As a manufacturing and
mining country and a producer of olive oil Attica supported
three or four times the population she could have fed if
devoted to producing her own food supply; the latest
estimate of the Athenian population in the fifth century is
of the order of 300,000. Of course Athens was in a rather
exceptional position as owning at Laurion the richest silver
mines in the eastern Mediterranean. But other classical
cities of the Iron Age were immensely larger than their
Bronze Age forerunners and could compare with the Bronze
Age cities of the Orient, though not with Iron Age capitals
like Nineveh. At Samos, one of the most prosperous cities of
the sixth century, the walls enclose an area of some 400
acres, not all built over. Miletus in Ionia as replanned
in 480 B.C. covered 222 acres, of which 52 were parks and
gardens. In Sicily the original colony of Selinus had been
confined to an acropolis of $21\frac{1}{2}$ acres, but extension in the
sixth century gave it an area of over 48 acres. Megara
Hyblaea in the same island straggled over 150 acres.
Syracuse was still larger. Moreover, every Greek city
enjoyed amenities foreign to the Orient – an agora or
market square used for public assemblies, government
offices, a theatre, a gymnasium, and a fountain supplying

a constant stream of water to a basin. A large private house at Olynthos covered 85 ft by 56 ft, while a block 56 ft square contained a house and three shops, each measuring 16 ft by 14½ ft.

The manufactures that helped to pay for the imported foodstuffs were, like the olives and wines, mainly produced by small but independent working proprietors. Archaeologists have identified from their trade-marks no less than a hundred different makers of Attic pottery in the sixth and fifth centuries. Nevertheless, they were producing *en masse* and for the market. Accordingly several workers might be collected in a single workshop and different operations might be divided among them. In other words, classical Greece exhibits the germs of a factory system with specialization of labour – but hardly on a larger scale than is illustrated by the workshops of Egyptian mortuary estates depicted in Old Kingdom tombs (p. 130), or attached to a Sumerian temple (p. 103).

In the ceramic industry, for example, a vase in Munich shows a pottery employing four throwers, a painter, and a furnace-man in addition to the owner. At first the master potter was also the painter of the vases. Later vase-painting became a distinct branch of the craft. At Athens the firm of Hischylos published works of three different painters who each signed their own products. Conversely we know painters who worked in three or even five different 'factories'. These artists' pictures are now displayed in places of honour in European and American museums as masterpieces of classical beauty; judging by their names they were in most cases either slaves or enfranchized slaves (freedmen) and in no case 'citizens of Athens'. This factory system, of course, was adopted in other industries too. At the end of the fifth century the father of Demosthenes, the most famous Attic orator, owned a bedstead workshop, employing twenty slaves, and an arms factory with thirty-two. No less than a hundred and twenty artisans worked in the shield factory of a certain Kephalos.

Greek industry provided citizens with many amenities

and refinements – and the modern world with objects of great beauty. It secured for the cities supplies of food and real wealth. But it did not in practice offer an effective and expanding outlet for the overflowing rural population. Instead, as the cities grew rich from industry – and less legitimate pursuits – they invested their wealth in slaves and turned over to these craftsmanship and all sorts of manual labour. The typical industrialist in a rich city of the fifth century like Athens was no longer even a working craftsman assisted by slaves, but a capitalist like Kephalos, living on the produce of his slaves.

The number of slaves and their role in production must not be exaggerated. The number of Athenian slaves in the fifth century has been put as high as 365,000, four times the citizen population. But Gomme's recent estimate of 115,000 is more probable. Even that is a third of the total population on the same author's calculations. Still there were plenty of free craftsmen. Free citizens as well as resident aliens and slaves worked on piecework contracts for the Athenian State, at fluting temple columns, for instance. The silver mines at Laurion had been developed first by free labour, and there were still free miners in the fifth century, though the majority were slaves. On the other hand, slaves held official positions as policemen and in even more responsible posts. Nor did the competition of slave labour reduce wages to a subsistence level. On the contrary, working at the minimum wage of two obols a day an Athenian day labourer in the fifth century would earn in a hundred and fifty days enough to provide the subsistence minimum of food and clothing for the whole year. But a century later real wages fell catastrophically.

Still slavery did impede the expansion of industry. It restricted the home market, since slave producers, receiving little more than their bare keep, could not purchase their own products. It made industry appear degrading (*banausic*). So even successful industrialists instead of putting their profits back into industry invested them in the more reputable channels of farming and money-lending. On the other hand, the manufacturer in so far as he was producing not for local consumption but for a Mediterranean market was very much at the mercy of the merchant who bought his products and through his personal knowledge of foreign demands could make the larger profit. And just as in the Oriental Bronze Age (p. 166) merchants themselves as well as producers were liable to become indebted to financiers who collected the largest profits as interest.

Finally the Greek 'industrial cities' were not only cleft internally into contending classes, but were also opposed to one another as autonomous States continually dissipating real wealth in internecine wars that benefited only the slave-dealers. It is this state of perpetual internecine warfare, itself due partly to the class struggle (inasmuch as slavery prevented the productive employment of surplus population) and in turn aggravating it (by replenishing the slave-market), that appears in history as the occasion for the ruin of the classical economy and the collapse of the polity it supported.

Barbarians, entering civilization in the Iron Age, even when they lacked the outlet of sea-borne commerce, were not inexorably doomed to servitude in great households. Under its new money economy and with its cheap tools they could become small proprietors, especially where a diversity of soils favoured specialized farming more than did the alluvia of river valleys.

In Italy the conquering Etruscan landlords had supported, from their surplus luxury and armament industries, mining and reproductive engineering works. Their irrigation and drainage channels show what could be done with iron tools towards the reclamation of stony land. But the Romans, when they had expelled their Etruscan overlords, the Tarquins, found themselves civilized farmers, blessed with money, mortgages, and debt-slavery, but with no outlet in an exporting industry. The dangers of their situation are revealed by the historian Livy, who records famines in the years 490, 477, 456, 453, 440, 411, and 392 B.C.

In the sequel they developed two industries – usury and

war – even more successfully than the Assyrians. The bigger usurers became noble landlords and imitated the Phoenicians of Carthage in farming their large estates with slave labour which war provided. The evicted smallholders had the privilege of dying in glorious battles or, if they survived, were granted new allotments in a colony (*colonia*) on conquered territory.

In the barbarian fringe iron tools opened up virgin land to cultivation and armed fresh war-bands for conquest. From central Europe indeed, even in the later Bronze Age, cultivators, provided, by the innovations mentioned on page 180, with cheaper bronze equipment, had been spreading in all directions with the aid of ploughs and broadswords. At length mixed farming based on plough agriculture began to replace the régime of pastoralism combined with scratch agriculture (hoe-cultivation), even in southern England; the old aristocracies perished about 1100 B.C. But trade, even to the Mediterranean world, was intensified and extended; amber, for instance, was traded southward through Upper Italy along the old Bronze Age route (p. 179) throughout the Dark Age. Conversely the secret of iron working was diffused northward, mainly by the same route through Upper Italy, to regions rich in iron ore and fuel too.

North of the Alps, the first Iron Age, termed the *Hallstatt* period after a cemetery in Upper Austria, began about 750 B.C. In the British Isles, however, where local ores of copper and tin kept the older metal cheap, a Bronze Age lasted longer – in England till 500, in Scotland till 250, in Ireland even later. With iron tools the farmer could clear forested land and the population grew fast with the enlarged food supply; Hallstatt cemeteries contain over 1,000 graves in Upper Austria. Still, this very growth intensified the competition for land (further accentuated perhaps by a general deterioration of the climate and therefore warfare).

With their iron tools Hallstatt farmers fortified hilltops with deep ditches and stupendous ramparts of timber and stone or earth to serve as tribal refuges. War-chiefs rose to affluence. Some acquired improved war chariots from the

Etruscans to consolidate their power like Mycenaean heroes; other tribes learned to ride from the Scythians and became knights. And so Greek traders from Marseille found them. The wily Greeks found a key to unlock barbarian wealth – wine – the same charm as white traders use upon Negroes and Redskins. In Iron Age European settlements Greek wine-jars take the place of the Tsar's vodka-flasks in a Siberian encampment or gin-bottles in an African kraal. A later Greek writer, Diodorus, describes how cheaply the Celts sold the captives to get wine, 'exchanging a servant for a drink'.

But if the Greeks thus secured slaves – and of course tin, amber, and forest products too – they likewise armed and incited fresh and fiercer war-bands to invade the civilized world. In the Second Iron Age or *La Tène* period beginning after 450 B.C., Celtic warriors sacked Rome, ravaged north Greece, and carved themselves out a kingdom, Galatia, in Asia Minor.

In the meantime nomads, breeding horses both for milking and for riding, spread all over the Eurasiatic steppes. They worried the Chou state in China, raided Asia Minor, and even threatened Assyria. In south Russia such nomads, as Scyths, subjugated a Bronze Age peasantry and established feudal kingdoms, collecting a large surplus of grain and other produce from their subjects. With this they supported blacksmiths, goldsmiths, armourers, and other native craftsmen; they purchased gold from Transylvania and the Altai, and forest products from beyond the steppes, but also Greek wines and manufactures from the colonies on the Black Sea coasts.

The swiftly-moving nomads must have been important agents in diffusing ideas between the Far East and the West. They may have taught both the Assyrians and Europeans the military value of cavalry. Perhaps they introduced trousers to the Celts. But they no more succeeded in creating a civilized State than did their Hallstatt neighbours farther west.

10

GOVERNMENT, RELIGION, AND SCIENCE IN THE IRON AGE

THE economic changes of the Iron Age naturally found political expression. In the Orient indeed the Iron Age inherited the monarchical traditions of the Bronze Age. Assyria, Babylonia, and Egypt were just continuations of Bronze Age States and preserved divine kingship with minor modifications, as they preserved so much of the old economy. The new kingdoms like Israel, Lydia, Phrygia, and Armenia (Urartu) tried to imitate them. The Medes and Persians took over the imperial machines that they had conquered, though they improved them in details. The Chous created a feudal monarchy rather like the Egyptian Middle Kingdom.

In Mediterranean Europe, on the contrary, theocratic monarchy on the Oriental pattern had never become firmly entrenched, even in Crete. The Mycenaean kinglets in Greece were ruined before the barbarian invaders arrived (p. 193). Admittedly the conquerors themselves had acknowledged patriarchal monarchs and war-chiefs. But when peace returned they, ruling over a small and poor territory, could not aspire to the pomp of an Oriental court, and could not maintain their positions above the richer landholders among their vassals. For with iron weapons these were no longer dependent on royal arsenals, but could arm themselves and even equip pirate vessels to win as privateers booty for themselves and their clients. So monarchy withered away or was reduced to a purely ritual office in most Greek States and also in Italy and the Phoenician colonies.

The typical Greek State and many Etruscan and Phoenician States too were becoming republics before the end of the Dark Age; magistrates elected for a year took over executive power, while general policy was determined by a 'council' of elders (senate) and an assembly of leading families or clans. When barbarian kinship organization had broken down and a money economy had made land a commodity privately owned, the clan chief became the big landlord; the machinery of government fell into the hands of a hereditary landed gentry or *aristocracy* (rule of the 'best'). It was used to protect the creditor against the debtor and the landlord against the tenant and share-farmer with such effect that Attica was becoming de-populated and general strikes were provoked at Rome.

But in commercial and industrial cities the landed aristo-cracy was forced, not without a struggle, to share its power with a new plutocracy. Turned into cash the proceeds of industry were no less potent than rents from land, and the profits of trade appeared no less honourable than pirates' booty. First perhaps in Ionia, then in peninsular Greece, the new merchant class successfully challenged the prerogatives of the landed gentry. The qualifications for executive office, seats on the council, and assembly votes were reckoned in money as well as, or instead of, in areas of land owned. Aristocracy gave place to *oligarchy*.

In their struggles the middle class often sought allies among the poor – small freeholders in debt, tenants and share-farmers, even landless artisans and labourers. The development of tactics appropriate to Iron Age armament had given even these military value. Victory no longer depended upon the prowess of chariotry, the preserve of the rich landowner, but on the valour of an infantry recruited from yeoman farmers. Moreover, at sea – and in Greece sea-power was decisive – even a labourer, too poor to afford body armour, could serve his city in the fleet at an oar. In fact he could claim with justice and some hope of success a vote in the election of magistrates and in the legislative assembly. The concession of such claims would transform the State into what the Greeks called *democracy* (rule by the people).

The conflict between the several classes often broke out into open violence – *stasis*. It gave, moreover, ambitious individuals, generally men who had grown rich in commerce or manufacture or in the control of mines and manipulation of currency, the chance to make themselves dictators with the support of one of the contending parties. Such were termed *tyrants* – a pre-Indo-European word appropriate to a despot of the Oriental type. And in fact, like these, tyrants did often protect the weak against oppression by the strong (p. 168), and expend much of their private wealth on reproductive public works and the beautification of their cities, and encourage the development of new industries. But they never became divine kings, and seldom founded dynasties. Most were expelled by oligarchic or democratic revolutions.

In Athens – Athens means not only the city but the whole of Attica, a district larger and more diversified than the territory of most Greek cities – after the expulsion of the local tyrants, democracy was made completely effective. Industry was put on an equal footing with commerce and farming. The old clans were deprived of political influence. Property qualifications for magistracies were abolished, and most offices were filled by lot instead of by election. Every citizen was expected to attend assemblies and to sit on juries. To make this effectively possible, assemblymen and jurors as well as magistrates and councillors were paid, as we should say, 'for time lost'. Democracy was not only politically conceded but also economically established.

It worked. In the latter part of the fifth century countrymen did in fact attend the assembly and vote on questions of general policy. The leaders, who had at first mainly been landed gentlemen, were now often craftsmen or merchants – a tanner, a lamp-maker, a manufacturer of musical instruments. The democratic State provided for its citizens free dramas and public buildings. The cost of these services, as also of the navy, was defrayed partly by the richer citizens – no doubt under pressure from 'public opinion', but not under the compulsion of confiscatory taxation. The contracts for public works were divided up into small items for which any competent citizen or alien might compete.

Fifth-century Athens thus provides the first adequately documented example of a thorough-going popular government. Its popular character must not be exaggerated. In the first place women had no place in public life. The wives of citizens were almost as completely secluded as women in Mohammedan countries today, and at law were in a worse position than their Assyrian and Babylonian sisters. Secondly, citizenship was now a hereditary privilege from which resident aliens were rigorously excluded. Yet on Gomme's estimate these included a tenth of the total population and comprised most of the craftsmen and manufacturers. Finally industry was based on slavery; even the small farmer generally owned a slave or two, and the majority of the employees in mines and factories and even the policemen were slaves. Though citizens did work on their farms, ply crafts, take on small contracts for public works, work as wage-labourers for fellow-citizens and even in mines, they secured leisure for politics and culture largely at the expense of their wives, of aliens who had no share in the government, and of slaves who had no rights whatever.

Moreover, the revenues of Athens which paid magistrates, jurors, and assemblymen were swollen by two exceptional sources. The richest silver-mines in the Aegean lay in Attica at Laurion; exploited mainly by slaves under local contractors, they yielded a rich harvest of royalties to the State. Secondly, Athens was an imperial city, nourished by the tribute of subjects. It is true that the Athenian Empire began as a league of free cities against Persia. The tribute was a substitute for the ships that the allies had originally equipped and manned for the common defence. But after 450 B.C. the allies felt themselves subjects and tried to rebel; the imperial people were diverting some of their contributions to the adornment of Athens and their own support.

Thus the Athenian 'people' was in a sense only an exceptionally large and diversified ruling class. The appearance of economic democracy had been achieved not so much by an even distribution of the wealth it produced as by using the proceeds of exploitation to relieve the poverty of its poor sections. When external supplies were cut off by the loss of the empire, the conflict of poor and rich broke out again in violence. In the sequel Athens lost her full autonomy and returned to a moderate oligarchy with foreign support in the late fourth century.

Rome, on the contrary, illustrates the growth of oligarchy. On the expulsion of the Etruscan kings, the organs of government – the magistrates (*consuls*) and the council (*senate*) – fell into the hands of an 'aristocracy', the *patricians*, owing their power not only to landed wealth but also to the status of their ancestors as military conquerors. Like the Greek aristocrats, they used these organs against the *plebs*, who included both artisans and small farmers and also some members of defeated clans who had been enriched by the money economy. In the sequel the plebs by 'secession' – a sort of general strike – won not only safeguards for debtors and the right to intermarry with patricians and so obtain a share in their estates, but also certain political privileges – votes and magistracies.

In practice only large landholders and to a minor degree successful moneylenders profited by these concessions. The small farmers were ruined by compulsory service in continuous wars, and so forced to relinquish their holdings to their richer neighbours. Effective government and the interpretation of law were monopolized by the Senate which was now composed of ex-magistrates. While all citizens were entitled to vote in the election of magistrates, the voting was managed in such a way that the rich landowners with their dependents could control the election, while the expenses of office-holders were so heavy that only the rich could support them. Finally religious offices were reserved to the old families and could be used to invalidate any inconvenient decisions by the people; for public business could be transacted only when hereditary officials had declared the omens auspicious in accordance with a system of prognostication which they had learned from Mesopotamia through the Etruscans. (The Etruscans, for instance, had introduced the Babylonian method of divination from the livers of sacrificial victims which they had themselves learned in Asia Minor, probably through the Hittites.)

Under Senatorial government Rome would rise in three centuries from a modest country township to an imperial capital whose military power dominated the whole Italian peninsula, Sicily, Spain, North Africa, and even Greece. But the yeoman farmers whose arms had won this power would have lost their lands which would be absorbed by the great landowners and worked – scientifically – by slaves. The tribute from the conquered lands would enrich only the Senatorial oligarchy and new middle class of usurers, tax-farmers, and contractors, while hordes of captives would compete in the labour market with the dispossessed peasantry and native artisans.

*

The social ferment of the Iron Age began to dissolve the established ideologies that corporations of anonymous priests and clerks had wrought into dogmatic theologies in the Bronze Age. Even in the old Oriental States as divine kings were dethroned and empires broken up by barbarians, conceptions of an empire of gods in imitation of earthly empires must have been shaken. Though the Babylonian priesthoods celebrated the traditional cults more zealously than ever, the old Sumerian idea of Fate (p. 144) seems to have come to the fore again.

Still more among the new barbarian peoples in contact with civilization and under the corrosive influence of money did ideologies reflecting the old tribal structure of society disintegrate.

Cheap iron tools and weapons had offered release from complete dependence on the group to individuals who were neither divine kings nor war-chiefs, and were dissolving society into units as discrete as the coins into which social wealth was now divisible. Alphabetic writing opened the doors of learning to all without initiation through the conservative discipline of priestly seminaries or the schools of totalitarian States. The task of reconstructing society's spiritual equipment therefore fell on individuals unfettered by dependence on perpetual corporations with their conservative traditions.

All over the civilized world, but above all in societies that had recently emerged from tribal barbarism, men were venturing to seek new solutions to the questions posed by the old order's dissolution, and to seek them no longer through traditional channels and established institutions. Prophets dared to receive direct revelations from the deity – that collective soul substance of barbarians that had comprehended and transcended all the members of a tribe. Philosophers appealed to the 'reason' innate as they supposed in all their fellows – which also is in a sense just the collective experience of society transmitted and interpreted in accordance with commonly-accepted principles. Particularly in the sixth century did pioneers who dared to receive personal 'revelations' find popular support, or patrons on which to found new religions; bold reasoners found sufficient numbers reasoning like themselves to form schools of philosophy.

In China, Lao-tse and Confucius are supposed then to have taught a rational morality, founding Taoism and Confucianism in the sixth century. In India, Gautama the Buddha reputedly 'attained enlightenment' shortly before 500 B.C. He was certainly not a member of the priestly caste, the Brahmans, but allegedly the son of a small raja. He preached salvation as escape from the wheel of births and deaths into an indefinable state of *nirvana*. The doctrine of the wheel, the theory of the transmigration and reincarnation of souls, he took from the Brahmanic theologians. But the means of escape were no longer sacrificial bribes and magical ceremonies, but moral virtues, notably obedience to parents, respect for all living creatures, and truthfulness. By the conversion of the Maurya emperor, Asoka (273–231 B.C.), Buddhism was to become a rich established church with all the trappings of sacerdotalism and magic ritual. But it did bring forth monasticism, and its missionary zeal was one of the most potent instruments in diffusing civilization in Central and Eastern Asia.

Zarathushtra (Zoroaster), who lived somewhere in Eastern Iran some time between 1000 and 500 B.C., believed himself called by Ahura Mazda (Ormuzd) to purify Iranian religion from polytheism, devil-worship, magic, and ritualism. So the old tribal gods (the *devâs* of the Vedic Aryans) become in his hymns evil spirits, the commercial sacrifice is condemned, the will of the one god sustains the cosmic order – the idea of cosmic order itself may be the fruit of the Babylonians' astronomical observations (revealing uniformities in the movements of the heavenly bodies) fertilized by their notions of society as governed by known and established laws that had been current since the time of Hammurabi. As champion of 'the cattle-tending husbandman' against the nomads, Zarathushtra may be said to appeal to the Iranian peasant masses. But his success was apparently due to the patronage of a great landed nobleman, Vistaspa, and his teachings became the creed of a rich State church with a new priesthood and fresh ritualism, if not under Darius, at least under the Arsacid kings after 50 B.C.

The Hebrew prophets again – Amos, Hosea, Isaiah, and their successors – relied on revelations. But they moralized the barbaric tribal god of the patriarchs, Yahveh, and denounced polytheism, idolatry, and magic. Their Yahveh had no need of the flesh of goats and the blood of bulls offered as bribes. 'What doth the Lord require of thee but to do justly and to love mercy and to walk humbly with thy God?' At the same time the prophetic movement reflects a reaction of a free peasantry against the economic and political absolutism of kings who from Solomon on were trying to ape Egyptian and Assyrian monarchs.

The prophets thus spiritualized old gods and moralized existing cults. The deity became personal, but in a spiritual sense incapable of being confined in carvings of wood and stone, however skilful and ornate. He is no longer just one among many gods with whom he contends on behalf of, and with the aid of, his tribal worshippers, like Amon-Ra,

Marduk, or the old Yahveh. He is exclusive. God of gods; potentially at least he is God of all men, not only of Assyrians or Egyptians (p. 169).

An element of commercial magic, indeed, survives, in as much as even the prophetic religions promise the devotee rewards in this world or the next. But these rewards are no longer to be obtained by compulsive magical rites; the deities' favour is not to be wooed by draughts of beer as in Sumer, or of intoxicating soma as in Vedic India. The way to salvation is to act morally – to do justly, to speak the truth, in general to behave towards one's fellows in the way most societies, even barbarian and Bronze Age, recognize as right.

But of course any doctrine that promises salvation as the reward for righteousness must also threaten damnation as the penalty for evil doing. In the inspired vision of the prophet the negative sanction is overshadowed by the positive message. But as the religions become more and more institutionalized and sacerdotalized, the sufferings of the damned are dwelt on with increasing gusto. So, like the Egyptian papyri of the second millennium (p. 165), later Buddhist and Zoroastrian scriptures and paintings give lively descriptions of hells and their torments.

Finally, as the one God is now maker of all men, mankind becomes potentially one society. It is no longer to his fellow-tribesmen or his fellow-citizens alone that the God-fearing righteous man owes justice, truth, and mercy, but, if not to all men, at least to a community of the faithful that should embrace all men, irrespective of race or political allegiance. These fruitful ideas are certainly implicit in the teachings of Gautama, Zarathushtra, Amos, and the rest. They became explicit in Buddhism, Mithraism, and other religions after 300 B.C. The idea of humanity as a single society, all of whose members owe one another common moral obligations, is an ideological counterpart of an international economy based on the interchange of commodities between all its parts, such as became effectively manifest in the second phase of the Iron Age.

In Greece during the Bronze Age minstrels who had been welcome at the heroes' courts, instead of priestly corporations, had defined a theology depicting the gods in the likeness of their warlike patrons, acknowledging the suzerainty of Olympian Zeus as did the turbulent war-lords that of the King of Mycenae. In the Iron Age the appropriate commercial sacrifices or bribes were still publicly offered to the Olympian gods, and temples were still built for them by the cities. But when the Mycenaean castles were vacated by their mortal models, the Homeric 'gods left the earthly Olympus and vanished into the sky. Nature, dispeopled of gods, was left free for Science' on the one hand, for the vaguer magic forces 'controlled' by the old peasantry and the new barbarian tribes on the other.

From the old magic rites were begotten 'mystery religions' – the cult of Dionysus or Bacchus, the god of wine, imported from barbaric Thrace, Orphism, the Eleusinian mysteries – and mythical philosophies, including those to Pythagoras and Plato, all appealing to individuals as such rather than of society as an organized whole. Mystery religions provided an ideology for the masses – the dispossessed peasantry, the miners, and even the slaves – promising them salvation, spiritual balm for their material and economic woes. Bacchus offered union with the deity through divine frenzy, 'Orpheus,' like Buddha, release from the wheel of births and deaths (p. 219), Elusis immortality. But the paths to salvation were mainly magic rituals – initiations and purifications taken straight from totemism – dramatic fertility rites of rustic barbarians such as had procured immortality first to pharaoh and then to all Egyptians who could pay for it (pp. 145, 165). Naturally the impure, the uninitiated, were threatened with hell. The Orphics contrasted gloomy Tartarus with the Elysian fields to which the initiates travelled after death. By the fifth century the fear of hell was a potent factor in Greek life, though scarcely alluded to in classical literature. From the Italian and Sicilian colonies the doctrine spread to the Etruscans, whose tombs are sometimes adorned with pictures of the tortures of the damned. But the aim of the mysteries was not 'to teach their votaries a body of dogmas, but to put them in a certain emotional state'.

The philosophical mystics for their part appealed to a more sophisticated clientele with a subtler magic. Pythagoras of Samos (flourished about 530 B.C.), for instance, for escape from the wheel of life prescribed, in addition to taboos and rites taken straight from barbarism, civilized sciences and art; his disciples formed brotherhoods that are more akin to barbarians' secret societies and the Orphics' church than to scientific schools; the same is true of the Brahmanic philosophical schools of Iron Age India. But the Pythagoreans, regarding the contemplative life as the greatest purification, incidentally studied arithmetic, geometry, and astronomy as a means thereto, not without practical results. In the meantime other philosophies, originating in Ionia, had been leading more directly to Natural Science.

The founders of what is termed Natural Philosophy – Thales (?625–540) and Anaximander (?600–530) of Miletus, Herakleitos (?550–475) of Ephesus – were in fact primarily concerned with the social questions that commercial contact with the Orient and the new currency had made urgent in Ionia. At first at least philosophers were no more concerned with an abstract 'nature' unrelated to human society than the theologians of Sumer and Egypt. 'The principal object of Greek speculation', according to Cornford, 'is not external nature as revealed by the senses, but a representation of reality as a supra-sensible extended substance which is at first both alive and divine.' ... 'Its aim is to create a new tool, a conceptual model of reality,' just as the aim of the Sumerian lists may have been (p. 144). The model was, as in Mesopotamia, provided by the order of society, but of a society emerging into Iron Age, not Bronze Age, civilization. The Greek name for the order of nature, *cosmos*, is derived from a root that in the earlier Greek of Homer is applied to the marshalling of clans for war and the settlement of tribes on the land.

The Iron Age, in fact, presented the problems of society

in a new light, and the agents and the instruments for their solution were different. The morality and the cosmogony of the Bronze Age Orient had been the collective speculations of corporations of priests or temple households; Brahmanical philosophy in India, too, was elucubrated by a priestly caste. Greek philosophy of the Iron Age was the personal speculation of individuals emancipated from complete dependence on the group by iron tools and coined money.

In Iron Age philosophy – in India as well as in Greece – the problem of the individual and society, the One and the Many, occupied the forefront. It had, indeed, begun to appear on the horizon when the first magician emerged from the horde in the Old Stone Age, and was clearly discernible in the Bronze Age when divine kings and warlords acquired individuality and 'souls'. But it fully dawned only in the Iron Age society of pirate captains, merchant shipowners, currency jugglers, and tyrants.

So Bronze Age speculation had taken nature as a whole, as society was a whole, manifestly united in dependence on the divine monarch, and as the temple estate was a whole collectively exploited in the interests of the household and its divine head. But Iron Age philosophy broke nature too into parts, as the community was divided into individuals and the city's territory into private holdings and estates. In Ionia Anaximander already explained qualitative differences as due to 'thickening and thinning', i.e. as quantitative like the differences in political status based on the property qualifications of citizens (p. 214). Finally between 500 and 420 B.C. the atomists, Leukippos (of Miletus) and Demokritos (of Abdera), set out to resolve external nature into discrete indivisible bits or particles (*atoms*), just as the new currency resolved wealth into discontinuous particles – coins. Thus they created the atomic theory that proved such a superb instrument of discovery in modern chemistry and physics.

What was really distinctive in Greek speculation was that the philosophers appealed again and again not to the wisdom of the ancients or divine revelations, but to facts of common experience, and the practice of the crafts. (Their Hindu contemporaries were hampered by inheriting from the Bronze Age the sacred hymns of the Veda (p. 176) and ritual manuals verbally remembered.)

The natural philosophers diligently observed natural phenomena and systematized their observations. Anaximander outlined a vague idea of organic evolution based upon accurate observations of the habits of fishes and animals. Xenophanes (of Colophon, ?565–475 B.C.) observed and correctly explained fossils. Moreover, they applied measurement to their observations, if only to a limited extent, more than their Bronze Age precursors; did not coins enable Greek society to measure even rank more accurately than the unminted money of the Bronze Age? By measuring the chords of the lyre Pythagoras (or one of his disciples) not only laid the foundation for the theory of music, but also was led to discover the mathematical properties of what we call harmonic progressions.

But the Greek philosophers did not have to rely exclusively on their own observations; they were admittedly acquainted with the genuine achievements of Babylonian and Egyptian science. In arithmetic, geometry, and astronomy Greek science built on foundations laid on the Nile and the Euphrates. Thales, the first natural philosopher, was reputedly half a Phoenician, and is said to have studied geometry in Egypt. Pythagoras too is reputed to have learned his geometry in Egypt.

He and his disciples certainly pursued the study of mathematics, albeit often for mystical and magical ends. Pythagoras seems to have thought that the 'nature' of things was somehow expressible in numbers, much as the Sumerians may have supposed that a thing's 'nature' could be grasped with its name; after all, in contemporary Greece a man's function in society and so his 'nature' was officially determined by the number of coins he owned. At the same time the constant and uniform properties of number appeared to reveal a permanent and changeless Order in which men might find refuge at a time when the structure of society was manifestly in a state of flux.

In any case, many interesting and curious properties of numbers were discovered. These discoveries seemed to reveal magical properties, and the numbers possessing them were given fanciful names like 'amicable numbers' by the Pythagoreans. But even these, to say nothing of progressions and the like, have turned out to be helpful in the modern theory of probability.

But the Greeks could not advance very far in pure arithmetic owing to clumsy systems of numeral notation. For the practical business of accountancy they used the counting-board, or *abacus* – a device probably invented by the Phoenicians and still employed in Russia and Oriental countries today. But neither the abacus nor the notations devised to record results obtained thereon lend themselves to higher mathematics; for fractions, for instance, the Greeks were confined to aliquot parts like the Egyptians (p. 127). They overcame the obstacle by using geometry. And geometry, like pure number, seemed to reveal a permanent and changeless order.

The Greek geometers generalized truths familiar to their Oriental predecessors. For instance, Pythagoras may have learned from Egyptian architects (the ancient writers speak of cord-knotters, *harpedonaptai*) the trick of constructing an accurate right-angle with the aid of a cord divided in the proportions 3, 4, and 5, or 5, 12, and 13; it was demonstrably used by the Brahmans of India for constructing altars a little, if at all, later. With this would go the converse fact, familiar to the Babylonians in the second millennium (p. 187), that in a right-angled triangle whose sides are in these proportions the square on the side opposite the right angle (the hypotenuse) is equal to the sum of the squares on the two sides containing it. Then Pythagoras is credited with having established by the sort of construction still used in school geometries that in *any* right-angled triangle the square on the hypotenuse is equal to the sum of the squares on the sides containing the right angle – what is still called, probably erroneously, the Theorem of Pythagoras.

In fact the Greek geometers by 'pure geometry', i.e. by laboratory experiments, by tracing out figures in the sand or with strings, and by cutting up globes and cubes and cones, did find out constant properties common to *any* triangle or other figure that they could construct. (The 'proof' of a theorem begins, e.g. 'Let A B C be *any* triangle ...' and then directs you to try out certain constructions on it.) Hence they inferred that these properties held good of *all* triangles or other figures. So by *induction* they generalized observations, many of which must have been familiar to Babylonians and Egyptians, and discovered new geometrical properties of the same kind.

With their aid the Greeks were enabled to obtain approximations to surds and other irrationals (e.g. $\sqrt{2}$) and to solve quadratic equations that had defeated the Babylonians. They found, too, that the stars did appear to trace out in the sky figures that men could describe in the laboratory with compasses, and that applications of geometrical rules would help them to locate planets in the heavens and ships at sea and to divide sundials more accurately. With the aid of geometrical figures engineers could plan a tunnel to convey water a third of a mile under a mountain, as at Samos in the sixth century.

It did not therefore matter so much that the foregoing discoveries had been made in pursuit of magical and mystical ends. Yet the baleful effects of their origin still persist. The Greek philosophers thought that the 'universal' truths of mathematics revealed to them an immutable and eternal reality behind the changing panorama of historical appearances, that geometry would provide a model of timeless Nature as a Sumerian temple or Egyptian pyramid had. Some, indeed, like Plato, inferred that the truths of geometry were not inferences from experimental facts – from figures that men drew and constructed – but 'memories' of the properties of ideal triangles apprehended by reason. Upon this confusion was based the theory of a suprasensible eternal world of ideas independent of observation that has haunted idealist philosophy ever since. But even experimental scientists today, despite Einstein and Darwin, seem loath to abandon the search for an eternal changeless unhistorical reality of which pure mathematics could be the model.

Astronomy the Greeks, like other farmers, had to study first for the regulation of the calendar. Even before 700 B.C. Hesiod's poem, *Works and Days*, illustrates the role of the stars as guides to agricultural operations and the early transmission in literary form of this rural lore. But the Greeks were perforce a sea-faring people. Lacking a compass, they had to rely on the stars to steer by. They had therefore a very practical incentive to observe them accurately and, moreover, opportunities to note phenomena that a priest, permanently stationed in the same temple, would lack.

For instance, a sailor would notice that as he sailed south the pole star came nearer and nearer the horizon. By measuring its altitude (as an angle) he could get a good idea as to how far he had progressed on his voyage across the Mediterranean.

In their study of the stars the Greeks doubtless benefited also from the results collected by the Babylonians and Egyptians. By the second millennium the Babylonians had compiled a great catalogue of stars. Copies of it found a place in the Royal Library of the Hittite capital in central Asia Minor, so that knowledge of its contents had spread well towards the Aegean before 1200 B.C. After 1100 the list had been revised in Assyria, while after 800 Babylonian texts begin to give the stars' positions and heliacal settings on a system like our 'equatorial coordinates'. Moreover, from 747 B.C. the Babylonians had begun to reckon years from a fixed conventional point, as we do 'from the Birth of Christ', and to date events from the 'Era of Nabonassar'. Hitherto celestial as well as terrestrial events had been dated at best to 'the nth year of King N'.

With the data thus collected the Babylonian astronomers were able to calculate in advance the relative positions of the sun and moon and of the planets; in other words, they could predict when eclipses were to be expected. Now Thales is reported (by a tradition going back to Herodotus in the early fifth century) to have foretold an eclipse of the sun, almost certainly that of 585 B.C. His prediction cannot have been based on his own observations alone, so he presumably based his deductions on data derived from Mesopotamia.

His success does not, of course, mean that either he or his teachers understood the 'cause' of eclipses. That was clearly stated by Anaxagoras (of Klazomenai, ?500–430 B.C.) a century later. The explanation seems to have been due to a purely Greek development in which the new geometry was bodily applied to accurately measured and recorded observations. Some Greeks had freed themselves from traditional superstitions sufficiently to treat the heavenly bodies as objects to be measured and weighed instead of (or as well as) the vehicles of a deity or symbols of a supernatural Fate. Nevertheless, about 450 B.C. Anaxagoras was condemned for impiety in democratic Athens, and in 413 an Athenian general postponed for a month a vital military operation because an eclipse of the moon occurred as an evil omen!

At the same time scientific astronomy was preparing the way for a mathematical geography. With the immense enlargement of the civilized world and the intensification of intercourse throughout it, men of the Iron Age needed more than ever to know about the planet on which they lived. Conquerors, generals, merchants, and mariners wanted to know not only what sort of people and lands they might conquer or trade with, but also how to reach them and how far off they were. Assyrian and Persian officials drew up itineraries giving roads and distances. The pharaohs of a temporarily revived Egypt sent out exploring expeditions: one crew rounded the Cape of Good Hope and were astonished to find the sun on the right as they sailed westward – a report that the credulous Herodotus refused to believe!

Much of this information thus gathered remained locked up in the confidential archives of Oriental monarchies or as the trade secrets of private merchants or individual cities. But the new class of travelling Greek philosophers picked up scraps here and there and added to them their own observations. They could sell such knowledge to a wide circle anxious to take advantage of the new facilities for travel, business, or even pleasure. Anaximander is reported to have made the first Greek map. Some even wrote down their information for the benefit of the new reading public. The results were both descriptive works and also scientific treatises in which the foundations of a mathematical geography were laid with the aid of astronomy and spherical geometry.

The Iron Age improvements in the applied sciences due to the cheaper metal tools and the need of new classes are too numerous even to mention. They did not as yet involve new methods of transmission. Despite the alphabet, craftlore in general was not committed to writing and so did not become fully scientific. Athenian potters' traditions, for example, still taught them to fear the demon who cracked pots in the kiln and to mount on it a Gorgon mask to scare him away! The illiteracy of craftsmanship (craftsmen could sign their names all right) is presumably due to old-fashioned contempt for the mechanic arts. The exceptions prove this.

The craft-lore of the medicine-man, like that of the magician, had been committed to writing even in the Bronze Age and continued to be transmitted in the Iron Age. In the Oriental schools this scholastic tradition all too faithfully preserved the magical theory of disease as due to possession by evil spirits. The Assyrians added only a few new spells and drugs for their expulsion to the Sumerian and Babylonian recipes. In Greece, too, there were healing gods, like Aesculapius, who wrought miraculous cures in their temples. But outside the temples there grew up a school of private physicians who discarded the magical paraphernalia of the medicine-man, but not his drugs, and relied on manipulative and chemical remedies.

Judged by the extant writings beginning with Hippocrates

(of Chios, ? 460–350 B.C.), the Greek medical tradition was characterized by freedom from demonology and by an accuracy and objectivity in the observation and recording of symptoms quite foreign to Assyria and Egypt. Even before 500 B.C. Greek medicine had gained such a reputation that Darius summoned to his court a Greek physician who cured his queen.

Agriculture again was a reputable pursuit in the Iron Age, and treatises on scientific farming were written both in Greek and in Phoenician. Even before 700 B.C. Hesiod was putting into verse a farmer's almanac replete with maxims for the application of practical botany, geology, and zoology. Thereafter migration overseas and the switch over to specialized farming broke down the routines of agriculture and made experimentation compulsory. A Phoenician or a Greek, transplanted to Italy or North Africa, could hardly help noticing the effect of the new soils and climates upon the seeds, cuttings, and young animals he took with him. Experience showed that a vine-stock from Lebanon produced different grapes on the slopes of Vesuvius or the plain of the Rhône valley. Comparison and selection of soils and stock were inevitable. Moreover, new plants and animals were introduced, as well as new methods, as part of the general diffusion already described on page 206; thus the Persians introduced lucerne into the Mediterranean when they invaded Greece in 490. Conversely they themselves learned to cultivate rice after their conquest of India.

The collation of such experimental results and the formation of a written, and therefore abstract and fluid, tradition of agricultural science may have been prompted by a demand for manuals on the part of large landowners; handbooks for 'gentlemen farmers' existed among the Carthaginians.

But with the data collected for practical purposes by farmers and physicians the new leisured class of natural philosophers in Greece were enabled to lay the foundations for modern descriptive botany, geology, and zoology. Their work differs from the Sumerian lists firstly in containing accurate descriptions instead of bare names, and secondly in drawing upon the observations of a much wider circle of educated persons. Their classifications too are more 'scientific' in that they are no longer based upon similarities of conventional names or written signs but upon real and often significant similarities in the actual plants, minerals, or animals classified. The results can best be judged from the lectures of Aristotle who died in 321 B.C.

In Aristotle culminate in a sense all the philosophical and scientific tendencies of the Classical period. A man of comprehensive interests and encyclopedic erudition, he lectured on the theory of knowledge, logic, ethics, politics, psychology, mathematics, astronomy, geography, botany, zoology, anatomy, chemistry, physics, and meteorology. The vast Aristotelian corpus consists of notes of these lectures, edited by the author or his pupils, and treatises of disputed authenticity. As a pioneer in formal logic, positive psychology, comparative anatomy, and systematic biology his contributions to later science are invaluable.

Inevitably Aristotle went wrong – sometimes stupidly wrong – for instance, in claiming that the heavenly bodies are incorruptible and that the sun goes round the earth, in denying the sexuality of plants, accepting spontaneous generation, and locating the intelligence in the heart. It is his misfortune and ours that his authority grew so great among his Hellenistic successors that his theories were sometimes preferred to observed facts. By the Middle Ages Aristotle's system with all its blemishes was virtually incorporated in the sacred canon of the Catholic Church. The schoolmen appealed to Aristotle rather than to experience; the Church condemned the heliocentric system of Copernicus as contrary to Aristotle's teaching that the Church had accepted. A champion of oligarchy and a defender of slavery, Aristotle appears as the mouthpiece of the class from which his patrons and pupils were recruited and as the victim of the contradictions in the economy of the City-state which were all too apparent by his day.

Compared with the stagnation of science in the Bronze

Age, in spite of the endowment of research institutes in temples, the progress achieved in Greece between 600 and 450 B.C. is amazing. It was moreover due not to clerks and priests assured of leisure by rich States or Churches, but to private individuals living either by their own industry or on the generosity of patrons and disciples.

Nevertheless, at least after 500, this superb effort of pure science did not, as the comparable efflorescence of modern theory did after A.D. 1600, find expression in technical inventions that not only enriched human life and guaranteed the workable truth of the theories but also provided instruments for fresh discoveries. On the contrary, except in the domains of agriculture and military engineering, natural philosophy became increasingly divorced from practical life as the Greek cities grew richer, wealth more concentrated, and slaves more numerous.

The wealthy slave-owners and landlords who welcomed to their banquets the natural philosophers and on whose patronage the latter had to rely, did not want labour-saving devices and despised craftsmanship as degrading (*banausic*) and servile. The pursuit of abstract knowledge for its own sake or as the 'greatest purification' became a consolation to the rich slave-owner who was relieved by his slaves of any need to exert himself productively and was yet jostled out of his employment in running the State by the vulgar mechanics in the Athenian assembly or by the equally vulgar tyrants of other cities.

Then the private merchant, loyal citizen of one of several competing States, would hesitate to disclose the geographical and astronomical observations he had made to any cosmopolitan scientist who might betray his secrets to enemies and rivals. Moreover, slavery made a real science of man and so scientific history impossible. To justify the institution Aristotle propounded the doctrine of the 'natural slave'. It means in effect that a man of any race except the Greek found the highest expression of which he was capable in serving the kindly Greek as an intelligent instrument. The Semites and Egyptians who had created civilization, the Celts, the Teutons, and the Jews who were to re-create it, were thus summarily labelled and dismissed.

Finally Farrington has argued that the freedom of thought and teaching was deliberately restricted in the interests of the propertied classes and by their influence in the State. Certainly the criticisms of the natural philosophers assailed the religious and superstitious pillars of the established order. That could be tolerated while the economic system was expanding so that an absolute increase in wealth hid the inequalities in its distribution. But after 450 the market was no longer expanding at the old rate; the profits of usury and slave-holding on the one hand, the ruination of small farmers through war and the congestion of the labour market on the other, were revealing nakedly the contrast between rich and poor. Disturbances occurred already in several cities. In the fourth century demands for the abolition of debts and a redivision of the land became widespread and chronic.

In these circumstances philosophers of the right recognized the value of superstitious supports for the existing order. Plato frankly recommends teaching the citizens 'a noble lie'. Later Polybius commends the Roman aristocracy for having done so successfully. 'The foundation of Roman greatness is,' he asserts, 'superstition. This has been introduced into every aspect of their private and public life with every artifice to awe the imagination. For the masses in every State are unstable, full of lawless desires, irrational anger, and violent passion. All that can be done is to hold them in check by fears of the unseen and similar shams. It was not for nothing but of deliberate design that the men of yore introduced to the masses notions about God and views on the after-life.' And Farrington can in fact point to the condemnation of Anaxagoras for 'impiety' and later of Socrates for 'corrupting the youth' as concrete examples of intolerance of criticism of precisely those notions and views.

In any case the development of classical Greek science was in fact limited by the peculiar social and economic conditions of the classical *polis*. The same limitations may have affected classical art.

Throughout the Bronze Age the conventions established as canons in the third millennium (p. 147) had remained fixed; only new technical processes had been introduced and styles had been modified. Even in the Iron Age Orient the venerable and sanctified traditions of the past dominated the taste of customers drawn from essentially the same social classes, albeit of different 'races', as before, though new media – glazed bricks and tiles, for instance – might now be effectively employed.

The Greeks, abandoning the stiff barbaric styles of the Geometric age about 700 B.C., began to copy the approved models of Oriental art as successfully as the Phoenicians had done in the second millennium, but always preserving something of that balance and restraint that distinguished the Geometric style. And then they broke away from the old conventions, as the Classical economy expanded, and with its expansion the market constituted by appreciative buyers deepened.

The sculptor and the painter were no longer dependent on the patronage of priestly corporations and despots' courts. Their most profitable and most honourable duty was therefore no longer to turn out idols of a pattern approved by sacerdotal tradition as divinely sanctioned and magically effective. Portraits of divine kings, still fulfilling a magic function (p. 146) no longer set a standard for the delineation of the human form. Sculptors were commissioned by cities or private individuals to execute statues of athletes and warriors or of deceased relatives none of whom made any pretence at divinity any more than the statues themselves worked magic. They were thus free to abandon sacred conventions and depict what they saw. And incidentally the frequent gymnastic contests gave them opportunities of seeing the human form naked which were less common in the Orient.

Thus Greek artists were the first, since the nameless masters who had worked in prehistoric India (p. 136), to present the human figure in a naturalistic manner; they were allowed to treat even the gods in the same spirit. So by the fifth century the Greeks had established canons of beauty in portraiture at least that are still generally accepted.

Architects too in translating into the lovely marbles of their homeland the wooden structures of their barbaric ancestors were very likely inspired by Egyptian and Asiatic models. But they created architectural forms that, however depressing they may seem when copied in dirty stone under a grey northern sky, in Mediterranean sunlight are still things of ineffable beauty even when in ruins.

Similarly in literature epics dealing with the warlike deeds of gods and kings had been recited in Asiatic and Egyptian courts; magic dramas were performed in Bronze Age temples; the barbarian ancestors of the Indo-Europeans composed chants in metric verse. But out of the epic lays sung by minstrels at Mycenaean heroes' courts some Iron Age 'Homer' created epics that not only describe incidents and scenes, but also reveal the personalities of human characters for the delectation of Ionian aristocrats and plutocrats. The choral ode accompanied by music and dance was created for the country gentry and the commercial tyrants of the sixth century. Finally, for the democratic citizens choral ode and epic recitation were combined for public performance as dramas that were no longer magical. The literary conventions thus perfected have been models not only to later Europeans, but to the Persians and Arabs and perhaps Indians too.

But the most original creative period of Greek art was over before 400 B.C. Decadence sets in precisely at the point when economic expansion had slowed down, the general level of prosperity was declining, and real wages were falling, though individual fortunes were bigger than ever and the number of slaves relative to the total population had increased.

Now to us classical Greek sculpture is represented not by statues of gods carved by the most celebrated masters (these are lost), but by tombstones and similar works turned out by humbler artists for patrons of more modest means. Greek painting is not known by renowned artists' pictures in temples and public buildings – for these have perished – but by the designs on vases manufactured in mass in factories for popular consumption and executed by craftsmen who were seldom citizens and sometimes slaves (p. 208). After 500, as the number of slaves increased, the social and economic status of such executants had declined, as had that of other craftsmen. Aristotle in the fourth century mentions the profession of a musician (flute-player) as typically degrading (*banausic*).

The fatal outcome of contradictions in the political and economic structure of the world of Greek *poleis* was fully exposed after 400 B.C. 'The social and economic life of the fourth century', according to Rostovtzeff, 'was marked by two dominant features – the lapse of the mass of the population into proletarianism, and closely connected therewith the growth of unemployment, and secondly a shortage of foodstuffs.'

Many small peasants were being driven off the land by prolonged military service in continual wars, by the actual devastation of their farms by hostile armies, and by the debts these circumstances forced them to incur and prevented them from repaying. Industry offered no outlet to such as these. For the small craftsman could not compete with the slave-manned factory (p. 208). The internal market for industrial goods contracted; for usury and slave-owning concentrated wealth into fewer and fewer hands. The external market contracted too; for in true Bronze Age fashion industry exported itself instead of its products. For example, not only in Italy but also in the colonies on the Black Sea, local potteries, presumably staffed in the first instance with emigrant craftsmen, were successfully imitating for the local market vases that had formerly been imported from Athens. The emigration of the ceramic industry is just an index of what was happening in other domains. By reducing the export market it of course made it increasingly difficult to cover the cost of imported food-stuffs, like the wheat from the Black Sea.

So in the fourth century there was no outlet for the over-flowing and dispossessed rural population save to sell their bodies as mercenaries to the King of Persia or other 'barbarians' or to take to piracy and brigandage; one pretender to the Persian throne alone hired without diffi-culty 10,000 Greek mercenaries, while pirates became bolder and more numerous, aggravating (by increasing the slave-supply) the foregoing evils. No wonder that violent social struggles became endemic in most cities. Such were the consequences on the one hand of the economic con-tradictions exposed on page 209, on the other of the paro-chialism of the City-States that split Greece into tiny units, each clinging to local autonomy with suicidal fanaticism.

All Greeks were indeed conscious of a common Hellenism. They spoke dialects of a common language hardly suffi-ciently divergent to prevent mutual understanding alto-gether. All acknowledged a common pantheon of Olympic gods, despite local differences in cult. They even partici-pated in pan-Hellenic festivals like the Olympic games. In fact most Hellenic cities had joined forces to oppose aggression by non-Hellenic powers like the Persians and Carthaginians though even in old Greece there were cities that supported Darius and Xerxes. But otherwise each city fought with its neighbours almost continuously – first to be able to maintain the ideal of self-sufficiency by stealing other people's land, later to win a political or commercial hegemony.

No doubt passionate devotion to the *polis* provided a conscious motive for self-sacrificing moral action such as a barbarian tribe did not need and an Oriental State could not evoke. It inspired its citizens to deliberate valour, triumphant art, and noble generosity. But in practice it squandered the man-power of Greece, dissipated its wealth, brought Greeks to the slave-market to reduce the status of free craftsmen and in the end forfeited the autonomy of the *poleis* themselves. Such local patriotism in fact sums up the ethical ideal of the Classical moral philosophers like Plato and Aristotle. It could not provide an ideology compatible with an economic system based inexorably on international trade on at least a Mediterranean scale.

II

THE CLIMAX OF ANCIENT CIVILIZATION

In the three centuries beginning in 330 B.C., the frontiers of civilization were further enlarged until a continuous zone of literate States extended from the Atlantic to the Pacific. The new economy, hitherto realized only in the eastern Mediterranean, came to dominate Atlantic Europe and Hither Asia, and at last found political expression for the unity it created in the Roman Empire. This result was achieved in two main stages.

In the first the Greeks themselves, under the leadership of Alexander of Macedon, took over the whole Persian Empire as a going concern, extending the *polis* economy right to the Indus and the Jaxartes. At the same time the Syracusans established a smaller Greek Empire in the west (under Hiero) while the Romans were uniting Italy on Greek rather than Oriental lines and enlarging the sphere of the new economy at the expense of the Phoenicians of Carthage. In the second stage the Romans, having conquered the Greeks in Italy and Sicily, annexed the Carthaginian Empire and slowly swallowed Old Greece and its new appanages in the East, brought barbarian Europe by force of arms into the Mediterranean economic system. In the meantime a large part of India had been united, albeit for only a century, in the Maurya Empire, while the Chinese Empire advanced its frontiers to the Tarim basin.

The conquests of Alexander opened up Asia to Greek trade and Greek colonization, thus temporarily relieving the economic crisis sketched on page 238. They made Egypt and Hither Asia a province of the cultural and economic system of Hellas. Throughout this new province a single dialect of the Greek language was everywhere understood, so that ideas could and did circulate freely. Unity of currency, new roads, improved harbours and lighthouses, and larger ships facilitated intercourse and trade. The political and monetary unity created by Alexander did not indeed survive him. After his death in 321 his overseas empire became the prize in a prolonged contest between rival generals and was eventually decomposed into from three to five major monarchies.

Egypt fell to the Ptolemies who at first held also the coasts of Palestine, southern Syria, and Cyprus. Asia became the kingdom of the Seleucids; they rapidly lost their eastern provinces to the Indian Mauryas, independent Hellenistic kings, and eventually the Iranian Parthians, but after 200 acquired Palestine and Syria in compensation. Minor Greek kingdoms arose in Bactria (eastern Iran), and eventually recovered parts of India too for Hellenism, while native dynasts in Asia Minor, notably the Attalids of Pergamon, successfully imitated these Greek models. Finally the cities of peninsular and insular Greece mostly recovered their cherished autonomy, which meant for them the privilege of fighting with and enslaving their neighbours and rivals. This political disintegration did not, however, obliterate the cultural unity created by Alexander.

The annexation of the Persian Empire had meant not just a change of monarchs, but the opening up of a new world to Greek colonization. Alexander himself began founding in his new domain military colonies for his veterans and cities of Greek type. His successors founded many more. The new *poleis* all enjoyed at least municipal self-government and civic institutions of classical type. The Hellenistic cities of the East, like contemporary foundations in Old Greece and the West, were endowed with the amenities indispensable to the classical *polis* – market-place, theatre, official buildings, schools, fountains. Most new foundations were scientifically laid out on the grid system. All were adorned with statues and works of art. Few were larger than their classical models. Priene covered only 52 acres, Pergamon, though the capital of a kingdom, not more than 222. At Heraklea on Latmos the fortified area covered 245 acres in 295 B.C., and was reduced to 148 ten years later, while the

walls of Demetrias in Thessaly enclosed 645 acres. But by
100 B.C., Alexandria, the capital of Egypt, occupied 2,200
acres, while the population of Seleucia on the Tigris is said
to have numbered 600,000. The component houses, however, were commodious. Even at Priene, a small and predominantly agricultural city, the built-up area was divided
into blocks of 155 by 116 ft, each normally containing
four to eight two-storeyed houses; only a few richer dwellings measured as much as 65 by 60 or even 100 by 52 ft,
and boasted on the ground floor eight to ten rooms round
a pillared court or peristyle.

These *poleis* in the Orient were inhabited by Greek or
Hellenized officials, bankers, merchants, craftsmen, and
farmers plying arts and crafts in the Greek fashion and
worshipping Greek gods. On the other hand, the old
Oriental cities with the native commerce and industry,
religion and science, laws and institutions that animated
them were not suppressed. Alexander himself had planned
to rebuild the great temple of Marduk at Babylon, and his
successors actually endowed similar buildings in Erech and
other cities. So the old Sumerian cults were still celebrated
in the Babylonian temples, which continued to function also
as observatories and research institutes. In Egypt the
Ptolemies showed themselves no less solicitous for the
temples and their priesthoods.

Naturally the Hellenistic kings stepped into the niches in
the Oriental pantheon previously occupied by the king of
Babylon and the pharaoh of Egypt. At their death or even
during their lives they were deified. By the titles they
assume, Benefactor (Euergetês), Saviour (Sôtêr), they lay
claim to the same ideological role as their Bronze Age
precursors who, as 'the Good God', 'The Waterer of
Babylon', advertised their real services in promoting reproductive public works and protecting the weak from
oppression by the strong. 'Monarchy', as Glotz says,
'appeared a necessity to hold together the opposing classes,
to govern the relation between different races and to define
the rights and place of each.'

The Hellenistic monarchs carried on the traditions of their remote precursors in developing the resources of their kingdoms, but now with the experience of Iron Age Greece behind them. In Egypt the Ptolemies revived the ancient doctrine of Pharaoh's eminent domain over the Nile valley and its resources. Egypt was once more the 'king's household' (*oikos*), its territory his 'estate' (*chora*), the prime minister his 'steward' (*dioikêtês*). Its whole economic life was scientifically planned on strictly totalitarian lines to make the country self-sufficing.

The land, apart from estates belonging to temples or granted to royal favourites and to soldiers, was cultivated for the king and under strict supervision by 'king's peasants'. These were 'free' tenants, but bound by minutely-defined contracts as to what they should plant, and obliged to use seed provided by the State and to deliver to royal storehouses a high proportion, probably at least a half, of the yield, as well as to maintain canals and dykes and perform other specified services. The productivity of the land was enhanced by the introduction of superior varieties of plants and animals (seed corn from Syria and Greece, fig-trees from Asia Minor, vines from the Greek Islands, sheep from Asia Minor and Arabia, pigs from Sicily), by the supply of efficient iron agricultural implements to replace the wooden equipment that had survived scarcely changed from the days of Menes, and by the installation of irrigation machines like the Archimedian screw.

Mines and quarries were exploited by criminals and slaves for the profit of the State. Secondary industry was conducted by private firms under licence, by monopolies, or most often in State factories manned once more by 'king's peasants' working as free wage-earners under contract, but bound to remain at work during the stipulated period. Here too Greek techniques and methods of organization were grafted on to native traditions, and the output of each branch was regulated in accordance with the Plan.

The ambitious edifice was supervised by a hierarchy of officials and inspectors and controllers. The higher ranks in this bureaucracy were staffed, at first exclusively, always mainly, by Greeks; the minor officials must have been recruited from the old clerical class, but would of course have to learn Greek. As an additional check the Ptolemies farmed out the various taxes to underwriters who paid down a lump sum in advance, recouping themselves from the collection, but not personally doing the collecting – for that there were permanent officials.

No such grandiose experiments in planned economy were attempted elsewhere, and more play was left to the initiative of landowners, industrialists, and merchants, though the Hellenistic monarchs claimed a substantial share in the proceeds and the autonomous cities a more modest slice.

Specialized farms producing for the market were spread by the Greek colonists right to Russian Turkistan and India. In Sicily and the Carthaginian domains large estates worked by slaves or serfs were run on scientific capitalist lines, profitably if brutally. The same methods were adopted by Roman landlords in Italy. They tended to correct the balance between crops and livestock that is so hard to maintain on small peasant holdings but is yet necessary to preserve the soil. Under these conditions the experiments in acclimatization that had begun empirically in the preceding epoch were tried out on a larger scale and more deliberately. Cotton, apricots and citron, geese and buffaloes were introduced into European Greece, sesame and improved stocks of horses, asses, and swine from Europe into Asia as far as India, lucerne, oriental fruit trees, melons and beets, and barnyard fowls from Greece into Italy.

At least, in so far as sea or river transport was available, each natural region could concentrate on raising what was best suited to the local soil and climate, exporting the surplus, and receiving in exchange a variety of foods and materials that could hardly be produced at home. In the third century all the Greek cities were frankly dependent on imported corn, and even Rome had sometimes to supplement Italian supplies from Egypt. Egypt now imported olive oil, salt fish, pickled pork, honey, cheese, dried figs, nuts, and melons. The distribution of Rhodian jars (which archaeologists happen to have studied) as far afield as Susa in Elam, Erech and Seleucia in Mesopotamia, north Syria, the north coasts of the Black Sea and the Lower Danube, Carthage, Italy, and Sicily is one archaeological index of the export of oil and wine from Greece.

Secondary industries developed along the classical lines. Specialization was further advanced – in Delos, for instance, the joiner who fits a door does not set up the doorposts, and stonemasons do not sharpen their own tools. As a productive unit the small factory or workshop employing ten or twenty hands as described on page 208 was more typical than in the previous period. Such factories might be attached to the larger landed estates as they had been in the Bronze Age, to temples or to palaces. The kings of Pergamon in particular owned large factories for parchment and textiles, manned by masses of slaves. Workers were not normally collected into factories to make use of machinery, or even to facilitate the cooperation between specialist craftsmen performing different operations, but simply for convenience in supervision.

To this there is at least one exception. The development of the milling industry in Hellenistic times was revolutionary in two ways. Since the neolithic revolution each household had had to convert its grain into flour for itself, even though it had long abandoned its neolithic self-sufficiency. After 330 monuments and literature disclose special milling establishments, often attached to bakeries. And in them the grains were no longer ground by hand by pushing the rubber up and down a saddle quern (p. 65), but in *rotary mills* driven by donkeys or, after 100 B.C., sometimes by water-power. This new industry not only began to alleviate domestic drudgery, but also initiated the first extension in the employment of non-human motive-power since the Copper Age and the first fresh application of rotary motion since the potter's wheel. At the same time baking and milling are just instances of a number of new branches of industry that were now specialized to cater for the needs of the masses.

Trade was simplified by the political unification of large areas, monetary reforms, improvements in shipping, the construction of lighthouses and harbours and road-building. Alexander established for his whole empire a unitary currency based on the Attic standard on which the Roman denarius was also based. His policy was followed by his successors, except for the Ptolemies, who adopted the Phoenician standard for the Egyptian coinage. Meanwhile the Roman denarius spread in the west at the expense of Carthaginian and other currencies and competed successfully with the Greek coinage of the east. Moreover, the money economy finally ousted a natural economy from many strongholds where barter had persisted throughout the first Iron Age, spreading, for example, even among the Celts north of the Alps.

Ships were larger and faster. We even read of a ship of 4,200 tons burden, built for Hiero of Syracuse. Though she was not a success, she gives a hint of what Hellenistic shipbuilders could do. Rigging and steering gear were also improved, and captains now ventured to sail direct instead of hugging the coast more frequently than in earlier centuries. A veritable new era in navigation was initiated by the construction of lighthouses, inaugurated under Alexander by the Pharos of Alexandria, where a tower over 480 feet high was erected, in the lantern of which burned a fire of resinous wood. Improvements in ports were scarcely less important. Here again Alexandria led the way, but later contributions by the Romans – hydraulic cement, the coffer dam, pile-driving in deep water – were momentous.

Despite these improvements, the journey from Rhodes to Alexandria still took four days, as in Classical times. You might get from Alexandria to Sicily in six or seven days, but the voyage thither from the port of Rome (Pozzuoli or Ostia) normally occupied twenty to twenty-seven days. In fact it took longer to cross the Mediterranean than it now does to cross the Atlantic, and the chance of reaching your destination was immeasurably less; for the risks from ships wreck and still more pirates were really grave. Outside the

Mediterranean traffic was still slower. A journey by sea and river from the Indus to Seleucia on the Tigris could be accomplished in forty days. Till the trick of using the monsoons was discovered, four to six months might be consumed on the long sail of 2,760 miles from Berenice, on the Egyptian coast of the Red Sea, to peninsular India.

Land transport was also expedited. The caravan routes in Asia were more or less policed and equipped with khans and post stations by the Hellenistic monarchs, the Arabian States, or the merchant companies themselves. The Persian road system was extended and improved by the Seleucids. Profiting from their example, the Romans, as they united Italy under their leadership, began to bind their domains together with military roads. As pioneers of communications in a temperate zone, they were forced to face problems that do not arise in the arid lands east of the Mediterranean. Dust may be unpleasant, but it does not paralyse traffic; mud does. In Hither Asia rain falls in sufficient quantities to bog the roads for only brief seasons every year. In northern Italy rain and therefore mud may impede transit at almost any time and for long spells. The Roman engineers solved the problem thus created magnificently. Their roads are feats that have not been surpassed till the nineteenth century. According to Ptolemy, for instance, the roads radiating from Rome had been so graded that 'a wagon could take the load of a barge'.

None the less, land traffic was slow and costly. It took fifteen days for a messenger to get from Seleucia on the Tigris to the coast of Syria, and at the beginning of our era twenty-seven to thirty-four days from Rome to Britain. The journey from Rome to Naples might occupy three to five days – a train does it in as many hours. For bulky or heavy goods land transport was almost prohibitively costly. In the second century Cato, a celebrated Roman statesman and writer on scientific agriculture, bought an oil press at Pompeii for 384 sesterces. To transport it from the town to his farm, a distance of about seventy miles, cost him 280 sesterces!

Under such circumstances it is not surprising that industry often migrated to its market instead of sending its products thither. Pottery again illustrates the tendency. After 330 B.C. the ceramic industries of Athens and the Greek islands found new export markets in Alexander's empire and recovered old markets by offering new wares. Before and shortly after 300 vases in the new style decorated with patterns in relief made in a mould were imported in large quantities into Alexandria, Europus in north Syria, and all the ports of Syria, Palestine, and Asia Minor, as well as to south Russia and Italy. Soon after 300, however, local potteries, often at least manned by immigrant craftsmen, began making imitations which soon closed the Egyptian, Asiatic, and Russian markets to Old Greece. After 200, potters trained in the new tradition settled round Calles in Italy to supply the Roman market. In the same way glassworkers migrated from the ancient centres of that industry in Syria and set up glass-houses in Italy after 100 B.C.

Nevertheless, the volume of trade was greater than ever, both within the Mediterranean world with its Hellenistic extensions into Africa and Asia and beyond its borders. Of course commerce handled largely 'luxuries'. Still, the large-scale importation of foodstuffs, alluded to on page 244, and the exportation of pottery just mentioned will suffice to suggest how extensively a variety of popular consumption goods were transported over considerable distances – from the Crimea to Athens and from Egypt to Rome, for instance. Again, raw materials, such as tin, can hardly be called luxuries, yet after 300 B.C. Cornish tin was being regularly shipped across France to Marseille on the Mediterranean. Moreover, many exotic luxuries were becoming necessities. Arabian frankincense was regarded as an essential for public worship and actually cost five shillings a pound in Old Greece.

So caravans and flotillas brought to the Mediterranean world perfumes, spices, drugs, ivory, and jewels from Central Africa, Arabia, and India; gold, furs, or forest products from Siberia and central Russia; amber from the Baltic; metals from the British Isles and Spain. After 114 B.C. a dozen caravans a year loaded with silks crossed the deserts of central Asia from China to Russian Turkistan, whence the fashionable stuff was sent to Seleucia, Antioch, Alexandria, and Rome. A citizen of Rhodes, Alexandria, or Syracuse could be familiar with elephants, monkeys, parrots, cotton, silk, tortoiseshell, furs, myrrh, pepper, ebony, coral, amber, and lapis lazuli.

Thus materials and manufactures were diffused. Persons were diffused, too. Slavery in its Hellenistic–Roman development brought to the great international mart on Delos victims from Britain and Ethiopia, south Russia and Morocco, Iran and Spain, Greeks, Jews, Armenians, Germans, Negroes, Arabs, to be redistributed to Seleucia, Antioch, Alexandria, Carthage, Rome, Athens, or Pergamon – human cattle indeed, but comprising highly educated doctors, scientists, artists, clerks, and craftsmen as well as prostitutes and labourers. As in the Bronze Age Orient, merchants not only travelled about, but needed permanent offices and agencies in foreign cities. In every port and capital alien colonies were established, Jews being ubiquitous. We read of an Indian merchant resident in Egypt and actually holding a priesthood there. A guild of Syrian merchants maintained a regular hostel on Delos, providing lodgings, stock-rooms, a council chamber, and a chapel. A contract survives between a Massiliote and a Spartan who were partners on a trading voyage to Ethiopia. Free labour, too, was as mobile as ever. An Italiote bronze-worker transferred his business from Luciania to Rhodes, while a silk manufacturer from Antioch died in Naples.

The migrants, slave and free, brought with them to their new homes the fashions, techniques, and cults of their native countries, and established shrines where the deities of their nation or city were worshipped with appropriate rites on foreign soil. Their spontaneous efforts were supplemented by the proselytizing of Assoka, the recently-converted emperor of India, who sent missionaries to the courts of Egypt, Syria, and Macedonia. Finally the standing armies maintained by the Hellenistic kingdoms, Syracuse, Carthage, and Rome were not only consumers of industrial and rural produce, but also agents for training barbarian mercenaries in civilized ways and familiarizing farmers' sons with foreign lands.

So Oriental and Mediterranean civilizations, having fused, were joined by commerce and diplomacy to other civilizations in the east and to the old barbarisms of the north and south.

In the Far East the feudal anarchy into which the Chou empire had relapsed was at length suppressed by Shih Huang Ti (246–210 B.C.), a prince of the Ch'in state. This conqueror is credited with establishing the centralized rule by the Son of Heaven and a bureaucracy recruited not by birth, but by examination; the subjects of examination were theology and polite literature, without those concessions to science and modern languages that have been extorted from the Oxford mandarins in Britain. The frontiers of Chinese civilization were advanced into the tropical forests of the south and against the nomads of the arid north. Built as a defence against the latter, the Great Wall, 1,500 miles long and fifteen to thirty feet high, dwarfs the Great Pyramid, Hadrian's Wall, and Radio City as the largest alteration in the world's surface effected by man.

Then in 115 B.C., under the Han Dynasty, the Chinese army occupied, albeit only temporarily, the Tarim basin. At length the civilizations of the Far East and the Near East were in contact directly, no longer through intermediaries. Glass beads of the type fashionable in the Mediterranean during the fourth and third centuries had already found their way to China and had been imitated in home-made glass containing barium; Chinese silk had reached India before Alexander. After 115 the silk caravans, equipped by the Empire, travelled on roads protected by blockhouses and police. From their Chinese neighbours the Greeks of Bactria learned of a new element – nickel; like the Chinese, they used an alloy of it with copper for their coinage. The

Chinese for their part acquired vines, lucerne, and a superior breed of horses that 'sweated blood'.

In barbarian Europe preparations were made for the civilization that was to be imposed by Rome. The Scythians in south Russia had already come under the influence of colonial Greek civilization, which was now reinforced by that of Hellenistic Bactria on their kinsmen further east. The Celts in Central and western Europe were reached by Etruscan traders and Greeks from Marseille (p. 212), and bartered slaves, metals, and forest products for wine and manufactured luxuries.

Their rural economy, growing wheat and barley on small square fields tilled with a light plough, and breeding cattle, yielded a small surplus which was concentrated to some extent by numerous petty chiefs and nobles. These kept up the life of a Bronze Age chivalry, still fighting from chariots like Homer's heroes. Their clients, scattered in lone steadings and small villages, used iron tools, but could otherwise be self-sufficing; their surplus young sons sought fresh land for farms at the expense of their neighbours in neolithic fashion.

As internecine warfare was therefore endemic, the La Tène Celts fortified hill-tops even more strongly and ingeniously than their Hallstatt ancestors. Many of these hill forts were just refuges to which tribesmen retired with their cattle during a war. Others were permanently inhabited, but even these were economically just villages occupied by farmers living in squalid one-roomed round huts without any appreciable admixture of artisans, shopkeepers, and merchants. As late as the first century A.D., for instance, iron equipment was not brought from such fenced villages, but the metal was smelted and forged on a tiny scale in farms and hamlets, even though these might be in sight of a permanently-inhabited hill fort.

Only chiefs disposed of sufficient real wealth to be able to support specialist craftsmen such as wainwrights and artists in metal or potters using the wheel. These experts probably wandered from court to court just as in Homer's Greece. But they created a very attractive decorative style by taking

naturalistic Greek patterns and converting them into complicated geometric designs.

With such an economy and a growing population the
Celts inevitably overflowed. Ambitious war lords led the
younger sons of their tenantry in quest of land and booty.
In the fourth century Celts had flooded across the Alpine
passes, occupied the Po Valley, and sacked Rome herself in
390 B.C. So in the third other waves spread down the
Danube valley to the Balkans, devastated Macedonia and
northern Greece, and established a barbarian kingdom in
Asia Minor – Galatia. Other Celtic bands turned westward.
They laid hands on the metalliferous regions of north-
western Spain, Brittany, and the tin-lodes of Cornwall, thus
securing materials both for their own needs and to barter
for wine with the Greeks. And part of the tribe called Parisii
moved from the chalk-lands of the Marne across the sea to
the Yorkshire Wolds, while the rest settled on the Seine to
leave their name in Paris.

Farther north the Germans, though they too had acquired
from the Celts the secret of iron working, remained in barbarism. But they did apparently invent a system of tillage
appropriate to the heavy clay lands of the north European
forests – deep cultivation with a heavy plough drawn by
eight oxen and equipped with mould-board and coulter to
turn over the sod instead of just scratching the soil as the
Mediterranean and Celtic ploughs did. This new technique
and equipment unlocked fresh sources of food, which in
their turn stimulated a growth of population. Among barbarians that meant territorial expansion. A great horde of
migrants with wives and household belongings – the Cimbri
(from Denmark, the Cimbrian Peninsula) and the Teu-
tones – invaded Celtic France, only to be annihilated by the
Romans in Italy in 101 B.C. Filtering across the Rhine,
Germanic colonists introduced the new rural economy to
the Celts of Belgium and north-eastern France and formed
a mixed nation, the Belgae – Celtic in speech, but Germanic
in appearance (according to Caesar) and in burial rites
(according to archaeologists). Some of these occupied south-

eastern England about 75 B.C., and for the first time opened to the plough the richest soil in Britain. By 50 England was even exporting corn to France.

So the economy of barbarian Europe throughout the La Tène phase of the Iron Age was still dominated by subsistence farming, supplemented by a minimal development of specialized industry and by trade in metals, salt, and a few luxuries, not different in kind from that which had been conducted ever since the beginning of the Bronze Age. This rural economy, as far as it went, was in fact well adapted to the conditions of the temperate zone of woodland. Emphasis was rightly laid on pastoralism, especially on cattle-breeding, and that to such an extent that classical writers sometimes missed the agricultural aspect altogether. But the cattle were small, and the growth of herds restricted since the lack of winter made it necessary to eat too many of the calves. Lacking industry and a diversity of crops, this barbarian economy could not support a really sedentary, still less an expanding, population. Endemic warfare kept down numbers all too effectively till the Roman legions introduced urban life and peace.

The channels of intercourse just surveyed thus diverted into the Hellenistic cities traditions and discoveries accumulated by diverse societies in varied environments. From this great pool of human experience the natural philosophy of classical Greece united with Babylonian and Egyptian disciplines could distil a truly international science which need not remain pure theory. The Hellenistic scientists – many were Greeks only in name and culture – were no longer dependent on the patronage of the parochial bourgeoisie of a *polis* nor confined in a theological seminary. Research was encouraged and endowed by the heads of powerful States, eager to develop the resources of new domains.

Alexander himself was a pupil of Aristotle. His army was accompanied by surveyors and observers to map out the country and note its resources. His fleet was expressly sent to explore the Arabian Sea. These traditions were worthily maintained by his successors in Egypt and Asia while the Phoenicians of Carthage performed similar work in the Atlantic. Ptolemy I of Egypt in particular fostered learning. The *Museum* that he founded at Alexandria functioned as a University with the accent on research. All the Hellenistic kings and their officers indeed saw chances of political and commercial profit from applications of systematized knowledge more clearly than had the small factory owners and petty traders of any city state.

If private merchants were chary of disclosing trade secrets, the captains of royal fleets felt no such scruples. Ministers of State and capitalist farmers were developing kingdoms and estates as practical experiments in botany and zoology, genetics, and geology. Continuous warfare, conducted now by standing armies, permitted changes in tactics and strategy. In particular sustained sieges became feasible and demanded new weapons of attack and defence.

At the same time the cosmopolitan populations of the great Hellenistic metropoles were likely to be more tolerant, if no less superstitious, than the Athenian people that had expelled Anaxagoras (p. 234). As pointed out already, the foreigners in each city brought with them and celebrated there their own native cults. With these religions and their officiants spread new brands of magic and philosophy – a motley horde of quacks, astrologers, alchemists, and oracle-mongers – competing with traditional beliefs and legitimate sciences. Polytheism could easily find room both for new gods and new rites. All were tolerated with equanimity both by the States and by the less tolerant masses. Even Asoka, who with the zeal of a new convert was establishing Buddhism in India, professed and enjoined toleration to other creeds. Only Judaism remained exclusive; only Yahveh would accept no partner. The State of the Maccabees gave the first practical demonstration of religious intolerance and spiritual totalitarianism.

The proliferation of often ridiculous cults, the motley pantheons of polyglot deities, the dissemination of magic rituals and pseudo-sciences do not necessarily imply an absolute increase in superstition; they were but indications of the free interchange of ideas. They broke the absolute authority of old-established priesthoods and left sensible men free to discuss practical science without interference either from sacerdotal interests or mob fanaticism.

At the same time the ancient temple research institutes in Babylonia were still functioning. Mathematical texts and astronomical observations were written down in cuneiform as late as 20 B.C. Greeks from the west frequented these ancient seats of learning and would then take the title 'Chaldaean' as an equivalent to our Ph.D. Alexander's conquest, in fact, inaugurated two centuries of fruitful collaboration between Babylonian and Greek scientists, by which the substantial achievements of the Bronze Age Orient were conserved for transmission to the modern world. So close, indeed, was this collaboration that we cannot now always decide which party was in the lead; it is an open question whether the Babylonian Kidannu or the Greek Hipparchus first recognized the phenomenon termed the *precession of the equinoxes*.

To Alexandrian science the Orient contributed Babylonian mathematical processes, examples and all, and astronomical data. With the latter the Babylonian system of sexagesimal fractions (p. 186) was transmitted to the West, and that in an improved form; for the Babylonian mathematicians by the third century had at last agreed upon a sign for zero. The Alexandrians at first used the sexagesimal notation for tables of angular measurements, presumably themselves borrowed from Babylonia; but by the second century A.D. the device was used in preference to the clumsy aliquot parts of Egypt and Classical Greece for other quotients, approximations to square roots and to π. The idea of a zero sign in the form of an o (for *ouden*, nothing) was adopted too, but only in connexion with sexagesimal fractions.

So through its adoption by the Hellenistic mathematicians the most ingenious contribution of the Bronze Age to the mastery of numbers was preserved, transmitted to the

Arabs, and then brought back to Europe to come to fruition in our decimal notation in A.D. 1585. But of course the Greeks, in adapting sexagesimal fractions to their alphabetic notation, sacrificed their greatest charm – place value. ᚠᛗᛏᛋᛖᚲᛏᚲᚲᛏᛏ became $\rho\gamma$. $\nu\varepsilon'$ $\kappa\gamma''$ (103° 55′ 23″). By the Roman period Greek mathematicians were using distinctively Babylonian methods for the solution of quadratic equations (e.g. multiplying both sides by a instead of dividing as we generally do). They must even have adopted Babylonian examples. At least one example in an early medieval arithmetic book, the *Liber Abaci* of Leonard of Pisa, based upon Arabic, and so eventually Hellenistic, material, copies almost verbatim a problem set out in two cuneiform tablets, one early Babylonian and the other Hellenistic in age.

Still the greatest achievements in pure mathematics during the Hellenistic age were developments of the classical Greek geometric methods. Euclid (? 323–285 B.C.) not only systematized theoretical geometry and expanded previous work on curvilinear spaces, but also made practical use of it in the theory of optics. About the same time Aristarchus of Samos began to use what we term trigonometrical ratios. A generation later Apollonious at Alexandria developed that branch of higher mathematics known as conic sections. The name itself reveals how these figures of 'pure geometry' are derived from actual man-made objects; the curves it studies 'theoretically' include the parabola that the projectiles of the Hellenistic artillery followed and the hyperbolas traced by the shadow on contemporary sundials.

At Syracuse Archimedes (287–212) laid the mathematical foundations of mechanics, on the basis of empirical principles already verified in practice. Such achievements take us into the realm beyond the comprehension of the ordinary man, but they had practical results in yielding good approximations to ratios, π and other 'irrationals'. In an age which was using water-wheels, mapping the earth, and measuring the sun an accurate evaluation of π was more essential than in the Bronze Age, when the issue had been the circumference of a well or a cart-wheel; in constructing a water-wheel 10 ft 6 in. in diameter like that found at Athens, the Babylonian value of 3 might well cause trouble.

Even more fruitful were the collaboration between Greek and Babylonian astronomers and the cooperation of observers in different countries. After the more speculative adventures of the Ionians the Hellenistic astronomers boldly set out to measure the earth by strictly scientific methods. From observations on the sun's altitude at the summer solstice made respectively at Syene on the Tropic of Cancer and at Alexandria, Eratosthenes (Director of the Museum from 240 to 200) calculated the globe's circumference as 252,000 stades, probably 24,662 miles, and if so, only 4 per cent out! Later Poseidonius, apparently from observations on the meridian transit of Canopus from Alexandria and Rhodes respectively, reached the figure of 180,000 stades. Unluckily the later pundits of Alexandria accepted this smaller figure and handed it on to their Arab successors.

Still bolder, the astronomers proceeded to measure the divine Sun and Moon by perfectly rational methods. Aristarchus devised two ingenious and perfectly correct methods, which, however, were not practicable with the instruments at his disposal. Owing to unavoidable errors of observation, he made the sun's diameter only between six and seven times that of the earth and its distance twenty times that of the moon. More than a century later Hipparchus of Alexandria, using other methods, deduced that the moon's distance was between sixty-seven and seventy-eight times the earth's radius and its diameter about one-third of the earth's. He put the sun some 13,000 radii away from the earth. Though not much more than half the true distance, such figures were a shattering blow to common sense and theology alike. So equipped with instruments of its own devising, man's mind burst the bounds of terrestrial space and launched out on a voyage into the limitless inane not on the wings of fanciful speculation, but guided by strictly practical geometry. The fruits were not delusive superstitions, but maps that generals and merchants could use.

An even more subversive theory was in sight. The theory of concentric spheres, revolving round the earth, propounded to explain the movements of the heavenly bodies as plotted by the Babylonians and classical Greeks, was proving increasingly difficult to reconcile with accumulating observations. To escape the impasse Aristarchus advanced the revolutionary theory that looks so patently absurd that the earth itself and the planets really revolve around the sun. Seleucus, the Babylonian, shortly after 200 B.C., espoused the same *heliocentric* hypothesis.

Unfortunately, it was not only contrary to common sense, but ran up against perfectly genuine theoretical and observational difficulties. Hipparchus rejected the hypothesis on the quite reasonable scientific ground that he could not observe the parallax of a fixed star from the opposite poles of the earth's orbit round the sun – a phenomenon that only a high-power telescope can in fact disclose. So he returned to the geocentric view, embellishing it with a theory of epicycles. It became then the 'party line' on which all subsequent Hellenistic astronomers and their Arab successors worked and which was embodied in the sacred dogma of the medieval Church. But Aristarchus was never quite forgotten, and Copernicus, with very little fresh observational data, reverted to him – and was condemned for heresy!

Such epoch-making astronomical achievements were possible in the Hellenistic age not because 'a spirit of inquiry' was abroad, nor because men had leisure to pursue the contemplative life as the greatest purification, but because, in spite of all conflicts of political loyalty, men using a common language were cooperating all over the enlarged world; for they pre-supposed observations on star-transits and declinations in different cities and the communication of the results. They were not inspired by mere curiosity, however divine, nor only by the vain hope of foretelling the destinies of mortals, but by the urgent need of finding one's way about an expanding world. Their results were not only to liberate humanity from the bonds of space and the terrors of solar myths, but also to define the form of the inhabited globe and to guide armies, merchant ships, and caravans on unprecedented journeys.

For astronomy was applied to geography. Once Eratosthenes had fixed the value of a degree, angular measurements on the elevation of the Pole Star and on meridian transits gave a much more accurate idea of distances north and south than any calculations from marching or sailing times. By correlating such observations the positions of places could be plotted on a terrestrial sphere divided up, like the sky, into parallels of latitude, numbered 0 to 90 to indicate the angular distance from the Equator. Latitude just means 'width', and so the word reveals how the system started with sailors' observations in crossing the long Mediterranean.

To find astronomically how far one had progressed westward, sailing *along* the Mediterranean, one's *longitude* in fact, was not so easy. Longitude expresses the difference between local sundial times. With a modern accurate chronometer it is easy enough to compare your local noon, the moment when the sun crosses the meridian above you, and 'Greenwich time', and so fix your position, an hour being equal to 15°. The ancients had only sundials and water-clocks. Hence only a celestial event, independent of the earth's diurnal rotation on its axis, an eclipse, or an occultation, permitted the comparison of local times. As early as 331 B.C. the times of an eclipse seen at Arbela in Syria and at Carthage had been recorded and compared. Hipparchus had the idea of fixing the longitudes of various places by cooperative observations on the relevant phenomena. By the second century A.D. his idea had borne such fruit that Ptolemy was able to construct a skeleton map of the globe on a frame of astronomically fixed latitudes and longitudes, such as has been used ever since.

Unfortunately cardinal errors were accepted and repeated again and again till they acquired the authority of 'facts'. For instance, Eratosthenes had taken as his meridian a line through Alexandria, Rhodes, Troy, Byzantium, and the mouth of the Dnieper, a line that is anything but straight. Yet it remained the basis of all subsequent ancient maps.

Theoretical advances in biological science were less dramatic. The substantial achievements of Hellenistic botany and zoology are to be found in the agricultural experiments of the Ptolemies and of the Romans. But Crateuas, physician to the king of Pontus (120-63 B.C.), introduced a fruitful innovation in method when he illustrated his herbal with realistic pictures of the plants he was describing and classifying. In physiology and anatomy Herophilus and Erasistratos of Alexandria made important discoveries between 300 and 275 by dissecting human bodies. In a later age when men were devoting all their ingenuity to torturing their slaves and theological opponents, these Alexandrian physicians were accused, particularly by the Christian fathers Tertullian and Augustine, of practising vivisection on condemned criminals. There is some evidence for the existence of a public medical service in Egypt, rather less in the Seleucid kingdom and Pergamon, but its benefits were probably confined to the Greek citizens and the army; the natives were left to their fate. Of effective measures against epidemics, such as campaigns against fleas, lice, and mosquitoes, we hear nothing, while human excrement was still regarded as the best manure.

Hellenistic science was not divorced from the practical life of the producer, as Bronze Age learning and Natural Philosophy after 450 had been. The two centuries beginning in 330 B.C. brought forth a crop of mechanical inventions that cannot be paralleled in any comparable period till A.D. 1600.

Besides laying and experimentally testing the mathematical bases of pure mechanics, Archimedes of Syracuse showed how the principle of specific gravity could be utilized in daily life; in fact he stumbled upon the principle itself in trying to unmask a fraud practised upon his patron by a goldsmith who had adulterated the metal entrusted to him. For an earlier tyrant of Syracuse his forerunners designed engines of destruction far more potent than the slings, bows, wheeled towers, and battering rams that formed the strongest items in the Assyrians' equipment, despite that nation's preoccupation with wars and sieges. The propulsive force in the new artillery was provided by torsion and levers, and they could hurl missiles weighing sixty pounds for 200 yards.

Archimedes not only studied the geometrical properties of the screw, but also applied the results to the construction of a machine for raising water. This was made of wood, gave a lift of from six to twelve feet, and was generally driven by human motive-power – a man working a treadmill. Greater lifts were subsequently effected by buckets attached to an endless chain on a rotating drum. Irrigating machines of the latter type seem to be referred to in Egyptian papyri of the second century B.C.

Finally Ktesibios, who probably lived at Alexandria in the third century, invented a perfectly good pump equipped with valves and cylinders and pistons and embodying the same pneumatic principle as old-fashioned hand-pumps. Funnily enough there is no evidence for its use during our period for raising water – perhaps owing to the unsuitability of lead pipes, the cost of bronze ones, and ignorance of cast-iron. A similar fate befell a number of ingenious pneumatic and hydraulic devices described by Hero of Alexandria, a writer whose date cannot be fixed within four centuries.

The significance of the use of rotary motion in corn-mills and of the application thereto of water-power was emphasized on page 245. Now it must be insisted that these water-mills were complicated machines involving the insertion of gears, both to convert horizontal into rotary motion and to increase power by reducing speed. They were, of course, made of wood, as was mill machinery as late as the eighteenth century A.D. Gear-wheels, this time of metal, were also employed in a water-clock described by Hero which forms the starting point for all subsequent developments in clockwork mechanisms and chronometers.

In applied chemistry glass-blowing, supplementing and superseding the older processes of casting and moulding (p. 189), was probably invented in Syria during the second century B.C., and had momentous consequences. It seems likely, too, that distillation was practised in Alexandria before the beginning of our era. Retorts are described in treatises on alchemy that can hardly be later than A.D. 300. But just when alcohol opened a new chapter in the history of inebriety is still unknown. The use of lime mortar was popularized by the Hellenistic builders of the third century B.C. And the Romans or their employees discovered an almost indestructible cement made by mixing lime with a volcanic ash (first found near Puteoli and hence still called 'possolana') which would set even under water.

Hydrostatics were effectively applied to the supply of water to cities, notably at Pergamon, in the second century, and also at Rome. There an aqueduct constructed in 312 B.C. flowed underground for no less than ten miles through tunnels the construction of which was a remarkable feat of surveying and levelling. But though the syphon was perfectly familiar to the Alexandrians, as Hero's book shows, the Roman engineers never applied it to large-scale undertakings (of course their lead pipes could not stand high pressure). They preferred to build those superb viaducts that still survive to testify to their mastery of the arch and other architectural devices inherited from the Bronze Age Orient.

Strangely enough, as it seems to us, mechanical inventions found little application in practice – save in warfare – during the Hellenistic age. In that period water-power was not apparently applied in any industry save corn-milling. Even water-mills for corn were still so rare at the beginning of our era that geographers mention them specially as curiosities. Antipater of Salonica blithely sang in the first century B.C.:

'Mill girls touch the quern no more; for Demeter hath bidden the Nymphs perform your work,
They rush on to the top of a wheel and make its axle turn.'

But landlords and capitalists preferred to invest their profits in living instruments rather than costly machines of wood; slaves were cheap.

Similarly the pneumatic and hydraulic devices of Ktesibios and his successors were not demonstrably applied to draining mines or watering gardens. What Hero describes are water-organs, automata, parlour toys to divert guests at a rich man's banquet, and temple furniture to mystify the credulous.

The failure to exploit productively the inventions offered by science was a consequence of the structure of Hellenistic society and of contradictions in its economy. These reacted on theory too. The most original and creative activity, the epoch-making discoveries, and the great constructive hypotheses all fall within the later fourth and third centuries – precisely the period when the economic system was expanding triumphantly. Though the lines of research then laid down were fruitfully pursued subsequently, the output of genuinely novel ideas virtually ceased after 200 B.C.; the compilation of data from records began to take the place of fresh observation and experimentation (Strabo and subsequent geographers, for instance, are constantly repeating the reports of Alexander's observers and third-century ambassadors, adding relatively little later information). But by 200 economic contradictions were becoming manifest in an arrest of the market's expansion externally, and a slowly growing impoverishment internally.

The system described in this chapter undoubtedly yielded a genuine increase of real wealth. But an excessive proportion of the yield was concentrated in the treasuries of a few kings; most of the balance was annexed by Greek and other ruling castes; very little was left to the 'natives' who tilled the soil and less to the slaves who manned the factories and mines.

The planned economy established in Egypt by the Ptolemies was planned to produce revenue for the king just as much as the pharaoh's systems under the Old and New Kingdoms had been. Inasmuch as it was more scientific, it increased Egypt's prosperity; even the natives benefited in securing better tools, perhaps a more varied diet, on paper a freer legal status. But it added to the old antinomy between nobles and peasants a new contrast between Greek rulers and native subjects. Perhaps the natives preferred the old rulers 'who had been their compatriots, who spoke their own language and had the same religion and mode of life' to the 'bureaucratic machine in which foreigners played the most important part, foreigners who regarded themselves as far superior to the natives, who did not speak their language and had no intention of learning it'. This suggestion of Rostovtzeff's is borne out by the letter of a literate Egyptian who writes bitterly about being 'despised because I am a barbarian', and the readiness of the peasantry to support the native priests in revolt against the conquerors.

The machine produced revenue all right. Ptolemy II enjoyed an income of 14,800 talents, and even his father's prime minister had secured a rake-off of 6,000. But, however excellent the intentions of the rulers may have been, the machine soon became oppressive. The Rosetta Stone, inscribed in 196 B.C. with a decree in Greek and Egyptian which first gave the clue to the decipherment of hieroglyphics, implies 'pressure of taxes, rapid accumulations of arrears and concomitant confiscations, prisons full of criminals and debtors, public and private, many fugitives scattered all over the country and living by robbery, compulsion applied in every sphere of life'. The decree in question was designed to remedy this situation, but like equally humane decrees by later Ptolemies was frustrated by the administrative officials. For complaints in Hellenistic papyri prove that corruption and extortion were as rampant in the civil service then as they had been under the New Kingdom (p. 167).

The natives had one recognized remedy – the strike; they left their work and retreated *en masse* to the asylum of a temple till intolerable grievances were remedied. They resorted to it so frequently that many later contracts include a clause binding the tenant not to strike. The natural results were scarcity of labour, the gradual depopulation of the villages, abandonment of fields, neglect of dykes and canals. One complainant writes that his village had shrunk from 140 to 40 souls. Such were the results of a planned economy run in the interests of a governing class – even from the biological standpoint the reverse of progressive.

In the Greek cities the principal beneficiaries from the new opportunities afforded by Alexander's conquests were the bourgeoisie. Its composition may be defined with Rostovtzeff as: landowners whose land was tilled by tenants, hired hands, or slaves; tenant farmers employing the labour of the latter classes; owners of workshops, directing their employees, slaves or freemen; owners or tenants of shops or ships and warehouses; money-lenders and slave-hirers. To such belong the nice houses we have admired at Priene (p. 242) for instance.

All over Greece, as also in Italy, the number of peasants who worked their own land was declining to make room for capitalist farms. After 300 B.C. contracts for temple building (at Delos) were not taken by independent craftsmen who performed small jobs themselves as in the fifth century, but were let to contractors in the modern sense who supplied labour, free or servile.

The profits of the bourgeoisie were – at first – large. The Alexandrian Zeno left a fortune of 2,000 talents, while the richest man in Athens before Alexander's day had possessed only 160. On the other hand as compared with fifth-century Athens, real wages fell. On Delos a skilled artisan made at best four obols per day per annum and an unskilled worker only two obols, though the price of wheat had doubled, wine had gone up two and a half times, and rents nearly five times. Rich citizens were certainly generous in helping their cities with gifts or loans – loans from private citizens to the State are a common feature in Hellenistic finance – and contributed handsomely to the adornment of the city and the upkeep of schools and other public institutions. Yet the concentration of purchasing power restricted the internal market for popular goods.

For a while the opening up of new export markets and the distribution to Alexander's soldiers of the hoarded wealth of Oriental kings masked the disequilibrium; purchasing power was widely distributed through a finely-graded middle class. But soon the migration of industry (p. 248) narrowed the export market once more. The ravages of war, debt, and the competition of slave-manned factories relegated the smaller producers and retailers to the ranks of the proletariat. Demands for the cancellation of debts and the redistribution of land broke out in open civil war in Sparta and other States of Old Greece. But everywhere the bourgeoisie stubbornly and successfully resisted reform, sometimes with the aid of Rome.

Of course in Rome itself a similar class struggle developed as the outcome of tendencies outlined on page 217. But there loot from imperialist wars and an expanding market in the barbarian west staved off the crisis. Two efforts at a resettlement of peasants on the lands of great estates initiated by the Gracchi in 131 and 121 B.C. were defeated by the Senatorial oligarchy, at the cost of concessions to the new middle class of contractors, tax-farmers, and usurers and of doles of free corn to the urban proletariat.

Finally Alexander's expeditions, the wars between his successors and between the still autonomous city states, the intensified activity of pirates, inroads by barbarian Celts, and Roman imperialism enormously augmented the slave supply till industry and agriculture in Hellenistic times were really run by slave labour except in Egypt. Of course only in mines and quarries were slaves systematically and rapidly worked to death. Most were allowed opportunities of earning money for themselves; many might hope to buy their freedom (when they were too old to work!). Materially even the slaves on a capitalist farm lived better than most barbarian peasants; Cato provided the slaves on his estate with sheets, blankets, mattresses, and pillows, and the slave-quarters on excavated farms compare favourably with the Celts' round huts. Many professional men – clerks, doctors, tutors, factory managers, and farm bailiffs – the equivalent of our 'black-coated proletariat' – were actually slaves like labourers and artisans, particularly but not exclusively in the Roman Empire. As slaves of kings and ministers, these might rise to positions of responsibility and amass large fortunes, holding slaves themselves.

Hence slavery hardly created a class conscious of a solidarity of interests against its exploiters. Rather did it cut across the division of the free population into bourgeoisie and proletariat. Yet slave revolts did actually occur and assume serious proportions for the first time in history after 134 B.C. in Attica, Macedonia, Delos, Sicily, Italy, and Pergamon. The rebels were often joined by small peasants and tenants and even by 'free' proletarians. But all these efforts were brutally suppressed in the end by the armies of Rome and other States.

Incidentally the institution of slavery impeded the proclamation of an ideology appropriate to the international economy that was already *de facto* in existence. Nevertheless, some Hellenistic philosophies did begin to transcend the narrow bounds of the *polis* and even the time-honoured contrast between Greek and Barbarian, and present the conception of the unity of the human race adumbrated by Alexander himself after his victory over his country's traditional foes.

Zeno, a Phoenician from Cyprus who lectured in Athens in the *Stoa* – hence the name *Stoics* applied to his school – dreamed of one great Polis where all were citizens and members one of another, bound together by their own willing consent or, as he put it, love. Zeno accordingly denounced slavery as unnatural, but he regarded it, like sickness and other material ills, as an irrelevant external accident over which the wise man could triumph in his spiritual power; the wise man, though he serve in slavery, is yet a king, though he be a pauper, possesses all things. Such a doctrine was too sophisticated to be a rallying cry for the oppressed masses but might soothe the consciences of the bourgeoisie. The later Stoics in fact, doubtless as a concession to rich patrons, revived Aristotle's doctrine of the 'natural slave' (p. 233).

Religion too, though not of course the official cults of the States, began to reflect, in a striving after one god, the world unity realized in the economic sphere. Astrology, the most widespread cult of the age, was on its theological side a catholic version of the old Sumerian doctrine of Fate as a power superior to all tribal, civic, and national deities. But it was amoral and in practice purely magical. Other religions, celebrated by unofficial congregations, did inculcate a morality that recognized no distinctions of race or civil status. One quotation must suffice.

The ordinances of a private shrine to Agdistis at Philadelphia in Asia Minor read: 'Let men and women, slave and free, coming into this shrine swear by all the gods that they will not deliberately plan any evil guile or baleful poison against any man or woman; that they will neither turn to nor recommend to others nor have a hand in love-charms, abortives or contraceptives or doing robbery or murder; that they will steal nothing but be well-disposed towards this house.' Of course such cults were not concerned with reforming abuses in earthly society, but with securing admission to an imaginary society where such abuses did not exist. Still, admission thereto is obtainable by moral action and open equally to slave and free.

But if philosophy and religion could avoid the impediments of slavery, the institution continued to obstruct the progress of science (p. 184) by making labour-saving machinery unprofitable, and contributed to the impoverishment of all producers by keeping down the purchasing powers of the internal market. For by 200 the failure of the classical economy even in its amended version was in fact becoming apparant. At least in Old Greece the results of this failure could already be measured by purely biological standards. The population was actually declining. Citizens, rich and poor alike, were deliberately restricting their families by abortion and infanticide. And slaves had no chance to rear large families.

But the purely economic factors in this catastrophe were reinforced, and in the literary record are quite overshadowed, by purely political factors incompatible with the economic system itself. The Hellenistic world, throughout which language and culture were so nearly uniform, was split up into three or more major kingdoms and a varying number of city-states and confederacies. All these units fought one another continually with senseless ferocity. 'Barbarian' States – Parthia, Armenia, Arabia, Rome, Carthage – joined eagerly in the mêlée. Engrossed in self-destructive wars the States allowed or even encouraged pirates and robber bands to nest in the disputed frontier zones. The multiplication of these parasites was only a symbol of social disorders which denied an adequate livelihood to peaceable peasants and artisans and extolled violence and slaughter in the name of patriotism as the highest expressions of manly virtue. But by replenishing the slave market it exaggerated the evil.

The conflict between these economically futile political entities was at length terminated in the most brutal manner by Rome. Having made herself head of an Italic alliance (390–264 B.C.), and annexed first the foreign domains of Carthage (Sicily, 251, Spain, 210) and then the city and her African domains (154), Rome proceeded to absorb Macedonia, the Greek city-states, and the Hellenistic kingdoms in Asia Minor, Syria, and finally Egypt.

THE DECLINE AND FALL OF THE ANCIENT WORLD

CONQUEST by Rome brought to the war-scarred Mediterranean world peace, but not at first prosperity. Quite the reverse. The original kernel of the Roman domains, the peoples and cities of Italy, had been organized as a nation of allies; eventually after 88 B.C. all Italians were admitted to Roman citizenship. The annexed territories overseas on the contrary were treated as estates to be exploited by tribute like the conquests of an Oriental monarch. But Babylonian, Assyrian, and Persian kings seldom quite forgot that their revenues depended in the last resort upon the prosperity of their subjects. They generally saw to it that their governors acted accordingly. The elected magistrates, sent out for a year as governors by Republican Rome, were not thus cramped.

The Senate, composed of time-expired governors, did not aspire to be hailed as 'Saviour' or 'Benefactor' by its subjects. Laws against extortion were indeed enacted. But after 121 a governor, if impeached, would be tried before a jury of capitalists and contractors who owed their wealth and rank to the exploitation of the Provinces by tax-farming, usury, and concessions. At the same time election could be secured only by bribes to 'the Roman People'. The governor had to make three fortunes out of his Province – one to pay the election expenses, another to secure acquittal on his return, and a third to live on. No wonder he joined forces with the tax-farmers and money-lenders who might try him in an unparalleled exploitation that completed the impoverishment of the Hellenistic world.

In the last century of the Republic Senators and capitalists amassed vast fortunes: Pompey was worth 11,000 talents, Crassus 7,500, the Stoic Brutus who murdered

Caesar, 1,700. These figures can indeed be surpassed by the fortunes of some Hellenistic officials and financiers. That does not mean that the noble Romans pocketed less of the loot, but (as Heichelheim points out) that there was less loot to pocket; depredations and mismanagement had destroyed so much of the accumulated wealth. In any case these fortunes had been acquired, not as the rewards for organizing industry and commerce, but as the plunder of war and the proceeds of extortion, usury, and financial manipulation.

In Rome itself the empire enriched only a relatively small class. Debts and conscription had driven from the land a large proportion of the peasantry; their small holdings were replaced by capitalist farms worked by slaves. (These were not always very large; Cato's ideal in the second century was a farm of some 60 to 150 acres, worked by 13 to 16 slaves.) The dispossessed peasantry could find no rehabilitation in industrial employment; for the urban working class too were being impoverished and socially degraded by the competition of slaves who were poured upon the market by each imperialist war. The imperial city contained within her the material for civil war, just as inflammable as what caught alight in some Hellenistic cities.

This situation helped Julius Caesar, after he had added to the Empire the Celtic lands to the Rhine and the Channel, to seize supreme power like a Greek tyrant. Two years later he was murdered in the name of liberty. But after twelve more years of civil war, his grand-nephew, Augustus Caesar, became in fact emperor, though called only *princeps* (first citizen). Julius was duly deified, and in the east Augustus accepted divine honours in his own lifetime, thus proclaiming himself the spiritual successor of the Ptolemies and Seleucids and their Babylonian, Sumerian, and Pharaonic forerunners. But he was now monarch of a single State extending from the Euphrates, the Black Sea, the Danube, and the Rhine to the Atlantic, and from the North Sea to the Sahara and the Arabian desert. As thus completed the Roman Empire is the best instance of a geographical area large enough to be completely self-sufficing that enjoyed a common culture as well as political unity.

Julius and Augustus put an end to the worst excesses of Senatorial governors. They gave the Empire a reasonably efficient and honest administration. Above all they gave it peace. For nearly two hundred and fifty years the great unit enjoyed internal peace to a degree never hitherto enjoyed by so large an area. After the victory of Augustus the Roman Peace was seriously disturbed internally only in the terrible year A.D. 68, when 'a secret of empire was divulged that emperors could be made elsewhere than at Rome', and three provincial armies warred in Italy to win for their generals the imperial dignity. Even external peace was not long nor deeply troubled by remote local wars that added to the Empire Britain (A.D. 50–80), Transylvania and Rumania (as it was in 1938), Armenia, and parts of Mesopotamia.

The immediate result was a revival of prosperity and, at least in the new western provinces, an increase of population. All over the new provinces in Gaul (France and Belgium), Germany (the Rhine valley), and Britannia (England), as well as in Spain and North Africa, cities of the Greco-Roman pattern were established. In size Roman cities were quite like Greek *poleis*. As laid out in A.D. 100, Timgad in North Africa covered only some 30 acres; Caerwent in South Wales measured 44 acres, and Herculaneum, near Naples, had not outgrown 26. Pompeii and many similar towns occupied 150 to 160 acres. Even at Naples itself the walled area did not exceed 250, and Cirencester, in England, was about the same size. But Roman London was already 300 acres, Capua 440, and Autun, in France, 490, while New Carthage reached 1,200 acres, Alexandria 2,275, and Rome by the third century 3,060.

In themselves these figures do not imply any substantial increase of population. Today the sixty-four closely built-up acres of St Malo house only 7,262 souls, and the ancient cities were hardly more densely populated. The significant fact is the addition of a number of such cities in formerly barbarian lands to those of Italy and the Hellenistic east. All but the smallest exceed in area the hilltop forts and villages in which Celts had lived in La Tène Britain, and all were far more closely built over. As the capital of a Belgic kingdom Colchester is disclosed by excavation as a disorderly huddle of squalid huts. As a provincial city its successor appears as a well-planned array of commodious dwellings.

For all Roman cities, like the Hellenistic *poleis*, enjoyed the amenities of a public water supply, now often laid on to every block, handsome public buildings, baths, theatres, colonnades, market halls, and assembly places adorned with statues and fountains. The private dwellings were tasteful and commodious. In a provincial watering place like Pompeii with at most 30,000 inhabitants archaeologists have uncovered street upon street of mansions with mosaic pavements, frescoed walls, colonnaded courts, glazed windows, running water, bathrooms, and latrines.

A good middle-class house with a terrace garden might occupy a block 108 ft square, the main reception room being 48 ft long. More sumptuous houses with a colonnaded central court are of the order of 200 ft by 40 ft. These, though very numerous, are doubtless the dwellings of the bourgeoisie as defined on page 265, and occupied a space disproportionate to the numerical strength of that class. The larger body of small retailers, artisans, and labourers would live in flimsier houses of one or two rooms or, in the larger cities, in tenements that might run up to 60 ft in height. Still a baker's house (two-storeyed) at Pompeii with the ovens and four donkey-mills on the ground floor forms a block 90 ft long and nearly 60 ft wide. At Caistor by Norwich in distant Britain, houses adjacent to potters' kilns, and so presumably occupied by master potters, are resplendent with tessellated pavements.

Moreover, Roman cities like the Hellenistic *poleis* enjoyed municipal self-government. Election posters discovered at Pompeii show how keen the competition for magistracies was before the eruption of Vesuvius overwhelmed the city. Rich citizens were as public-spirited as in Greece and the Hellen-istic world, and delighted to adorn their city with parks and buildings and to finance gladiatorial shows and other enter-tainments for the benefit of their fellow-citizens.

Rostovtzeff once called the new cities 'hives of drones', but they were also hives of industry and trade. The handi-crafts pursued in them supplied not only the citizens and rural population of the vicinity with manufactured goods, but also barbarians far beyond the frontiers of the Empire. Bronze casseroles made in Capua for instance have turned up in Scotland, Denmark, Sweden, Hungary, and Russia. Artisans and industrialists from Italy and the Hellenistic east migrated westward and established factories in the new provinces. Fine red-glazed moulded ware in the Hellenistic tradition was produced now by potteries established in France, 'Germany', and even at Colchester in England. Syrians established glass-houses in the Rhine valley and northern France; an 'artist in glass of African nationality and a citizen of Carthage' has left a tombstone at Lyon.

Trade circulated freely throughout the Empire. The cities were united by a network of superb roads. Harbours were everywhere improved or constructed, and the seaways were now free from pirates. Pottery manufactured in Italy has been found in Asia Minor, Palestine, Cyprus, Egypt, North Africa, Spain, and southern Russia; the products of the factories in France reached North Africa and Egypt as well as Spain, Italy, and Sicily.

But the Empire, though self-sufficing, was not a closed economic system. The barbarians of the north supplied slaves, amber, furs, and other materials. In return they acquired wines, pottery (mostly from French and Rhenish kilns), metal-ware, glass vessels, and coins, which are dug up all over Germany to East Prussia, Sweden, Denmark, and Norway, as well as in the distant isles north of Scotland. Trade routes radiating from the Black Sea ports distributed similar commodities across the south Russian steppes to the forest belt beyond.

Regular caravans of camels brought spices, aromatics,

unguents and jewels across the deserts from southern Arabia and Mesopotamia. Their western termini, Petra, Jerash, Baalbek, Palmyra, and Dura-Europos, became rich and prosperous entirely as a result of this traffic. Under Roman auspices direct sea trade between Egypt and India was intensified, partly cutting out the Arabs who controlled the caravan traffic.

From Egyptian ports like Arsinoe and Berenice the India-men sailed down the Red Sea, and then at first coasted along southern Arabia, across the mouth of the Persian Gulf and so coastwise to the Indus delta. But at least after A.D. 50 they began to exploit the discovery of a Greek sea captain, Hippalos, that the monsoons provided a reliable means of transit direct across the ocean to peninsular India, enormously economizing time. The south-west monsoon in August provided both the motive power for the crossing and a guide as reliable as a compass, which was still unknown. The north-east monsoon in January ensured the return voyage.

By using the monsoons the 2,760 miles from Berenice might be covered in less than six months, the return voyage could be accomplished within ninety days. In fact, by leaving Italy with the corn-ships in May, and taking Nile boat and caravan from Alexandria to the Red Sea, you might be back in Rome again in just over a year. A regular fleet was engaged in the traffic, and we read of a boat 180 ft long, 45 ft wide, and 44 ft deep.

The fleet brought to the Roman market not only Indian goods but also Chinese products carried so far overland or by sea in Indian and Chinese bottoms. The imports were mostly 'luxuries' – dancing girls, parrots, ebony, ivory, pearls and precious stones, spices and perfumes from India, silks and drugs from China – but some, such as pepper, were becoming necessities to quite large circles.

Owing to the limitations of transport and to the structure of Middle and Far Eastern societies these imports could not be paid for in the products of mass manufactures or agriculture. High-class textiles, glass and metal ware, parchment and papyrus and such substances as coral were in fact exported eastwards from the Empire. But the balance of trade between Rome and India was adverse, and the deficit was made up by exporting coin – and good gold coin at that. Roman *aurei* still turn up in numbers all over India and have been found as far away as Ceylon and China. From the falling ratio of silver to copper and to gold it has been calculated that two-thirds of the stocks of gold and half the silver in the Empire had crossed its frontiers, mostly eastwards, by the fourth century A.D. (Under Augustus the ratio of copper to silver was as 1 to 60, of silver to gold 1 to 12; after 300 the respective ratios are 1 to 125 and 1 to 14 or 18.)

Finally, Greco-Roman agricultural science was fruitfully applied to the undeveloped soil of the western provinces, as of North Africa. All over France, the Rhine valley, and southern England Romans and provincials established capitalist farms. On them Mediterranean techniques were applied, vines and other new plants cultivated and acclimatized. The farm buildings, the so-called *villas*, afford a pleasing contrast to the squalid and untidy steadings of the La Tène Celts, such as we know on the English Downs. Even the slaves' quarters are more hygienic than the hovels of contemporary native villagers. The owners' apartments are adorned with mosaic pavements. To meet the unaccustomed rigours of a northern winter, Italian proprietors even installed an ingenious system of central heating.

The Roman Empire formed a unique reservoir for the pooling of human experience. The intensity of commercial intercourse between all its scattered parts and with civilized and barbarian worlds beyond its frontiers has already been indicated. Besides traders, craftsmen, and slaves, civil servants and military officers were continually travelling to the remotest outposts of the Empire. The huge standing army needed to guard the long frontiers against barbarism without was a great educative force. Soldiers were recruited in every part of the Empire, but the normal practice was to send them to serve away from their home country. Finally ambassadors and missionaries came from the East to Rome, and conversely Marcus Aurelius is said to have sent an embassy to China.

In the scientific arrangement of the vast mass of information thus made available hardly any progress was made. No original creative hypothesis for reducing to order a number of scattered facts was advanced. Not a single major invention was suggested by all the data accumulated. Despite the existence of a large leisured class of cultivated and even learned men, Imperial Rome made no significant contribution to pure science. Rich amateurs like Seneca and Pliny, with the aid of an army of Greek clerks, compiled voluminous encyclopedias of natural knowledge. Though a number of true and novel observations were therein recorded, their arrangement is astonishingly unsystematic, and the critical judgement of Aristotle is conspicuously absent. While Pliny rejects magic verbally, his credulity is deplorable. Only in Alexandria was the tradition of Hellenistic science still active, but subject to the limitations mentioned on page 263.

In applied science, too, the advances made under the Empire are disappointing in comparison with the resources available. Roman architects and engineers applied and amplified processes and techniques inherited from the Hellenistic world and Republican Italy without any revolutionary innovations. Medical studies were encouraged and supported by the Emperors, and military hospitals were admirably organized, but the results were hardly novel. Even in the highly respectable domain of agriculture the writers of the Empire have little to add to Cato. It may be questioned whether the Romans and their provincial disciples appreciated the difficulties of applying a system of farming evolved in the Mediterranean to the very different soils and climates of temperate France and Atlantic England, whether in fact the villas were so scientific after all.

If the sciences did not profit much from the facilities for intercourse offered by the Empire, religions did. Slaves, emigrant artisans, merchants, and soldiers carried with them every variety of Oriental cult, not only to the capital but to the uttermost bounds of the Roman world. Altars dedicated to the Egyptian Isis and the Iranian Mithra have been dug up even in remote frontier posts in Scotland and Germany. Of the many sects and rites thus diffused Judaism and Christianity were alone destined to have a permanent world significance. Judaism was too nationalistic to make many converts outside those accruing to it by birth. Christianity, on the other hand, provided the truly international ideology that a world economy had long demanded.

Christianity began as a small Jewish sect whose members saw in Jesus the Messiah of the Scriptures and expected his immediate return to set up the Kingdom on earth. But Jesus' doctrine of love and His life, at once an example of, and object for, such love, combined with the promise of salvation and resurrection, gave the faith an infinitely broader appeal. After the journeys of Paul the religion spread rapidly, if at first principally among slaves and proletarians. As their one God, like Yahveh, would tolerate no other deity, least of all the divine Emperor, to share the worship due to Him, the Christians, like the Jews, were persecuted by a State that would still tolerate any cult provided only that loyalty to its deified head were publicly proclaimed by conformity to the prescribed ritual. But love for the Master inspired them to suffer and to die for an ideal with an unprecedented fortitude. In the end they won not only toleration but also endowment from the State – but only when that State needed an ideological support to reinforce its failing powers.

In the meantime Christianity had acquired a priesthood, a sacred book, and several theologies. The first disciples and their immediate followers had no need of an organization, an elaborate ritual or a philosophical formulation of their faith; they expected the Messiah hourly. But when the second coming was found to be delayed, adjustments became inevitable. Leaders were forthcoming to organize the brethren's meetings, to conduct their devotions, and to proselytize the heathen. The very growth of the Church and above all the pressure of persecution made organization imperative. The Church evolved a hierarchy, modelled on the imperial administrative system. Reminiscences of the life and sayings of Jesus must early have been recorded. Collected and edited and combined with writings attributed to the apostles, these came to form a canon to which the bulk of the Hebrew Scriptures was prefixed. Missionaries were thus equipped with a sacred book to compete with those of the Jews, the Zoroastrians, and the Orphics.

To defend and explain their faith before imperial officials and the middle classes, the leaders were obliged to formulate in terms of analytic reasoning the emotional content of religious experience. They inevitably used the terminology of Greek philosophy and Aristotelian logic, helped out by references to approved or tolerated and familiar Classical and Oriental doctrines. The inherent difficulties of the task inevitably provoked controversies which would split the Church into sects, each branding as heretics all its opponents, as soon as the pressure of persecution relaxed. At the same time a tincture of dogmas derived from Judaism, Neo-Platonism, and other heterogeneous sources was infused into the simple teachings of Jesus. In fact, the scientific mythology of the Jewish book of Genesis, Greek science as expounded by Aristotle, and even the geocentric astronomy of Hipparchus became incorporated in the tenets of the most successful sect.

In the same way ritual was enriched by borrowings from the ceremonial of mystery cults and the vestments of priest-kings, while converts were conciliated by the adoption as saints, martyrs or virgins of local heroes and mother-goddesses of neolithic antecedents. Increasing emphasis came to be laid on the negative sanctions for piety and morality, implicit in the teachings of Jesus as in any other doctrine of salvation. If Christianity as a religion of love surpassed all others in stimulating positive virtue, it came to match the Egyptian, Zoroastrian, Orphic, and Buddhist faiths in deterring from evil by terrifying descriptions of hell.

Finally, with their hopes and fears focused upon the coming Kingdom and the life beyond the grave, the early

Christians accepted the social order as they found it here, except in so far as it conflicted with their ritual duties. In the Kingdom there would be no distinction between slave and free, but here slavery was an established institution, and the slave must submit himself to his master.

Nevertheless the Christian conception of the Brotherhood of Man and its command, 'Love thy neighbour as thyself', provided a motive for moral action more universal than loyalty to tribe or *polis*, and yet more potent than Stoic philosophy or Roman law. But for the moment the new religion, like older cults, made life significant and livable for the masses to whom the resources of the Empire and the fruits of natural science offered no prospects in this life. It spread through the middle and upper classes precisely in the measure that these too were forcibly convinced of the vanity of earthly hopes by the growing impoverishment of the economic system. And this disillusionment was not long delayed.

The multiplication and beautification of cities and the lively bustle of commerce that we have described give an impression of limitless prosperity. Yet the Empire had not removed the contradictions of Hellenistic economy. Rome had not released any new productive forces and did not materially extend the use of those already available in the Hellenistic age. Not even the structure of industry was radically reformed. 'The step from the "manufactory" to the factory and the machine as the fundamental means of production was not made.'

No doubt the size of the productive unit was increased. For example, the ceramic industry of Arretium (Arezzo in Tuscany) was organized on a larger scale than the same industry in Athens five centuries earlier. Out of twenty-five potteries operating there between 25 B.C. and A.D. 25, two employed more than 30 artists who 'signed' their products, ten had from 10 to 14 artists, and only six so few as 7 to 10. The largest firm that in the fifty years sold vases signed by 58 artists must have had at least a hundred slaves engaged at any one time in the less skilled operations. So in the textile industry we read even at Pompeii of a workshop employing 25 weavers.

The multiplication of employees under unitary management does not, however, imply any greater specialization of labour than we have already encountered in classical Athens and Corinth. Still less was it dictated by any sort of mechanization. Water-mills, for instance, were hardly commoner in the first century after our era than in the last century before it. The 'aristocratic' tradition, inherited from the Republic, discouraged the investment of capital in industry. A Senator was forbidden by law to engage in trade. Even more than in classical Greece 'agriculture and to a lesser extent commerce were the only "respectable" occupations; the sphere of industry was left to freedmen and others of humble birth' and slender means. The new rich accordingly hastened to invest in land, like the freedman, Trimalchio, in the famous satire of Petronius. Having made a fortune in shipping and money-lending in the days of Nero, he proceeds to buy up estates and farms. At best such a capitalist might buy slaves to man a workshop, but he would not even fulfil what economists call the entrepreneur function since the works would be managed by a freedman or a lessee.

Hence we find at Pompeii forty little bakeries with mills, like the one described on page 273, and about twenty fullers' shops to cater for the needs of the 30,000 inhabitants of this little town. So in the ceramic industry at Lezoux in southern France, which after A.D. 70 took the place of Arretium in supplying the western market, eight distinct firms are known by their trade marks.

The real increase of wealth attested in the early days of the Empire was the result of the superficial expansion of civilization and the suspension of attritional warfare. But 'the expansion of urban civilization was a system of exploitation which organized the resources of the newly conquered lands and concentrated them in the hands of a minority of capitalists and business men.' In other words, the market for goods was made wider, but not deeper. 'The purchasing power of the very large lower class was still small. Buyers for wares of somewhat superior quality were derived from the middle and upper classes and from the Army,' as in Hellenistic times.

On the land the position of the peasantry was not improved and probably deteriorated in the old provinces; in Egypt, for example, Tiberius suppressed the right to strike by abolishing the immunity of refugees in temples (p. 264). In Celtic lands like Britain the natives lived in the same squalor and cultivated their lands by the same inefficient means as before their annexation to the Empire.

In industry the remuneration of artisans and manual workers was kept down by the competition of slave labour. Admittedly slaves did not oust free workers from employment. Of the artisans mentioned in inscriptions of the first and second centuries, 27 per cent were free-born, 66 per cent freedmen (emancipated slaves), and only 7 per cent slaves at Rome; in the rest of Italy the proportions are 46 per cent, 52 per cent, and 2 per cent respectively. Of course slaves were less likely than others to be honoured with tombstones or offices in religious clubs – and it is to those that our inscriptions mainly refer – so that these figures do not give actual proportions of the employed population. Nevertheless even in a brickworks the bricks are stamped with the names of 22 freedmen, as against 52 slaves and 22 employees of uncertain status. In the potteries of Arretium before A.D. 25, out of 132 known workers, 123 were slaves. But in the ceramic industry of France and the Rhine valley the employment of slaves is not thus attested. In inscriptions from Dijon woodworkers, smiths, and other craftsmen are called 'dependents' (*clientes*), not slaves.

It must again be recalled that slaves were in practice allowed to earn and retain a 'peculium' over and above their bare keep. Clerks, tutors, and many other professional men were often slaves, and Caesar's slaves might actually fulfil the functions of ministers of State. Some authorities assert that wages actually rose till A.D. 200. Be that as it may, the share of the industrial worker in the produce of his labour was very small.

The fact is that for the masses the standard of living was, and remained, very low. 'The men of antiquity, if they did not live in opulence, had few needs. They lived mainly on wheaten bread, olives, and figs, consuming relatively little meat and wine, in miserably furnished rooms, heated only with braziers and lit with oil lamps.' Most men apparently accepted this standard, and no advertising propaganda aimed at raising it.

Hence the internal market was as restricted as it had been in the Hellenistic and Classical worlds. But now the external market could expand no more; by A.D. 150 the frontiers of the civilized world had been reached. Unable to expand, the whole system began to contract. Now in the Roman Empire no political disturbances intervened to mask the results of purely economic forces. Undisturbed we can observe the fatal results of the contradictions inherent in the Classical economy since 450 B.C.

They appear first as light shadows on the bright surface of first-century prosperity. Already we see the familiar tendency of ancient industry to export itself instead of its products. The demand of the new provinces was not met by an expansion of the manufacturers of Italy and Greece, but by migration of craftsmen to France, Germany, and Britain. Down to A.D. 25 the better-class pottery used in the west had been exported from Arretium. Thereafter craftsmen, expert in its manufacture, migrate first to South France, then to the north and Germany, finally even to Britain to set up potteries there to supply the local markets. The case of the glass industry, already cited, illustrates the same process.

The result was a reduction of inter-provincial trade, particularly in cheap consumption goods. Each province tended to become an economic unit that supplied its own needs as far as its natural resources would allow. That was not the consequence of any chauvinistic demands for self-sufficiency such as have inspired the tariff policies of Australia and Canada. It resulted rather from the deficiencies of the transport system already explained. Not even the splendid

Roman roads had made the carriage of bulky goods by land really cheap. So 'Rome, which imported everything from the provinces, never reimbursed them except with money from their taxes.'

Still graver was the tendency of capitalist farms to grow into self-sufficing 'households' of the old Oriental pattern. In the days of Cato only minor repairs were done at the farm; for major operations the local smith would be called in. Clothes for the slaves, burned bricks, and metal ware were bought in town. Under Augustus only very large and remote estates maintained specialist craftsmen. But after A.D. 50 Pliny assumes that on every estate there are weavers, fullers, smiths, carpenters, and so on.

Then the capitalist farms, scientifically run, albeit with slave labour, and producing for the market, began to be replaced by, or combined with, estates exploited by dependent tenants or share-farmers practising subsistence agriculture. The villa began to turn into the *manor* as familiar in medieval Europe. This meant the replacement of slave-cultivators and herdsmen not by free peasants such as had formed the backbone of classical Greece and early Italy, but by tenants dependent on the landlord for seed and equipment and paying rent often in kind and services as well – an old Oriental system already encountered more than once. The system offered the new bourgeoisie the opportunity to 'make fortunes out of unspecialized agriculture by absentee landlords'. It was definitely a step back towards the Oriental economy of the Bronze Age, indeed towards neolithic self-sufficiency.

The specialized farmer, large or small, relied on urban industry to supply the needs of himself, his family, or his slaves. The new type of tenant could cover a larger proportion of his needs by household industries. The landlords maintained on their estates small-scale smithies, potteries, tile-works, and brick-kilns worked by their slaves or the compulsory labour of their tenants. Only luxury products like glassware and exotic materials had to be bought in town.

The inevitable result was the decline of urban industries

and the impoverishment of the once-flourishing cities. The process can be measured by the actual contraction of urban areas. After A.D. 275 Autun had shrunk from nearly five hundred to less than twenty-five acres; in fact hardly any cities in France after A.D. 300 exceed sixty acres. Bordeaux is down to fifty-six, Nantes, Rouen, and Troyes to thirty-nine. In Britain, too, the decline of city life is no less clear in the last quarter of the third century. At Verulamium (St Albans) the town walls were partly in ruins and the theatre fell into disuse. At Wroxeter the town centre was burned and not rebuilt. These facts symbolize the ruin of the smaller bourgeoisie at least as a corollary of the exploitation of the primary producer.

Now, as Rostovtzeff says, 'the advance made in the Greek and Hellenistic periods in the sphere of industry was due to a constant increase in the demand for goods. After 125 the market for industry was limited to the cities and country districts of the empire. The future of industry depended on their purchasing power. And while the buying capacity of the city bourgeoisie was large their numbers were limited, and the city proletariat grew steadily poorer. The material welfare of the country population improved very slowly if at all.' 'When the limits of the *oikoumene* were reached, industry should have exploited the internal market more actively and should have extended its scope to include the lower classes. This would, however, have required a modification of the social structure of the Empire' (*Cambridge Ancient History*, xiii, 252).

Having failed to stimulate proletarian and peasant demand by advertising and to make it effective by a redistribution of purchasing power, the middle class of factory owners, merchants, and shopkeepers, who had reaped such benefits from the Roman peace, now found themselves doomed to proletarianism, too. No wonder they began restricting their families like their forerunners in Hellenistic Greece. Only the great landlords escaped, and that by a reversion to neolithic 'self-sufficiency.

By A.D. 250 all semblance of prosperity had vanished.

The bankruptcy of the Roman economy was nakedly exposed. It was proclaimed to the biologist by the decline in fertility that is notorious in all classes of the population of the later Empire. Economically, as well as scientifically, classical civilization was dead a hundred and fifty years before barbarian invaders from Germany finally disrupted the political unity of the Empire and formally initiated the Dark Age in Europe.

*

In these hundred and fifty years the later emperors made a heroic if vain attempt to rescue the machinery of civilization by reviving a régime of Oriental centralization, often miscalled State Socialism. A more appropriate term is now available since Nazional-Sozialismus employed almost identical methods for the same purpose of maintaining an antiquated social system.

The impoverishment of the Empire and the decline of its population naturally reacted on the State itself. A large standing army was essential to defend the vast empire from the prolific starvelings of the Germanic north and the envious nomads of the eastern and southern steppes. The army had to be equipped and paid, and its cost increased as the emperors were forced to hire barbarian mercenaries from abroad to make up the shortage of native recruits. Administration and the collection of revenue required a large and costly civil service. The emperors spent vast sums on public works that were either really reproductive, like roads, or at least added to the amenities of life, but also on quite wasteful luxuries. While the economic system was expanding it could easily stand the strain, but as it approached the limits set forth above, a discrepancy between revenue and expenditure became noticeable.

Nero already began to cover his deficit by debasing the currency. The drainage of bullion to the east to pay for the luxuries imported for the plutocracy (p. 275) further embarrassed the Treasury. In the third century the deficit was swelled by civil wars in which the armies were turned from defending the frontiers to support the claims of rival Caesars. Taxes had to be increased. The burden fell most heavily upon the city bourgeoisie, and that just at the time when its taxable capacity was declining owing to the growing self-sufficiency of the manorial estates. Magistracies that had been sought as honours became onerous obligations, both owing to the expenses they traditionally entailed and because magistrates were made responsible for the payment of their city's taxes. So magistracies were made compulsory on all who, in the eyes of the State, could afford them.

Then compulsion was applied to industry and commerce too. The guilds of craftsmen and merchants, originally free associations for religious and social ends, became organs of the State for ensuring a supply of artisans or ships. To secure the maintenance of public services the employees of the mint, the State arsenals, the State textile factories (there were seventeen in the west alone), the public post, the water supplies, and similar utilities were bound to their employment, often branded, and allowed to marry only into the families of fellow-workers. One was no longer free to adopt or ply a craft, but compelled by law to follow it. Crafts in fact became castes. All were brought under military discipline, which applied also to corporations of shipowners, teamsters, and others performing services 'affected with a public interest'.

The food supplies and amenities of the capital and a few more favoured provincial towns were thus maintained. At Rome there were 956 public baths and free shows were given on 175 days a year! The citizens now received the free corn, distributed to them since the days of the Gracchi, already ground to flour for them; water-mills became common in Rome after 300. Prices were fixed throughout the Empire by edict as by Babylonian kings, but wages were fixed too, and that not minimum but maximum wages as in the Bronze Age – for there was a real shortage of labour.

Finally the primary producers were reduced to the status

of serfs tied to the soil. That fate had overtaken the 'king's peasants' in Egypt already when Tiberius withdrew the right to strike, leaving banditry or beggary the sole resort of an oppressed tenant; in the third century the typical questions put to an oracle were: 'Am I to become a beggar?' 'Shall I fly?' 'Will my flight be stopped?' After 300 the same system was applied to Europe, primarily as a fiscal measure to make sure that the cultivator did not escape his poll tax. In 332 Constantine, the first Christian emperor, made the attachment of the share-farmer (*colonus*) to the manor enforceable at law. In 371 the Emperor Valentinian wrote: 'We do not deem that *coloni* are free to leave the land to which their condition and birth attach them. If they do, let them be brought back, put in chains and punished.' The tenant has become a serf.

But by favouritism and corruption the landlords of the great estates escaped the pressure of the machine. Though they might be compelled to provide contingents for the army from their tenantry, they were often able to protect these against the exactions of tax-gatherers and the rest of the swarm of officials. So ruined freeholders and urban workers sought refuge under the patronage of great landowners. These feudal lords were already on the way to vindicating for themselves a political independence corresponding to their economic self-sufficiency and so preparing the disruption that was consummated by barbarian warbands in the fifth century.

Finally, as the ideological expression of the totalitarian régime, the 'First Citizen' as head of the State became 'Master and God' (*dominus ac deus*). Only Christianity, as an exclusive monotheism effectively organized in a universal and independent church, offered for a time a spiritual refuge against absorption in the Nazional-Sozialist State. The conversion of Constantine is generally hailed as the final victory of the new faith. It may equally be regarded as the triumph of totalitarianism.

The Church no doubt won not only tolerance and relief from persecution, but also wealth and the right to persecute.

The price was clerical endorsement of the existing order on earth. The Emperor is indeed no longer 'Master and God', but he has become the 'Orthodox and Apostolic Emperor'. His rule was an earthly counterpart and representative of the Sovereignty of the Divine Word. In the 'Sacred Palace' at Istanbul the 'Divine Household' abode and issued 'Celestial Commands'; even the annual tax assessment was known as the 'Divine Delegation'.

It seems as if humanity has reverted from the Greek Iron Age back to the Oriental Bronze Age. The atmosphere of Byzantium is more like that of Babylon or Ur than of Athens or Alexandria. Nor could the relapse to Oriental centralization and despotism save even the physical unity of the Empire. Germanic hordes overran the western provinces and sacked even Rome itself. (The capital had been removed to Byzantium (Istanbul) under Constantine.) A flood of barbarism submerged all the new acquisitions of civilization, leaving only its ancient East Mediterranean core as an impoverished relic – the Byzantine Empire.

*

No, Byzantium is not Ur. Its citizens are not only far more numerous, they are still citizens of a world infinitely wider than any Sumerian dreamed of, however much its frontiers may have contracted since Augustus. Water-power now drives the mills that slaves had once pushed. There is more than a verbal difference between an 'Orthodox and Apostolic Emperor' and 'the divine Narâm-Sin, the mighty, god of Agadé'. The former acknowledges himself servant of a God who is Father of all men, not only of Akkadians. His universal dominion needs no extension by military victories.

In reality the cultural capital accumulated in the long ages here surveyed was no more annihilated in the collapse of the Roman Empire than smaller accumulations had been in the lesser catastrophes that interrupted and terminated the Bronze Age (pp. 158, 161, 194, 195). Of course, as then, many refinements, noble and beautiful, were swept away. But for the most part these had been designed for and

enjoyed by only a small and narrow class. Most achievements that had proved themselves biologically to be progressive and that had become firmly established on a
genuinely popular footing by the participation of wider
classes were conserved, even if temporarily fossilized.

So in the Eastern Mediterranean city life, with all its
implications, still continued. Most crafts were still plied
with all the technical skill and equipment evolved in
Classical and Hellenistic times. Farms were still worked
scientifically to produce for the market. Barter did not
entirely oust the money economy, nor did self-sufficiency
paralyse trade completely. Writing was not forgotten.
Indeed, at Alexandria and Byzantium scientific and literary
texts were studiously copied and preserved. Greek medicine
was practised in public hospitals with the blessings of the
Church.

In the newer provinces of civilization the losses were
comparably graver. But despite a reaction towards self-
sufficiency barbarized Europe did not relapse into the
Stone Age, nor even into the La Tène period. Where the
Mediterranean city vanished, it was not replaced only by
hill-forts. Around a cathedral or an abbey there grew up
a reincarnation of the Sumerian temple-city. But it was
more than a small replica of its Bronze Age prototype. Its
citizens knew themselves as inhabitants, not of one narrow
alluvial valley, but of a vast round world. However isolated
they were by the deterioration of the roads and the dangers
that infested them, pilgrims, missionaries, and merchants
could and did travel about a continent. The new arts and
crafts introduced under the Empire were not extinguished.
For instance, descendants and apprentices of the Syrian
glass-workers kept the Norman and Rhenish furnaces going
all through the Dark Ages. Water-wheels were built on
feudal estates and by 700 were at work even in England.

The foregoing pages have disclosed the formation of the
'main tradition' and have followed its course from sources
in Egypt and Mesopotamia to their confluence in the
Hellenistic Mediterranean. With the collapse of the Roman

reservoir the stream seems to be obstructed and lost. But the possibility of writing this book itself refutes that supposition. It would be for a sequel to show how the current flowed on to fertilize a new science and a new technology under a fresh economy in an Atlantic environment. The main lines are clear.

On the one hand, the body of classical theory and Hellenistic technology was preserved in a state of suspended animation at Byzantium and Alexandria in the sterilizing atmosphere of a theocratic State. It began to revive in the more tolerant atmosphere of Sassanian Iran (in the University of Jundîshâpûr, 530–580) and then under the khalifs of Baghdad (750–900), when the temporal conquests of Islam, realizing again the unity of a large area of the inhabited world, re-created an era of peace and prosperity. Before the old internal contradictions had destroyed the prosperity and disrupted the polity of the Arabic world, before 'the establishment of the Orthodox Faith about 1106 sealed for ever the fate of independent research in Islam', the blood stream of the old body, enriched with new experiences digested by the Arabs, was being transfused into a new vessel in Europe through the Moorish provinces of Spain and Sicily.

On the other hand, the barbarian hordes in Europe had not massacred all clerks, priests, craftsmen, and merchants. The Church kept alive not only the dogmas and rites of Christianity, but also the techniques of writing and ciphering, a respect for precise conventional divisions of time and machines for their determination (clocks), a demand for exotic products, some refinements such as glazed windows, vestiges of Classical art and Roman architecture, motives for travel such as pilgrims or missionaries, memories of rational medicine and scientific agriculture. Many craftsmen survived as indicated; old Mediterranean towns were replaced by new cathedral cities.

The rural economy of Europe did not revert to that of the pre-Roman Celts. No doubt even more than in the late Empire it was based on subsistence farming by unfree serfs.

Admittedly local famines were recurrent and could not be relieved by the distribution of a world surplus. Nevertheless, the feudal estates did permit of the establishment of methods of farming really suited to the temperate forest zone. Serfdom for the first time converted its half-nomadic cultivators into really sedentary farmers. And the lords' water-mills provided examples of the rational exploitation of resources with which our continent is exceptionally blessed.

These hints must suffice. Progress is real if discontinuous. The upward curve resolves itself into a series of troughs and crests. But in those domains that archaeology as well as written history can survey, no trough ever declines to the low level of the preceding one; each crest out-tops its last precursor.

MAPS

THE EXTENT OF THE CIVILIZED WORLD ABOUT
2500, 1500, 500, AND 100 B.C.

In these the reader sees the areas of literate urban civilization (horizontally hatched) grow from three little pools in Map I to a vast lake embracing the whole Mediterranean basin and extending continuously to India, where it almost joins on to a western bay of a second lake – in China – in map IV. Maps II and III indicate (by vertical hatching) also the remarkable growth of trade from Greece between 1500 and 500 B.C.

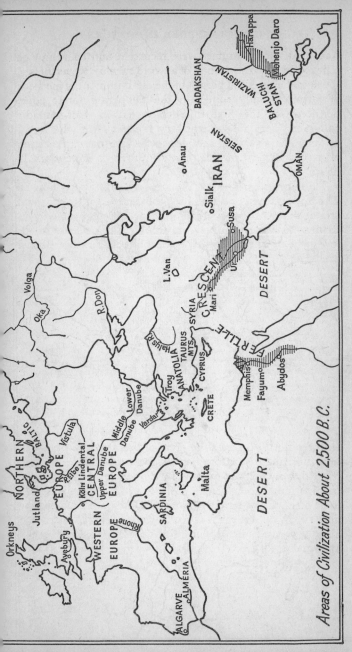

Areas of Civilization About 2,500 B.C.

MAP I

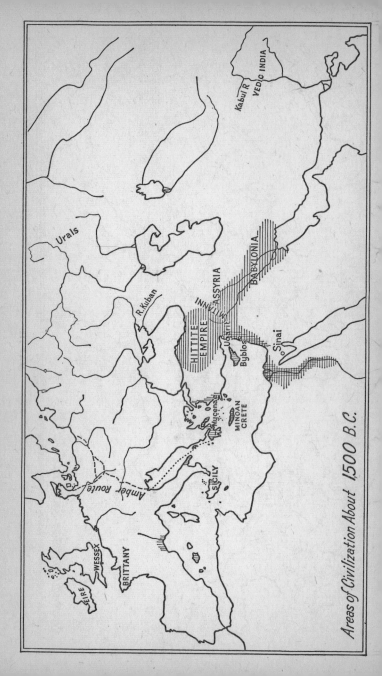

Areas of Civilization About 1,500 B.C.

Urals

R. Kuban

HITTITE EMPIRE

MITANNI

ASSYRIA

BABYLONIA

Ugarit

Byblos

Sinai

Kabul R.

VEDIC INDIA

MYCENAE

MINOAN CRETE

SICILY

Amber Route

EIRE

WESSEX

BRITTANY

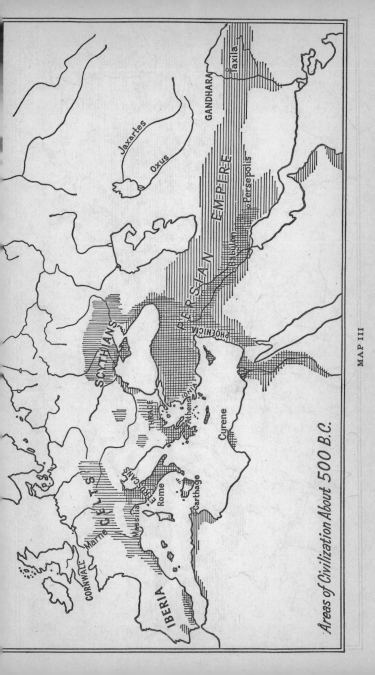

Areas of Civilization About 500 B.C.

MAP III

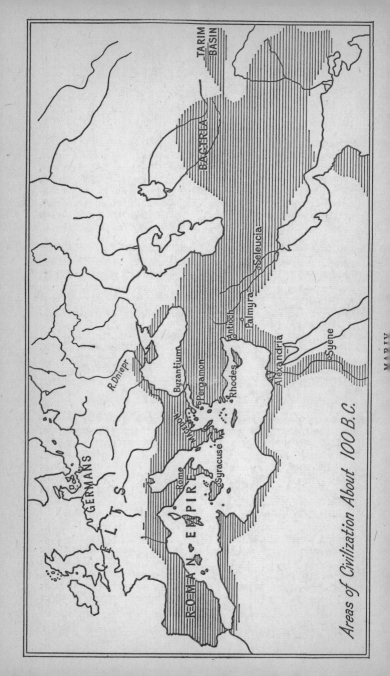

TARIM BASIN

BACTREA

GERMANS

C E L T S

R.Dniepr

Byzantium

Pergamon

MACEDON

Rome

Syracuse

Rhodes

Antioch

Palmyra

Seleucia

Alexandria

Syene

R O M A N   E M P I R E

Areas of Civilization About 100 B.C.

MAP IV

INDEX

Abstraction, 18–19, 21–2, 112, 141, 230

Agriculture: Bronze Age, 169; Copper Age, 78; feudal, 31, 292; Germanic colonists, 252–3; Greco-Roman, 276; Greek colonies, 243–4; Iron Age, 231; Neolithic Age, 30, 55–6, 59–62

Alphabet: Aryan, 201; Babylonian, 189; development of, 31, 200–201; Egyptian, 126; Greek, 195, 201; Phoenician, 189–90, 200–201

Aqueducts, 262

Architecture, 146, 236, 277, 291, *see also* Buildings, Houses, Temples

Areas of villages and cities: Asia Minor, 154, 181; Bronze Age, 173, 178, 181; Crete (Minoan), 173, 181; decline of, 285; Greek, 207–8, 241–2; Indian, 133; Iron Age, 203–4, 207–8; Mycenaean, 178; Neolithic Age, 61–2, 66–7; Nineveh, 203; Roman, 272–3; Sumerian, 102; Ur, 102

Arithmetic, *see* Mathematics

Art: Bronze Age, 136, 139, 146–7, 171–2, 174; Celtic, 251–2; Church keeps alive demand for, 291; Cretan (Minoan), 174; earliest, 21; Early Dynastic, 109; Egyptian, 146–7; Greek, 235–7; Greek colonial, 241; Mycenaean, 193; Palaeolithic, 38, 47–8, 49–50

Artillery, 256, 261

Aryans, 170, 175–6, 185, 191–2, 197, 200

Asses, 90, 149

Astronomy: Babylonian, 220, 228–9, 255, 257–9; Egyptian, 127, 141, 161; Greek, 228–9, 255–9; origins of, 40; Pythagorean, 223, *see also* Astronomy, Greek; Sumerian, 118, *see also* Astronomy, Babylonian

Beer, *see* Intoxicants

Boats and ships: Bronze Age, 122, 125, 134; Copper Age, 92–3; Egyptian, 92, 122, 125; Greek, 195–6, 241; Indian, 134; Mesopotamian, 98; Polynesian, 92; Roman, 275

Bows and arrows, 43, 59

Bribery and corruption, 167–8, 264, 270, 288

Bricks, 80, 81, 82, 99, 124, 133

Bronze and industrial metal: Bronze Age, 125, 130, 134, 139–40, 152–3, 154, 157–8, 169, 178, 190–92; in Central Europe, 157–8; in China, 169; in Cyprus, 153; earliest skill in, 85; economic methods of working, 191; in Egypt, 125, 130, 140, 164; in Greece and Mycenae, 178, 195; high cost of, 190–91; in India, 134; Iron Age, 204, 211; in Mesopotamia, 104, 110

Buddhism, *see* Religion

Buildings: in Egypt, 124, 125, 148, 181; in Greece, 208; in Greek colonies, 241–2; in India, 135; in Mesopotamia, 81–2, 99–100, 181, 203–4; in Mycenae, 178; in Persian Empire, 204; in

Rome and Roman Empire, 273

Burial rites: Bronze Age, 122, 124, 152–3, 156, 169, 178, 181; in China, 169; in Cyprus, 152–3; in Egypt, 122, 124; in Mycenae, 178; Neanderthal, 21; Neolithic, 71, 152, 169; Palaeolithic, 41–2, 47; in Sicily, 156, 181

Calendar: Egyptian, 128, 143; of Hesiod, 195, 228; Sumerian, 116–17

Camels, 91, 203, 274–5

Chariots, 91, 160, 162, 169, 170, 173, 178, 182, 212, 251

Chiefs, 53, 73, 94–5, 96, 154–5, 175, 251

Christianity, see Religion

Civilization, summary of earliest, 31–2

Clan organization: in Athens, 215; Bronze Age, 122, 123–4, 138, 153–4; Copper Age, 94–5; of craftsmen, see Guilds; Neolithic Age, 73, 75; Palaeolithic Age, 53

Class division in society: in Bronze Age, 124, 135; in Egypt, 124, 264; in Greece, 209, 216–17, 233–4, 265; in Greek colonies, 243–4, 265–7; in India, 135; in Iron Age, early, 203, 209; in Mesopotamia, 106–7; in Neolithic Age, 75; in Rome, 217, 266–7

Classification, 19, 115, 142, 144, 231–2

Clocks and sundials, 116, 161, 227, 256, 259, 261, 291

Coinage: debasing of, by Nero, 286; nickel used as alloy in, 250; Phoenician, adopted by Alexander, 246; retail trade facilitated by, 31, 202; Roman, competes with Greek, 246;

Roman, exports of, 276; usury encouraged by, 202

Copper, see Bronze, Metallurgy

Cotton, 66, 134, 244

Craftsmen: in Bronze Age, 31, 124, 130, 141–2, 152, 154, 159, 164, 173–4, 179, 184; Celtic, 251–2; in Copper Age, 85–7, 93; in Crete (Minoan), 173–4; in the Cyclades, 154; in Egypt, 124, 130, 164; in Greece, 195–6, 205–6, 215, 238, 265; in Greek colonies, 242; in Iron Age, 195–6, 204–6, 212, 215, 230; in Mesopotamia, 103, 109, 159, 164; in Mycenae, 179; nomadic, 212; in Persia, 204; in Roman Empire, 274, 282, 287; after Roman Empire collapse, 290–91

Cuneiform writing, 113, 120, 141, 183, 200

Dark Ages, 159, 161, 194, 211, 286, 290

Debts, 214–17, see also Usury

Democracy, 214–17

Dictionaries, 115, 142

Diffusion of culture: in Bronze Age, 170, 175, 179, 190; causes of, 27–8; in Copper Age, 86–7, 93–4; in Greek colonies, 242–3, 248; in Iron Age, 197–8, 211, 217–20; beyond Mediterranean, 248–9; in Mesopotamia, 105–6; in Neolithic Age, 68–70, 75–6; through Roman Empire, 276–8

Divergence of traditions, 24–5, 26–7, 37–8, 57–8, 69–70

Dramas, ritual, 48, 72, 108–9, 236

Election of magistrates, 213, 215, 217, 270, 273; Epics, 150, 178, 236

Experimental science, 227, 231, 244, 254, 259–60

Factories: in Arretium, 280; in Athens, 208, 216, 237, 245; in Lagash, 102-3

Faience, 123, 134, 172, 179, 188

Fate, 144, 229, 268

Feudalism, 31, 288

Fishing: in Byblos, 148; in Crete, 153; in Egypt, 122, 131, 138, 148; in India, 134, 138; in Mesopotamia, 97, 138; in Neolithic Age, 60; in Palaeolithic Age, 44-5, 46, 50, 53

Fortifications: Celtic, 251; China, Great Wall of, 250; Egyptian, 125; at Erech, 101; in Neolithic Age, 62, 66-7, 74

Fortunes, 236, 264, 265-6, 270-71

Fractions, 114, 127, 185, 186, 226, 255-6

Fruit trees, 78, 97, 155, 171, see also Olives, Vines

Geography, 229-30, 256-9

Geometry, see Mathematics

Glass, 164, 183, 188, 248, 262, 274, 290

Glazing, see Faience

Gods: Babylonian, 168-9, 218; Chinese, 219, 221; Christian, 278; Egyptian, 124-6, 144-6, 161, 168-9, 278; Greek, 222-3; Halafian, 81, 96; Hebrew, 220-21, 278; Hittite, 171; Indian, 136, 137; Iranian, 220, 221; Sumerian, 102-3, 144-6, 168, 218, see also Religion

Granaries, 60, 61, 65, 102, 135, 138

Guilds, 31, 87, 287

Harbours, 172, 240, 246, 274

Harness, 88, 89, 91, 182

Hell, 165, 221, 222, 279

Hieroglyphic writing, 124, 126, 141, 189, 200

Horses, 80, 90, 91, 162, 169, 170, 212

Households, great: in Asia Minor, 171; in Crete (Minoan), 172-3; in Egypt, 129-30, 140, 163-4, 243; in Mesopotamia, 103-4, 151, 163-4, 165-6, 170; Roman, 211, 284

Houses: Babylonian, 204; Bronze Age, 135, 173, 181; Copper Age, 80; Cretan (Minoan), 173; Egyptian, 181; Greek, 208; Greek colonies, 242; Indian, 135; Iranian, 80; Iron Age, 204, 208; Neolithic, 61-2, 63; Palaeolithic, 45; Roman, 273

Hunting: in Bronze Age, 122; in earliest times, 30; in Neolithic Age, 55, 59-60, 61, 68, 69; in Palaeolithic Age, 44, 50

Hydrostatics, 262

Immortality, 122, 129, 145-6, 156, 161, 165, 222, 278

Imperialism: Assyrian, 170, 197, 203; in Bronze Age, 149-50, 159, 162, 170, 173, 193; Cretan (Minoan), 173; Egyptian, 149, 162, 193; Greek, 216, 240-1; in Iron Age, 196-7; Persian, 197-8, 203; Roman, 269, 270 ff.; of Sargon, 150

Indo-Europeans, 93, 171, 176-7, 195, 196

Inflation, 167, 286-7

Innovations, summary of early revolutionary, 29-30

Intercourse between societies: in Bronze Age, 123, 177, 182-3; in Copper Age, 104-6; general, 27, 29; during Greek colonization, 249-50, 255; in Iron Age, 196; in Neolithic Age, 67-9, 74; in Palaeolithic Age, 38, 46; during Roman Empire, 276-7; after Roman Empire collapse, 291

Intoxicants, 65, 66, 175, 212, 222, 262, 283

Iron, 183, 190–2, 199–200, 210, 211, 213, 214

Irrigation: in Asia Minor, 154; in Copper Age, 78; in Egypt, 122–3, 166; in Mesopotamia, 98–9

Journey times: from Alexandria, 246; Byblos to Nile, 172; caravan routes in Asia, 247; Indus to Seleucia, 247; Sardis to Susa ('Royal Road'), 198; on Syrian steppes, 182

Judgement of souls, 145–6, 165

Kings, divine: Babylonian, 168, 213, see also Kings, divine, Sumerian; in Bronze Age, 184–5, 213, 224; Christianity opposes, 278, 288–9; in Copper Age, 95; 'corn', 72; Cretan (Minoan), 173; Egyptian, 121, 124–5, 140, 165, 168, 171, 213; Hellenistic, 242; Hittite, 171; Neolithic, 72; Roman, 271; Sumerian, 108, 140, 168, 213

Land tenure, 53, 75, 102, 128–9, 163, 205, 218, 224

Language: divergences in, 26–7; Indo-European, 176–7; origins of, 17–18; Phoenician, 189; 'Romance', 176

Law: Babylonian, see Law, of, Hammurabi; Egyptian, 164–5; Greek, 213–14; of Hammurabi, 160, 166, 220; Hittite, 171; Roman, 217

Lighthouses, 240, 246

Literacy, see Writing

Machines, 45, 46, 260–61

Magic: in Astrology, 268; in Bronze Age, 124–5, 129, 136, 143, 175–6; in Copper Age, 86–7, 95–6; in Egypt, 124–5, 129, 143; in India, 136, 175–6;

in Mesopotamia, 95–6, 143; in Neolithic Age, 70, 71–2; in Palaeolithic Age, 42, 47–8, 52–3; persistence of belief in, 23, 277; in prophetic religions, 221

Map, first Greek, 230

Mathematics: in Babylonia, see Mathematics in Mesopotamia; in Egypt, 126–7, 142; in Greece, 223, 225–7; Hellenistic, 225–7; higher, 185; in India, 135–6; in Mesopotamia, 116–18, 142, 185–8, 255

Measures, standardized, 115–16, 127, 225

Medicine: in Bronze Age, 230; Egyptian, 141–2, 260; Greek, 230–31; in Greek colonies, 260; in Iron Age, 230; Oriental, 230; public service of, in Egypt, 260; in Roman Empire, 277; Sumerian, 127, 230

Merchants: Egyptian, 140, 148–9, 163; Greek, 210, 215; Indian, 134–5; Mesopotamian, 104–5, 119, 151, 159–60, 163, 166; Mycenaean, 179; Neolithic, 68–9; after Roman Empire collapse, 290, see also Trade

Metallurgy: in Bronze Age, 122, 134, 169, 180, 190–91; in China, 169; in Copper Age, 81, 83–5; in Egypt, 190; in India, 134; in Mesopotamia, 190

Middle class, 31, 151, 161–3, 164–5, 172, 184, 203, 214, 218, 265, 285

Migration: after Alexander, 241, 249–50; in Bronze Age, 154, 155, 175, 177, 179; general results of, 28; in Iron Age, 194–5, 198–9, 205–6; in Neolithic Age, 74; during Roman Empire, 274, 283

Milk, 56, 91, 212

Mills, corn, 60, 245, 273, 281, *see also* Querns

Mining: in Cyprus, 153; by Egyptians, 125; in Greece, 207, 216; in Greek colonies, 243; improved methods of, 180; in Neolithic Age, 68; in Sicily and Central Europe, 156–7

Money: in Bronze Age, 118–9, 130, 135, 151, 163, 166; in Egypt, 130, 163; frauds, in early use of, 201; in Iron Age, 201–2, 210; in Mesopotamia, 118–19, 163, 166; after Roman Empire collapse, 290; small change, introduction of, 202

Morality: Buddhist, 219, 221; in China, 219; in Egypt, 145–6, 165; Greek, 238–9; Hebrew, 220, 221; Hellenistic, 268; Zoroastrian, 220, 221

Mortgages, 166–7, 202, 210–11

Music, 49, 147, 225

Natural Philosophy, 223, 234

Neanderthal man, 40–3

Numerals: Babylonian, *see* Numerals, in Mesopotamia; in Egypt 126–7; in Greece, 226, 255–6; in India, 135; in Mesopotamia, 101, 113–14, 127, 185–7, 255–6

Oligarchy, 214, 218, 232

Olives, 148–9, 153, 155, 174, 202, 206

Papyrus, 189

Piracy, 154, 155, 174–5, 179, 205–6, 213, 214, 238–9, 246

Plough, 88–9, 103, 211, 252

Population: Asia Minor, 155; Athenian, 207, 209, 268; Bronze Age, 131, 138, 152–3, 155, 180–1; Celtic, 252; Copper Age, 100; Crete, 153; Cyprus, 152; earliest, 35–6; Egyptian,

131, 138; Indian, 133, 138; Iron Age, 207, 209, 211; Mesopotamia, 100, 138; Neolithic, 66, 73, 152; Palaeolithic, 50, 51–2; Roman Empire, 272; after Roman Empire collapse, 285

Potter's wheel, 80, 83, 93–4, 99, 130, 133–4, 155, 169, 172, 177, 195

Pottery: Bronze Age, 130, 172–4; Copper Age, 80, 93–4; in Crete (Minoan), 172–4; in Egypt, 130; Geometric, 195; in Greece, 206, 208, 230; in Greek colonies, 248; Iron Age, 195, 206, 208, 230; Mycenaean, 195; Neolithic, 57, 61, 63, 70; in Roman Empire, 273–4, 280

Prices, 167, 191–2, 248, 287

Property, 53, 80, *see also* Land tenure, Money, Slavery

Pythagoras' theorem, 187, 188, 226, 227

Quadratic equations, 187, 227, 256

Querns, 60, 61, 65, 68, 245

Religion: Buddhist, 219, 221, 254; Christian, 279–80, 288–9; Confucian, 219; Egyptian, 129, 145–6, 168–9, 221; Greek, 222 234; in Greek colonies, 249–50, 254–5, 268; Hebrew, 220–1, 254, 278; Hindu, 136, 175; Indian, early, 136; Judaist, *see* Religion, Hebrew; Mesopotamian, 99–101; Palaeolithic, 49; in Roman Empire, 277–80; Taoist, 219; Zoroastrian, 220, 221, *see also* Gods

Retail trade, 134, 163–5, 172–3, 188–9, 201–2

Rice, 64, 169, 170, 231

Riding, 91, 212

Roads, 198, 203, 240, 247, 274

Rotary motion, 46, 57, 245, 261
see also Potter's wheel

Sacred books, 175, 225, 278

Sacrifices, 48–8, 219–20, 222

Sails, 92, 123

Schools: alphabetic writing helps
development of, 218; Egyptian,
126, 142; Greek, of pottery, 195;
in Greek colonies, 241; medical,
230–1; Mesopotamian, 114–15,
159, 185; Palaeolithic, of artists,
48

Science: Bronze Age, 127, 136–7,
139, 140–1, 143, 171; in Egypt,
127, 140–1, 143; in Greece, 222;
Hellenistic, 253–5, 260–1; Hittite, 171; in India, 136–7, 140–
41; in Mesopotamia, 111, 140–1,
143; Neolithic, 57, 65, 70, 85;
obstructed by institution of
slavery, 268; Palaeolithic, 39–
40; in Roman Empire, 277;
after Roman Empire collapse,
291

Seals, 80–1, 82, 83, 95, 99, 148,
153, 174–5

Secret societies, 95, 100, 129, 223

Self-sufficiency: in Asia Minor,
154; in Bronze Age, 132, 154;
Celtic, 251; in Copper Age, 82,
87; in Egypt, 132; feudal, 288;
in Greece, 205, 238; in Iron
Age, 203, 204; in Mesotopamia,
82; in Neolithic Age, 67,
75–6, 87, 132; in Palaeolithic
Age, 46; Persian, 203; in
Roman Empire, 283–4

Serfdom, 31, 131, 164, 203, 205,
243, 244, 284, 288, 291

Silk, 170, 250, 275

Slavery: in Bronze Age, 103, 105,
151, 163, 166, 184; Christian
view of, 280; in Egypt, 163; in

Greece, 208–9, 216, 222, 232,
233, 237; in Greek colonies,
243, 244, 245, 249, 266–7; in
Iron Abe, 31, 203, 208–9, 216;
in Mesopotamia, 103, 105, 151,
163, 166; revolts against, 267;
in Roman Empire, 266–7, 271

Sledges, 51, 89

Small change, 31, 201–2, 206–7

Specialization: in Bronze Age,
103, 124, 130, 133–4; in Copper
Age, 85, 87; in Egypt, 124, 130;
in Greece, 208; in Greek
colonies, 245; in India, 133–4;
in Mesopotamia, 103, 133; in
Neolithic Age, 67; in Palaeolithic Age, 48; among 'primitive man', 23; in Roman Empire, 281

Speech, *see* Language

Spinning and weaving, 57, 66–7,
103, 130, 133–4

Statues, 47, 71, 146, 235

Stock-breeding: in Bronze Age,
103, 122, 133, 148, 169, 175;
in Byblos, 148; in China, 169;
in Copper Age, 88; in earliest
times, 30; in Egypt, 122; in
Europe (barbarian), 251, 253;
in Greek colonies, 243; in
India, 133, 175; in Iron Age,
212, 231; in Mesopotamia, 103;
in Neolithic Age, 56, 59, 61, 62,
66, 73; nomadic, 212

Streets, 60, 66–7, 135, 273

Strikes, 217, 264, 282, 288

Surplus of food (wealth): in
Bronze Age, 122, 128, 139,
148, 152–3, 164, 165–6, 169,
172; in China, 169; in Copper
Age, 86; in Crete (and Minoan),
153, 172; in Egypt, 30, 122,
125, 128, 164, 165–6; in India,
30; in Mesopotamia, 30, 98,
100, 106–7, 109; in Mycenae,
178; in Neolithic Age, 67, 77;

nomadic, 212; in Palaeolithic Age, 48

Symbols, 18–20, 47–8

Temples: in Byblos, 148; in Greece, 236; in Mesopotamia, 82, 95–6, 98–103, 151, 242

Tin, see Bronze and industrial metal

Totemism, 52, 95, 106, 122, 124, 136, 222

Trade: in Asia Minor, 154–5; in Bronze Age, 122–3, 134, 148, 152–6, 159–60, 171–5, 179, 205–6, 210–11; in Byblos, 148, 152, 171–2; in Copper Age, 81, 82, 87, 92, 98, 104–5, 110, 120; Cretan (Minoan), 173–4; Cypriot, 153; Egyptian, 148; Greek, 205–6; Greek colonial, 244–6, 248–9; Mesopotamian, 81, 82, 98, 104–5, 110, 120, 134, 148, 159–60; Mycenaean, 179; in Neolithic Age, 68–9; in Palaeolithic Age, 46; Roman, 210–11, 274–6, 283, 290

Transport: Bronze Age, 133, 139, 172, 182–3; Copper Age, 105; during Greek colonization, 244, 246–9; Iron Age, 198, 203; in Roman Empire, 274–5

Usury: in Babylon, 166–7; coined money helps growth of, 202; in Greece, 234, 237; in Greek colonies, 265; in Rome, 210–11, 218, 266, 270

Vehicles, wheeled, 82, 90, 103, 134, 169, 170, 173, see also Chariots, Sledges

Viaducts, 262

Vines, 78, 153, 155, 171, 206, 231

Wages: effect of coined money on, 202; in Greece, 209, 236; in Greek colonial period, 243, 265; in Mesopotamia, 102–3, 118, 168; in Roman Empire, 282, 287

War: Bronze Age, 123–6, 149–50, 158; Celtic, 252–3; Copper Age, 88, 96, 107–8, 109, 120; Egyptian, 123–4, 125–6, 149, 162–3; Greek, 210, 212, 234; Greek colonization period, 240, 261, 266, 269; Iron Age, 193, 210–12, 252–3; Mesopotamian, 107–8, 109, 120, 149–50; Neolithic Age, 74–5

Water-mills, 256–7, 261, 281, 287, 290

Waterwheel, 92

Wheel: geared, 261; invention of, 46, 82; spoked, 160, see also Potters' wheel

Women, position of: in Athens, 216; in Copper Age, 88, 94, 103; in Mesopotamia, 103; in Neolithic Age, 55, 56, 57, 65–7, 70, 73

Writing: Cretan (Minoan), 172; Egyptian, 124, 126, 140–1, 149; Hittite, 171; Indian, 135–6, 140–1; Mesopotamian, 58, 95, 101, 111–15, 120, 140–1, 149, 151, 170–1, 183, 185; in Mitanni, 170–1; popularization of, 31; after Roman Empire collapse, 290, see also Alphabet, Cuneiform, Hieroglyphic writing

Yeast, 65

Zero signs, 255

Ziggurat, see Temples